God Loves You

HE ALWAYS HAS—HE ALWAYS WILL

Dr. David Jeremiah

Faith
Words

New York · Boston · Nashville

Published in association with Yates & Yates, LLP, www.yates2.com

Unless otherwise noted, Scripture quotations are from the New King James Version. Copyright © 1982 by Thomas Nelson, Inc. Used by permission. All rights reserved.

Scripture quotations noted KJV are from the King James Version of the Holy Bible; Scripture quotations noted The Message are from *The Message*. Copyright © 1993, 1994, 1995, 1996, 2000, 2001, 2002. Used by permission of NavPress Publishing Group; Scripture quotations noted NIV are from the Holy Bible: New International Version®. Copyright © 1973, 1978, 1984 by International Bible Society. Used by permission of Zondervan Publishing House. All rights reserved; Scripture quotations noted NLT are from the Holy Bible, New Living Translation, copyright © 1996, 2004. Used by permission of Tyndale House Publishers, Inc., Wheaton, Illinois 60189. All rights reserved.

FaithWords
Hachette Book Group
1290 Avenue of the Americas,
New York, NY 10104

www.faithwords.com

Printed in the United States of America

LSC-C

Originally published in hardcover by Hachette Book Group.

First trade edition: September 2014

10   9   8   7

FaithWords is a division of Hachette Book Group, Inc.
The FaithWords name and logo are trademarks of Hachette Book Group, Inc.

The Hachette Speakers Bureau provides a wide range of authors for speaking events. To find out more, go to www.hachettespeakersbureau.com or call (866) 376-6591.

The publisher is not responsible for websites (or their content) that are not owned by the publisher.

The Library of Congress has cataloged the hardcover edition as follows:
Jeremiah, David, 1941–
    God loves you : he always has—he always will / David Jeremiah. — 1st ed.
        p. cm.
    Includes bibliographical references.
    ISBN 978-0-446-56597-4 (hardcover)—ISBN 978-1-4555-2262-0 (large print hardcover)   1. God—Love.   I. Title.
    BT140.J47 2012
    231'.6—dc23
                                                                        2012021759

ISBN 978-0-446-56598-1 (pbk.)

For as long as I can remember Dr. Billy Graham has been telling people that God loves them. He has preached the Gospel in almost every country in the world and to more people in live audiences than anyone else in history. By conservative estimates he has proclaimed the good news of God's love to nearly 215 million people. And he has been doing this from before he was ordained in 1939—that's almost three-quarters of a century. Thank you, Dr. Graham, for your faithful life of ministry—and for always keeping the main thing, the main thing.

CONTENTS

ACKNOWLEDGMENTS

On more than one occasion I have been asked about the process of writing a book. As I was writing *God Loves You*, I discovered a phrase that is a pretty accurate description of the process: "relentless incrementalism"—taking each phase of the process seriously and pouring oneself into it. At each stage there is nothing more important than continuing to learn and move forward—whether the day's writing yields two pages or just two words.

I have found that the writing of a book can be divided into six steps: inspiration, incubation, investigation, creation, publication, and circulation. And at each intersection of the journey, there are people who help—each in their own and unique ways.

There is no greater source of inspiration than the Word of God and prayer. I am also inspired daily by the people I meet and the books I read. As a pastor, I write first of all to minister the Word of God to the people God has entrusted to me, the people at Shadow Mountain Community Church. But no one person inspires me more than my wife. Thank you, Donna, for the hours you have spent encouraging, listening, and sharpening my vision for this project. And thank you for loving me with the love of our great God.

Next comes a period of incubation. Once I have settled on a topic, I have found it necessary to take time to reflect on the message of the book and to truly understand the issues. This is a time of excitement, angst, and solitude. Thank you, Diane Sutherland and Barbara Boucher, for guarding my schedule and freeing me to pursue the things God has called me to do.

As ideas and thoughts begin to grow, the hard work of investigation is now in full bloom. During this time, articles flow in and books are piled high, as I try to read everything I can get my hands on. My friends Luke Thompson and Dr. Chuck Emert provided many articles, books, illustrations, and ideas during the writing of this book.

Next comes the creation of the manuscript. Here, there is much editorial work to be done. I would like to thank Tom Williams and Beau Sager for their attention to detail. And it has also been a pleasure to work with Rob Suggs and William Kruidenier one more time. Thank you for adjusting your schedules so that you could add your creative touch to this project.

As the book enters the publication stage, my literary agent Sealy Yates gets involved, coordinating the finished project with the publishing firm. This is the third book I have written for FaithWords, and I have enjoyed working once again with my editor Joey Paul.

The circulation of the book has become a very high priority for us at Turning Point. As a ministry, we believe it is our responsibility not only to produce the book but to promote it and see that it gets before as many readers as possible. My son David Michael oversees this process. Paul Joiner produces the incredible creativity that drives the process and Kevin Small is the genius behind the plan.

To all of you who have been a part of this "relentless incrementalism," and, most important, to the God who loves us relentlessly, thank you.

Dr. David Jeremiah
San Diego, California
June 1, 2012

INTRODUCTION

What the World Needs Now

❧

These last few years have been some of the most remarkable in my lifetime. I would guess the same has been true for you.

In 2008, I felt compelled to write a book about world events and what the Bible had to say about them. As I was completing that book, a worldwide economic crisis suddenly arrived. I knew the timing was providential.

Over the ensuing months, as current events continued to take new twists, I felt the need to respond with works that offered guidance through the most confusing, perplexing events of our generation. This meant writing about the world and the shape it was in, so I wrote about distressing events in government, distressing events in our culture, and distressing events on the world stage. I felt humbled that God would use me during such times as I worked hard to obey Paul's admonition to "preach the word! Be ready in season and out of season. Convince, rebuke, exhort, with all longsuffering and teaching" (2 Timothy 4:2).

As I finished those projects and stepped back from the chaos, I was reminded of a truth that seemed to have been marginalized during the confusing days I have just described: *God is love.* I stopped and thanked God that, with everything we were living through and all the cautions and admonitions I was responsible to deliver, we still served such a wonderful, loving God; that no matter how much despair burdens humanity, our God still loves us and counts us as His precious children—and *nothing* can change that.

And I thought, *Does everyone realize this? That God is still love? Has anyone told them lately?*

I did some checking on what kinds of books were being published, particularly books about God. And I was surprised that the simple message of God's love was being largely ignored. I knew what God wanted me to do. He wanted me to tell people, in the midst of such dark times, that God loves them; that He always *has* loved them; and that He always *will* love them. The title came together in my mind—something that doesn't always happen up front in the writing process: *God Loves You: He Always Has—He Always Will.*

I knew those were the right words. People needed fresh assurance of those truths. So I went to the Word of God one more time on this topic, looking at the love story that flows through the thousands of years of history that make up our Bible. I studied the love that God has for His children, following the rich pageant of His pursuit from Old to New Testaments, and time after time I was moved to tears by the majesty, the grace, the staggering insistence of His abiding affection for every citizen on Planet Earth.

Not only did all *people* in general need this message; *I* needed it.

As I studied to produce these chapters, I was reminded of what I've always known, but needed to be reminded of again: love isn't simply a Christian message—it's *the* Christian message. The Gospel—the "good news"—is that regardless of our human failings, God loves us.

There are plenty of details to teach about and preach about and write about and talk about, and each is important in its own way. But this is our headline news. This is what the world desperately needs to know, and we are responsible to tell them.

However, I also need to point out that, even if this is the greatest and most exciting news about God—it's not the *only* news about God. In this book, I've kept to the subject of God's love because there's plenty to say about the topic. But I want to be certain no one draws the conclusion that since God is love, this somehow rules out His other attributes, attributes that all orthodox Christians have recognized from the beginning. God's love cannot be allowed to obscure His holiness and His justice.

A popular song from several decades ago declared, "What the World Needs Now Is Love." And I have to agree—as long as the love the world is given is the true love of God. I don't know of anything the world needs now, or at any other time, more than the love of God. Only the love of God can remove the barrier of sin that separates mankind from God—"For God so loved the world that He gave His only begotten Son" (John 3:16). And only the love of God gives us hope in the face of disappointment and despair—"[Nothing] shall be able to separate us from the love of God" (Romans 8:39).

God desires to give you the gift of His love. But a gift must be received. If someone gives you a Christmas gift, and you leave it under the tree and never unwrap it, you haven't really received it.

My point is that the giving of a gift is one half of a transaction. The transaction doesn't become real and doesn't take effect until that gift is accepted, opened, identified, and appreciated. In the same way, it's not enough that God simply offers His love. He expects us to receive it.

This has been one of the more personally rewarding projects I've worked on, and I've worked on a few. As I delivered each of these messages to the church I pastor, Shadow Mountain Community Church in El Cajon, California, I was aware of the power of this topic as people interacted with the teaching. It has absolutely nothing to do with my preaching abilities, and everything to do with the eagerness of the Holy Spirit to comfort, encourage, and revitalize the human spirit with the message of God's eternal love.

As I retold the story of the prodigal son, I felt that our people were experiencing God's love in fresh and soul-freeing ways. Most of them had heard it as many times as I'd spoken it, yet that story never loses its power; it never fails to pull us in so that we become the characters and play out our own issues.

As I preached John 3:16, the thesis statement of the Gospel message, I could feel our people glorying in each word of the verse, each phrase, each implication. Again, I can't imagine there were too many people in that room who weren't familiar with "For God so loved the world…" And yet, there is special power in that simple, elegant, ageless sentence.

It's the same as singing "Amazing Grace" or hearing the "Hallelujah Chorus." There's no statute of limitations to prevent the hair from rising on the backs of our necks. We know we're on holy ground with certain verses (though all are inspired), certain pieces of music (though many are wonderful)—and certain messages.

The love of God is one of those messages. It's a basket of fishes and loaves that keeps replenishing itself. It's a feast for the heart, mind, and soul. My prayer is that these chapters minister to you in the reading, in the same way that they have ministered to me in the preaching and the writing.

> In praise of our God—
> who loves you,
> who always has,
> who always will,

> Dr. David Jeremiah

ONE

God Is Love

Because Your lovingkindness is better than life,
My lips shall praise You.

—PSALM 63:3

In the days when the great evangelist Dwight L. Moody was preaching in Chicago, a poor drunkard stumbled up the steps to the front door of Moody's church. The man pushed the door open, scanned the room, and saw no one inside. His eyes, however, were drawn to a large sign hanging above the pulpit that read "God Is Love." It struck him—with anger. He slammed the door, and staggered down the steps, muttering, "God is not love. If God was love He would love me, and He doesn't love a miserable man like me. It isn't true."

He went on his way, but those words were burning inside him, *God is love. God is love. God is love...* He couldn't resist, *Was it true... is it possible?* After a while he turned around, retraced his steps, and entered the church again—confused and desperate. By now the people had gathered, and as Moody began to preach the man slipped into a seat in the back corner.

He wept during the entire sermon as anger and confusion began to give way to joy and hope.

Afterward, Moody made his way to the door to shake hands with the people as they left. But the man didn't leave. He remained in his seat, weeping. Moody came over, sat down beside him, and asked, "What are you crying about, my friend? What was it in the sermon that touched your heart?"

"Oh, Mr. Moody, I didn't hear a word that you spoke tonight," the man responded. "It's those words up there over your pulpit, 'God Is Love,' that broke my heart." Moody sat down and explained to him the depths of God's love. The man listened and gave his heart to God, understanding for the first time that God really did love him.[1]

In her autobiography, *Over Mountain or Plain or Sea*, Trula Cronk, who served as a missionary in India for twenty-four years, tells of a little girl who visited her house one evening and stayed just a little longer than she intended. Darkness fell, and she was afraid to walk home. Trula explained that she should not be afraid, saying, "Dolan, God loves you and He will take care of you as you walk to your house." The little girl replied very solemnly, "No, memsahib, God does not love little girls."[2]

Trula Cronk was never able to forget that misguided statement, and it made her want to tell all little girls everywhere that God is love, and He does indeed love them.

There are many souls in this world who, like that little Indian girl and the drunken man in Moody's hall, believe for one reason or another that God does not love them. Maybe they have suffered misfortunes that convinced them that God does not care. Or maybe they believe they have committed sins that caused God to turn His back on them. Or maybe they believe that God simply favors certain classes or races or genders and does not love the others.

Like Trula Cronk, I have a burden to dispel this grievous misunderstanding. I have a burden to tell you that God is love, and that He deeply, stubbornly, and eternally insists on loving every individual on the face of the planet. It doesn't matter who you are or what you have done. As speaker and author Max Lucado has said, "You can't fall beyond His love."[3] God's love includes even people you may have trouble loving: That person who cut you off in traffic—God loves him. That woman who was rude at the grocery store—God loves her, too. That entire nation of people across the ocean that you deeply mistrust—God loves its every citizen. As a matter of fact, God loves *you*.

This is the most important fact in your life. *God* loves you. The eternal, self-existent Being who created and sustains everything that exists dearly loves you. The profound thought of God's love should begin and end your every day. It should define your every goal, your every action.

And He doesn't merely like you when you do well; He is personally and passionately committed to your good, even when you fail. God *loves* you. What would happen if that three-word sentence became the theme of your life—if you let it change everything about you and your world?

Let's see if we can find out.

The Declaration of God's Love

The Bible tells us that God is love. The apostle John writes, "He who does not love does not know God, for God is love" (1 John

4:8). He reiterates this truth a few sentences later: "God is love, and he who abides in love abides in God, and God in him" (v. 16).

It is important that we avoid two common mistakes when considering the statement "God is love." The first is to invert the equation and insist that "love is God." This is a serious error because there are many false loves that bear little or no resemblance to the perfect love of God. A man may "love" his mistress, but this is not God's love. These false loves must never be equated with His love.

Secondly, we cannot make the mistake of subordinating all of God's attributes to His love. There is more to God than love. For example, He is all-knowing, He is everywhere present, He is infinite, He is eternal, and He is just. And John can even write "God *is* light" (1 John 1:5). Any time we discuss His love, we must remember that God "may display one attribute or another at a given time, [but] no quality is independent of or preeminent over any of the others. Whenever God displays His wrath, He is still love. When He shows His love, He does not abandon His holiness."[4]

However, we must recognize the force of the apostle's declaration that God is love. In fact John Stott has called it "the most comprehensive and sublime of all biblical affirmations about God's being."[5] So what does the apostle mean when he says that God "is" love? He is telling us something about the nature and essence of God. It's not merely that God loves, it's that God *is* love. Everything He does is rooted in and motivated by love. He made the world because He is love. He formed human beings because He is love. And He rules the universe in love. In other words, John is reminding us that when we think of God and the world He created, we should never forget about His love.

Before we can go much further in this discussion, we need to do some additional disentangling. Just as people tend to be confused about who God is, they're also confused about what love is.

Bartlett's Familiar Quotations lists approximately thirteen hundred different definitions, reflections, and opinions on the subject of love, from the sappy to the abstract to the perverse.[6] Everyone talks about love, everyone experiences some form of it, and everyone is driven by the need to give and receive it. But false ideas of love are tearing the world apart—homes, hearts, even nations. Why does this happen? Christian philosopher Peter Kreeft points out that "the more important a thing is, the more counterfeits there are. There are no counterfeit paper clips, but plenty of counterfeit religions."[7]

Counterfeit ideas of love are all around us. Kindness is often a counterfeit for love. Discipline causes pain, which seems unkind, so parents withhold it in the name of love. But authentic love will administer discipline to achieve a long-term good for the child. Sex is often misused as a counterfeit of love, causing unmarried couples to be led down the dead-end path of temporary pleasures instead of the harder but more rewarding path of a long-term marriage commitment.

Those who have suffered from common abuses of love are often skeptical of love from any source, including God. If your heart is broken romantically, you face the danger of concluding that all love, including God's, is just as unstable. If you have a troubled relationship with your human father, you might conclude that your heavenly Father is just as unreliable. These mistaken ideas about God can be devastating, but they are not uncommon.

We cannot afford to make broad judgments about love or God from our limited personal experiences. Nor can we look to pop culture as any kind of authority—songs or sitcoms or soaps or cinema. We might as well get our idea of the beach from a child's sandbox. Better to go to the ultimate authority on both God and love. The Bible must be our guide.

In the Bible the love of God is like a multifaceted diamond: Each glistening facet reveals some blindingly beautiful truth about God. For this is where the quest for love leads—to an encounter with God Himself. To begin to understand love, we must begin to understand God. And to begin to understand God, we must begin in no other place than the revelation of His love in the Bible.

The Momentous Task of Describing God's Love

I am going to do my very best to describe God's love. But I must warn you, when I have said everything I can possibly say about the love of God, I will barely have touched it. In many respects I share the feeling of Frederick M. Lehman, who wrote these words to the well-known gospel song "The Love of God":

The love of God is greater far
than tongue or pen can ever tell;
It goes beyond the highest star
and reaches to the lowest hell.
Could we with ink the ocean fill,
and were the skies of parchment made,
were every stalk on earth a quill,

and every man a scribe by trade,
to write the love of God above
would drain the ocean dry.
Nor could the scroll contain the whole,
though stretched from sky to sky.[8]

In spite of our inability to fathom the full scope of God's love, He has revealed it to us in many ways that we can clearly understand. Exploring what He has said and demonstrated of His love will help us to grasp, within the range of our limitations, how dearly and passionately God loves us.

God's Love Is Uncaused

Our common experiences in life teach us that we must earn love. We must meet certain standards or conditions that will cause others to love us because of our good actions, attributes, or attractiveness. This is a weight we were not created to carry, a burden that leads to addictions and despair. Henri Nouwen explains:

The world says: "Yes, I love you *if* you are good-looking, intelligent, and wealthy. I love you *if* you have a good education, a good job, and good connections. I love you *if* you produce much, sell much, and buy much." There are endless "ifs" hidden in the world's love. These "ifs" enslave me, since it is impossible to respond adequately to all of them. The world's love is and always will be conditional. As long as I keep looking for my true self in the world of conditional love, I will remain "hooked" to the world—trying, failing, and trying again. It is a world that fosters addictions because what it offers cannot satisfy the deepest craving of my heart.[9]

In our human relationships, we generally do not love those who manifest unattractive or repelling actions or attributes. But God's love for us is not like that; it is free, spontaneous, unprompted, and uninfluenced. There is nothing we can do to cause God to love us, and there is nothing we can do to prevent Him from loving us. God loves us simply because He is God, not because we have done anything to cause it. Author John Ortberg brings this truth home to our hearts when he writes, "Nothing you will ever do could make God love you more than he does right now: not greater achievement, not greater beauty, not wider recognition, not even greater levels of spirituality and obedience. Nothing you have ever done could make God love you any less: not any sin, not any failure, not any guilt, not any regret."[10]

When writing to his protégé, Timothy, Paul described God as the One "who has saved us and called us with a holy calling, not according to our works, but according to His own purpose and grace which was given to us in Christ Jesus before time began" (2 Timothy 1:9). To the Ephesians he wrote that God's love for us is "according to the good pleasure of His will" (Ephesians 1:5).

Contemplative author and speaker Brennan Manning calls this concept "love without motive." He writes:

As a man, I love the Jersey shore, Handel's *Messiah*, hot fudge, and my wife Roslyn. I love what I find congenial or appealing. I love someone for what I find in him or her. But God is not like that. The God and Father of Jesus loves men and women not for what He finds in them, but for what He finds in them of Himself. It is not because men and women are good that He loves them, nor only good men and women that He loves. It is because He is so unspeakably, unimaginably good that He loves men and women in their sin. It is not that He detects what is congenial and appealing and He responds to us with His favor. He is the source of love. He acts: He does not react. He is love without motive.[11]

Because God is God, He does as He pleases, and it pleases Him to love us without cause. Think of the first days of the first man and woman ever to exist. God made Adam and Eve, so they brought Him no secrets or surprises. They could offer Him nothing He did not already have. He loved them simply because it was His plan to do so. From the beginning of time, God does not love us because we love Him. According to the apostle John, it is exactly the opposite: "We love Him because He first loved us" (1 John 4:19).

God's Love Is Unreasonable

Your first thought may be that it's blatantly presumptuous for me to call God unreasonable. But I am not using the term in the derogatory way we usually apply it. Indeed, as you will see, I am eternally grateful that God's love is unreasonable.

From the day Adam and Eve sinned against God, mankind has continued to rebel, to drift away from Him, and to break every commandment given to us for our good. It would seem that we have given back to God nothing but disappointment and heartbreak. Throughout the Old Testament, we see that if God had responded to us "reasonably" and reacted the way we do, He would have abandoned or destroyed humanity long ago.

Though God had countless reasons to have lowered the curtain on the human drama, He had none, humanly speaking, to press on with His love in the face of humanity's persistent failings. This is why I say that God's love is unreasonable. Though from a human perspective His love is beyond all reason, we simply need to remember that His thoughts and ways are as far beyond ours as the heavens are from the earth (Isaiah 55:8–9). So while His love is "unreasonable," it is not irrational; it bears divine reason, which our finite human minds cannot fathom.

In Romans 5:6–8, Paul brings the reality of God's "unreasonable love" down to a level we can all understand. He raises the question: "What would it take for any of us to die for another human being?" Very few people would give their lives even for a good man or a righteous person. But "God demonstrates His own love toward us, in that while we were still sinners, Christ died for us" (v. 8).

It is possible to consider—it is reasonable, though something of a stretch—that someone might be willing to die for a good person. In Charles Dickens's novel *A Tale of Two Cities*, we see this kind of noble sacrifice fictionally demonstrated when the British barrister Sydney Carton willingly goes to the guillotine in the place of Charles Darnay. Carton's sacrifice seems "reasonable" because he has led a somewhat dissipated life and has little to live for, while the falsely accused Darnay is a man of great honor, courage, and virtue.

In an extreme case and under certain dire circumstances and for an exceptionally good person, you or I might possibly find it in our hearts to make such a sacrifice. But for the vilest of criminals, a person who had made no contribution to society, and who seemed to delight in being an enemy of all that is good and right—would you die for that person? Your answer would probably be a quick and unmitigated "Hardly!" And that's a perfectly reasonable answer.

Yet that's exactly what Christ did! He died for you and for me, card-carrying sinners and enemies of God (Romans 5:10). It was in Christ's sacrifice that God demonstrated just how unreasonable His love is. His love is so great, so far-reaching, so overpowering that Jesus Christ, the only perfectly righteous person who ever lived, willingly died in the place of unrighteous men and women such as you and me. We should never cease to thank God that His love is so unreasonable.

God's Love Is Unending

Grappling with the magnitude of God's love forces us back to the basics of who He is. The unending nature of His love is inseparably connected to one aspect of His own nature, which the Bible reveals in several places: He is "the Everlasting God...the Alpha and the Omega, the Beginning and the End...who is and who was and who is to come, the Almighty" (Genesis 21:33; Revelation 1:8). He "inhabits eternity" (Isaiah 57:15). He is "the King eternal" (1 Timothy 1:17). Of Him, the psalmist wrote, "Even from everlasting to everlasting, You are God" (Psalm 90:2).

All of these passages speak of God's eternal nature. They

tell us that He existed always and will always exist. We know that God is a person, but that does not mean He shares the limitations of human personhood. Unlike us, He is not limited by time or space, because He created them both. Because He created time and stands above it, He has immediate access to the entire scope of time from beginning to end. Because He created space and stands above it, He can be at all places in the universe simultaneously. He transcends the ticking of the clock and pinpointing on the map. We cannot even imagine these mind-bending concepts because none of us have ever taken a step outside of time or space. Unlike God, we can occupy only one specific location and one fleeting moment.

God's love reflects His eternal absolutes. God's love is eternal, like He is: more durable than time, wider and deeper than the incalculable dimensions of the cosmos. As He tells us, "I have loved you with an everlasting love; therefore with loving-kindness I have drawn you" (Jeremiah 31:3).

God's perfect love for you existed deep in the depths of eternity even before time began. He created billions of wondrous galaxies, most of which no telescope will ever see; He created lovely, atomic-level worlds no microscope will ever penetrate; He knows all, He transcends all, and He is magnificent beyond human imagining. Yet His love for you is so close and intimate that it far outshines that of doting human fathers who, when they first see their newborn infant, often count the baby's fingers and toes. God actually numbers the hairs on your head. He knows and cherishes the tiniest details of your life, He watches over you every moment, and He has a plan for your life that has been in His heart longer than the world has existed.

In the modern classic *Knowing God*, J. I. Packer gives a beautiful explanation of what it means to realize that our lives are set within the perfect and constant love of God:

What matters supremely...is not...the fact that I know God, but the larger fact which underlies it—that *he knows me*. I am graven on the palms of his hands. I am never out of his mind. All my knowledge of him depends on his sustained initiative in knowing me. I know him because he first knew me, and continues to know me. He knows me as a friend, one who loves me; and there is no moment when his eye is off me, or his attention distracted from me, and no moment, therefore, when his care falters.

There is unspeakable comfort...in knowing that God is constantly taking knowledge of me in love and watching over me for my good. There is tremendous relief in knowing that his love to me is utterly realistic, based at every point on prior knowledge of the worst about me, so that no discovery now can disillusion him about me, in the way that I am so often disillusioned about myself, and quench his determination to bless me.[12]

In other words, there is incredible hope for those who are disappointed in themselves. God's love for you doesn't depend upon your perfection or achievement. It's not that He looks away or isn't concerned when you stumble. He sees it all, and He continues to love you with a love that is as eternal as eternity.

God's Love Is Unlimited

Solomon, the son of David and the wisest man of his age, built a majestic temple to the glory of God. It was a place for worshippers to experience the Lord's presence, a place where God had promised to meet His people in a special way. Even though this temple was a wonder of the ancient world, Solomon reflected on the inadequacy of anything built with hands to contain the magnificence of God. He said, "Behold, heaven and the heaven of heavens cannot contain You. How much less this temple which I have built!" (2 Chronicles 6:18).

Here is the paradox. We know that God is as far beyond us as the deepest reaches of the universe. Yet at the same time, "He is not far from each one of us; for in Him we live and move and have our being" (Acts 17:27–28).

Since God is both beyond us and beside us, His love also exists beyond us, beside us, and within us. His love is to us as the sea is to a fish: The sea is huge and expansive beyond the limited range of any fish, yet in it the fish lives, moves, and has its very being.

Psalm 139 is a hymn to the omnipresence of God, but its observations are true for His love as well. Where God is, love is. Allow me to illustrate this wonderful truth by replacing the terms for God with terms designating His love in this poem:

Where can I go from Your love?
Or where can I flee from Your love?
If I ascend into heaven, Your love is there.
If I make my bed in hell, behold, Your love is there.
If I take the wings of the morning,

And dwell in the uttermost parts of the sea,
Even there Your love *shall lead me,*
And Your love *shall hold me.*
If I say, "Surely the darkness shall fall on me,"
Even the night shall be light about me;
Indeed the darkness shall not hide me from Your love.

—PSALM 139:7–12

Psalm 139 reminds us that God and His love are always present with His people. As a pastor, I have listened to many people describe the same feelings as the drunken man at Moody's church and the young Indian girl in Trula Cronk's story. They are convinced that they have wandered beyond the reach of God's love. They say to me, "God could never love me because…" The truth is that there is no *because* that will fill in that blank. It doesn't matter how you complete the sentence, you come up with a wrong answer. *God could never love* is a false premise. It can never happen to you or to anyone else.

But we struggle to wrap our minds around that truth because, in our experiences with fellow humans, we can think of so many ways to complete the sentence "Bill could never love me because," or "Susan could never love me because." When we seek the love of other people, we factor in the assumed requirement that we have to be perfect. But divine math doesn't work the way human math does. When you add all of your flaws together and conclude that God cannot possibly love you, His answer is that He loves you anyway.

Since we encounter so few people who love without limits, we are prone to embrace doubts about God's love for us. I believe that is one reason why the apostle Paul prayed that believers would be "rooted and grounded in love...able to comprehend with all the saints what is the width and length and depth and height—to know the love of Christ which passes knowledge" (Ephesians 3:17–19).

We want to ask Paul, "How can we comprehend such a love? How can we measure something with no width or length or depth or height? How can we know that which 'passes knowledge'?"

The answer is that we cannot—unless we receive help from above. And we do. Here's Paul again: "The love of God has been poured out in our hearts by the Holy Spirit who was given to us" (Romans 5:5).

This does not mean that the Holy Spirit has been given to us so that we can love God. It means rather that God has poured out His Spirit into our hearts so that we might begin to understand how great God's love is for us. So great is His love for His own that it is necessary for the third person of the Trinity to be dispatched into our hearts that we might be able to comprehend it.

God's Love Is Unchanging

In a world that moves and changes as fast as ours, there is one thing that remains constant: the character of God. "I am the LORD, I do not change," God said through the prophet Malachi (3:6). The psalmist wrote that "the counsel of the LORD stands forever, the plans of His heart to all generations" (Psalm 33:11); and "You are the same, and Your years will have no end" (Psalm 102:27). James describes God as "the Father of lights, with whom there is no variation or shadow of turning" (1:17).

What a wonderful thought to know that because God is unchanging, His love is unchanging. God's love is constant in its faithfulness and continual in its expression; it neither diminishes nor disappears, regardless of our circumstances. In his book *The Pleasures of God*, John Piper writes:

Sometimes we joke and say about marriage, "The honeymoon is over." But that's because we are finite. We can't sustain a honeymoon level of intensity and affection. We can't foresee the irritations that come with long-term familiarity. We can't stay as fit and handsome as we were then. We can't come up with enough new things to keep the relationship that fresh. But God says his joy over his people is like a bridegroom over a bride. He is talking about honeymoon intensity and honeymoon pleasure and honeymoon energy and excitement and enthusiasm and enjoyment. He is trying to get into our hearts what he means when he says he rejoices over us *with all his heart*.

And add to this, that with God the honeymoon never ends. He is infinite in power and wisdom and creativity and love. And so he has no trouble sustaining a honeymoon level of intensity; he can foresee all the future quirks of our personality and has decided he will keep what's good and change what isn't; he will always be as handsome as he ever was, and will see that we get more and more beautiful forever; and he is infinitely creative to think of new things to do together so that there will be no boredom for the next trillion ages of millenniums.[13]

The thought of being loved forever as deeply and continuously as a newlywed bride should change who we are. How can that thought not make us eager to respond to God and love Him in return?

We need only look to Jesus for the model of unchanging, ever-enduring love. Toward the end of His three-year earthly ministry, Christ must have felt deep disappointment over the lack of spiritual maturity in His disciples. Thomas doubted Him. Peter denied Him three times. Judas betrayed Him into the hands of His enemies. His three most trusted disciples fell asleep when He implored them to watch and pray during His time of greatest crisis. While He was beginning to agonize over the Cross and its implications, they were arguing over which of them would be the greatest in the future kingdom.

On His last evening of freedom, Christ humbled Himself as a servant and washed the feet of His disciples. Then He sat down to speak quietly to them one last time before His execution. Even though He knew Judas was at that moment moving through the streets to betray Him to the authorities, Jesus expressed to His friends His deep love for them and urged them to love one another: "As the Father loved Me, I also have loved you; abide in My love" (John 15:9).

Even as these disciples demonstrated their characteristic misunderstandings, He called them His friends, not His servants. He knew his own execution was only hours away, yet He concerned Himself with comforting these flawed and stumbling men. He spoke of preparing them a place in heaven and about the coming of another comforter: the Holy Spirit. But again and again He returned to the theme of His constant love for them.

The apostle John summarizes: "Having loved His own who were in the world, He loved them to the end" (John 13:1).

It didn't matter that His soul was in turmoil, that He would soon perspire drops like blood as He agonized in prayer. He kept on loving—and not just the eleven disciples around Him. "I do not pray for these alone," He said, "but also for those who will believe in Me through their word" (John 17:20). As this prayer indicates, His love reached across time to this moment—to you, to me. In the shadow of the Cross, the power of His love never waned for a second. In a world that was condemning Him, and with excruciating pain and cruelty facing Him, His uppermost thoughts were of love for us—of helping us to understand the love of God.

Nothing that happened to Jesus could dislodge His tenacious attachment to us. He is a living picture of the unchanging love we're describing. His love is perfect and always has been perfect, meaning it never varies, grows, or diminishes. In other words, the love He will have for us in the future will never be greater or lesser than the love He has for us now. And His love for us now is no lesser or greater than it has been from eternity past. His love for us is nothing less than constant, unchanging, and eternal.

There is a good side and a better side to God's unchanging love. The good side is that God won't wake up in the morning and decide He's had enough of us. The better side is that even when we wake up in the morning and decide we've had enough of Him, He will still love us.

When the Bible tells us that God's love is unlimited, I think it means God's love is something like the love of the mother in this story told by Michael Brown:

A friend told me about a boy who was the apple of his parents' eyes. Tragically, in his mid-teens, the boy's life went awry. He dropped out of school and began associating with the worst kind of crowds. One night he staggered into his house at 3:00 a.m., completely drunk. His mother slipped out of bed and left her room. The father followed, assuming that his wife was in the kitchen, perhaps crying. Instead he found her at her son's bedside, softly stroking his matted hair as he lay passed out drunk on the covers. "What are you doing?" the father asked, and the mother simply answered, "He won't let me love him when he's awake."[14]

God's Love Is Uncomplicated

The crowning achievement of Switzerland's Karl Barth, one of the twentieth century's most prolific theologians, was his *Church Dogmatics*, a theological work containing more than six million words. It is told that when Barth made his only trip to the United States in 1962, a student asked him to summarize the broad-ranging biblical theology he had written in this vast work. His audience awaited his reply, expecting to be amazed by a profound statement from the learned man. After a short pause, he said, "Jesus loves me this I know, for the Bible tells me so."[15] The audience indeed got something profound, but they also got something uncomplicated. In a dozen simple words, Karl Barth summarized the essence of all Christian theology in a way that a child could grasp as easily as a world-class scholar.

John 3:16, the most beloved of all Bible verses, captures the essence of what God's love means for us: God loved and gave, so that we need only believe. We could write volumes of books about the subject and find new areas yet to be examined. Yet this vast tree of theological knowledge springs from a single seed, plain in its simplicity: *God loves*. Though He loves in profound ways we can never grasp, He has expressed that love in terms that all humanity can understand. We don't have to plumb the depths of theology to understand what "I love you" means when spoken in the language of the heart.

God's Love Is Unconditional

Most Christians are familiar with the word *agape*, which is a term used to describe God's unconditional love. For the writers of the New Testament, the idea of God loving imperfect people in a perfect way was so radical and new that only the relatively obscure word *agape* could capture it. J. I. Packer explains: "The Greek and Roman world of the New Testament times had never dreamed of such love; its gods were often credited with lusting after women, but never with loving sinners; and the New Testament writers had to introduce what was virtually a new Greek word, *agape*, to express the love of God as they knew it."[16]

This loving, pursuing God was clearly visible in the Old Testament, but for many who do only a cursory reading of the Old Testament, this can be difficult to see. In the New Testament, however, God's love is fully manifest through the revelation of Jesus Christ. It's no wonder that the message left Jerusalem and took hold of the Mediterranean world so rapidly. It said that God loves everyone—not merely a single nation, tribe, or a sect; it said that God desires to save every human being from the web of his or her own sin, and that He wants nothing in return but the joy of our fellowship. There had never before been such a message.

Unconditional love flies in the face of the most basic drives of human nature. We tend to love conditionally; we love only those we consider worthy. God's love is nothing like that. Christians see the unconditional quality of God's love displayed on the Cross. It is love for the utterly unworthy, a love that proceeds from a God who loves simply because He is love. Such a love could never be conceived by men. Only God would dare to love in such a way.

The Direction of God's Love

On the face of it, this is an easy question: Who does God love? All of us, of course. But "all of us" includes several identifiable groups. Let's explore these special recipients of God's love and how the Scriptures describe His love for them.

God Loves His Son

The preeminent recipient of God's love is His own Son, Jesus Christ. On two occasions—first at Jesus' baptism and again at His transfiguration—God the Father declared, "This is My beloved Son, in whom I am well pleased" (Matthew 3:17; 17:5).

In His final intimate conversation with His disciples, described earlier, Jesus acknowledged His Father's love: "You loved Me before the foundation of the world" (John 17:24).

Earlier in that same Gospel we read, "For the Father loves

the Son, and shows Him all things that He Himself does" (John 5:20). We cannot fully appreciate the meaning of John 3:16 and the sacrifice that verse alludes to unless we realize the deep and abiding love of the Father for His only Son.

God Loves Israel

One of the central themes of the Old Testament is God's love for His people Israel, whom He specially chose to bring His blessing to the world. Again and again almighty God expresses His enduring love for the Jewish people. For example, the prophet Jeremiah tells us that God will be faithful to Israel as long as the sun, moon, and stars shine, the waves roar, the heavens remain immeasurable, and the earth's foundations remain undiscoverable (Jeremiah 31:35–37).

The prophet Isaiah spoke often about God's special love for Israel:

> Can a woman forget her nursing child,
> And not have compassion on the son of her womb?
> Surely they may forget,
> Yet I will not forget you.
> See, I have inscribed you on the palms of My hands;
> Your walls are continually before Me.
>
> —ISAIAH 49:15–16

One of the most striking word pictures in all Scripture describes how God cares for and protects Israel. Two times Israel is called "the apple of [God's] eye" (Deuteronomy 32:10; Zechariah 2:8). The Hebrew term for "apple of the eye" actually means "the little man of the eye," referring to the tiny reflection one sees of oneself when looking into another person's eye. That "little man" in the pupil of God's eye is Israel. He is always looking upon the people of Abraham, Isaac, and Jacob. They are reflected in His eye, just as He desires them to be a reflection of Him.

God's love for Israel does not mean He loves everyone else less. But because He chose them to bear a special assignment to implement His plan to redeem all of us, they have a special place in His heart.

God Loves Those Who Believe in Christ

If we are believers in Jesus Christ, then the Father loves us as He loves His own Son. It's an astonishing concept. Yet in that Upper Room on the night of His arrest, Christ prayed this very truth (John 17:23; see also John 16:27).

The love of the Father for the Son is holy and unfathomable. Yet He has promised to love believers in Christ just as deeply and fully, making us His children and full heirs to His kingdom. The apostle Paul says of those who are led by God's Spirit, "These are sons of God" (Romans 8:14). In his Letter to the Colossians, Paul speaks of Christ's followers as "the elect of God, holy and beloved" (3:12). And in his Second Letter to the Thessalonians, he describes God as "our God and Father, who has loved us and given us everlasting consolation and good hope by grace" (2:16).

God's love for believers doesn't mean He doesn't love unbelievers. But as believers in Jesus Christ, we have become children of God. Now God loves us as His own family.

God Loves the World

The most profound expression of God's love is wrapped up in this truth: "For God so loved the world that He gave His only begotten Son, that whoever believes in Him should not perish but have everlasting life" (John 3:16). This world that God loves is a world that man ruined by his fall into sin. Yet man's failure did not quench God's unconditional love. In fact, as Paul tells us, "But God demonstrates His own love toward us, in that while we were still sinners, Christ died for us" (Romans 5:8).

We can also see that God still loves all the world, sinners and saints, in Paul's words to Timothy: "[God] desires all men to be saved and to come to the knowledge of the truth" (1 Timothy 2:4). The apostle Peter affirmed this truth, saying, "The Lord is not slack concerning His promise, as some count slackness, but is longsuffering toward us, not willing that any should perish but that all should come to repentance" (2 Peter 3:9).

No matter how wicked this world may become, no matter how deep into sin it may sink, God's love is unchanging. Jesus compares it to the love of a shepherd for a stray sheep. The shepherd goes into the wilderness to seek and save that lost animal (Luke 15:4).

Make no mistake: God hates sin. But He never stops loving sinners. He never stops going into the tangled wilderness of their failures to rescue them.

God Loves You

Against the backdrop of God's massive love for the world, we could doubt that God's love is also intimate and personal. But nothing could be further from the truth. In his spiritual classic *The Knowledge of the Holy*, A. W. Tozer writes: "The love of God is one of the great realities of the universe, a pillar upon which the hope of the world rests. But it is a personal, intimate thing, too. God does not love populations, He loves people. He loves not masses, but men. He loves us all with a mighty love that has no beginning and can have no end."[17] In a similar but more succinct thought, Saint Augustine is reported to have said, "God loves you as though you are the only person in the world, and He loves everyone the way He loves you."

In his book *The Wisdom of Tenderness*, Brennan Manning tells the story of Edward Farrell, a man who decided to travel from his hometown of Detroit to visit Ireland on a two-week summer vacation, where he would celebrate his uncle's eightieth birthday.

Early on the morning of his uncle's birthday, they went for a walk along the shores of Lake Killarney. As the sun rose, his uncle turned and stared straight into the breaking light. For twenty minutes they stood there in silence, and then his elderly uncle began to skip along the shoreline, a radiant smile on his face.

After catching up with him, Edward asked, "Uncle Seamus, you look very happy. Do you want to tell me why?"

"Yes, lad," the old man said, tears washing down his face. "You see, the Father is very fond of me. Ah, me Father is so very fond of me."[18]

In the moment Uncle Seamus experienced how much he was loved by his Father in heaven, an overwhelming sense of joy flooded his heart. And he began to dance along the shoreline. Have you ever had a moment like that? Have you ever awakened and said, "He really does love me"?

TWO

God Loved You Before You Were Born

❧

Oh, that marvel of conception…
What a miracle of skin and bone, muscle and brain.
You gave me life itself, and incredible love.
You watched and guarded every breath I took.
—JOB 10:10–12 (THE MESSAGE)

Billy Bigelow is a barker—a colorful, fast-talking character who attracts crowds at the gates of an old-fashioned carnival. He is the hero of the classic Rodgers and Hammerstein musical *Carousel*. Bigelow is rowdy, restless, proud, and given to fist-fights and carousing. But something good happens to him at the beginning of the story: He meets and marries Julie Jordan. Their marriage, however, is filled with quarreling. Bigelow has lost his job, and his shady friends invite him to help commit a robbery. Then, as he considers the offer, Billy Bigelow's world is changed. He learns that he and Julie are going to become parents.

To demonstrate Bigelow's deep joy and exhilaration, Rodgers and Hammerstein give their hero a lengthy song called "Soliloquy." It's about three times the length of a typical Broadway song. The macho Bigelow imagines a son, a namesake, who will be rough-and-ready, strong enough to do any job he takes on: "My boy Bill, he'll be tall and tough as a tree, will Bill!" The father-to-be glories over the wonderful possibilities. Maybe he'll be a carnival barker like his old man, or maybe he'll be elected president. Anything is possible for this child.

And then a sudden realization hits Bigelow—*What if the baby is a girl?* The song comes to a screeching halt. But not for long. As he considers the possibility of having a sweet little duplicate of his wife, he warms to the idea and begins to sing of his concerns about how to raise a little girl. But finally, with fists clenched in firm resolve, he bellows at the top of his range, "I'll try, I'll try, I'll try!" Whatever is required, that's what he will do, for a daughter needs a father.

Here's my point in relating this story: It doesn't matter whether Bigelow has a son or a daughter; he is already head-over-heels in love with a child who won't arrive for several months. His life has found a theme.

Tragically, Bigelow concludes that he will need money to be a good father, and he dies trying to steal it. Later, he returns as a spirit to see his little girl grown strong and proud, just as he predicted. *Carousel* gets its ideas of heaven and salvation all wrong, but its depiction of a father's love for his unborn child is right on the money. We recognize it from our own experience.

When a young couple announces that a baby is on the way,

everyone tells them, "It'll change your life!" But the fact is, they are already changed. From the first moment of anticipation, they see themselves in a different light. They find that it's possible to be deeply in love with a tiny human being they've never met. They brim with dreams of the things they'll do with their child—taking trips to the beach, getting a puppy, learning about God. Until that child is born, father and mother will think of little else; after the child is born, they will devote themselves fully to their precious offspring.

Where did this powerful love come from? The answer: It's an inherited trait. We are made in the image of a heavenly Father who felt the same deep joy before we were born, but His love is even more powerful, more boundless. You know that God loves you now, but do you realize that He always has—even before you were born? Even before the world was created? He has loved you from the very foundation of time. Let's explore what the Bible says about God's relationship with you before you were born.

Before You Were Born, God Knew Your Identity

My frame was not hidden from You,
When I was made in secret,
And skillfully wrought in the lowest parts of the earth.
Your eyes saw my substance, being yet unformed.
And in Your book they all were written,
The days fashioned for me,
When as yet there were none of them.

—PSALM 139:15–16

The primary purpose of this passage is to express a truth about God, but it also says something about the psalmist who wrote it. Clearly David considered himself to have been a person even before he was conscious of himself. He was saying, "I, as a person, was covered by Your hand, O Lord, in my mother's womb. I was made in secret and masterfully wrought in the inner recesses of my mother's body."

It is important to note that verse 16 contains the only use of the Hebrew word for *embryo* found in Scripture—translated here as "my substance, being yet unformed." As God was forming you, He was watching over you in love. We know this to be true because the Bible says that "God is love" (1 John 4:8, 16). Everything God does, including overseeing the development of an unborn human child, is carried out in love. Henri Nouwen explains:

> From all eternity we are hidden "in the shadow of God's hand" and "engraved on his palm." Before any human being touches us, God "forms us in secret" and "textures us" in the depth of the earth, and before any human being decides about us, God "knits us together in our mother's womb." God loves us before any human person can show love to us. He loves us with a "first" love, an unlimited, unconditional love, wants us to be his beloved children, and tells us to become as loving as himself.[1]

Think of a baby being born in a stressful situation—perhaps in a car on the way to the hospital. The parents have spent nine months planning for everything to be perfect for their little one's entry into the world. And then the unplanned happens—a late start to the hospital, a traffic jam, a fast labor for the mother. But the baby is born healthy; and once mother and infant are settled in the hospital, the mother coos her love to her baby and apologizes for the rough delivery. If that newborn could speak, he would open his little eyes and say, "It's okay, Mom, I'm fine. God has been loving me from the moment I was conceived. I've been bathed in His love for nine months, and I know you and Dad love me, too."

As far as I know, newborns can't even think such thoughts, much less speak them. Nonetheless, the words I put in the baby's mouth are true: God sees and loves infants in the womb from the moment of conception. That means He has already given them a human identity.

In the passage above, David writes with unmatched poetic eloquence about this loving and attentive heavenly Father who skillfully knits us together in the womb and oversees our development. We also learn that in His infinite wisdom and power, God designs us for our days even as He designs our days for us, writing our future in His book even before it comes to pass. Clearly God knew us and loved us as individual beings with a specific identity before we were born!

Before You Were Born, God Knew Your Complexity

For You formed my inward parts;
You covered me in my mother's womb.
I will praise You, for I am fearfully and wonderfully made;

Marvelous are Your works,
And that my soul knows very well.

—PSALM 139:13–14

Modern technology now allows us to see the astonishing complexity of a developing child with our own eyes. In a 2010 *TED* presentation titled *Conception to Birth—Visualized*, Alexander Tsiaras, mathematician and chief of Scientific Visualization at Yale University, presented a series of incredible images of a child's development in the womb. In his production you can see never-before-viewed videos and photos of the very first cell division, the development of the heart at only twenty-five days, the development of arms and hands at only thirty-two days, and the development of the retinas, nose, and eyes at fifty-two days.

Clearly astounded by what he witnessed in his own images, Tsiaras concluded his talk with these words: "The complexity of these things, the mathematical model of how these things are indeed done, [is] beyond human comprehension. Even though I am a mathematician I look at this with the marvel of, 'How did these instruction sets build that which is us?' It's a mystery, it's magic, it's divinity."[2]

And Bible scholar John Phillips describes the magnificent complexities of our bodies at the cellular level:

We know that every living creature is made up of microscopic cells so small that the letter O on this page would contain between thirty to forty thousand of them. Each microscopic cell is a world in itself, containing an estimated two hundred trillion tiny molecules of atoms. Each cell, in other words, is a micro-universe of almost unbelievable complexity. All these cells put together make up a living creature. Each cell has its own specialized function and each works to an intricate timetable which tells it when to grow, when to divide, when to make hormones, when to die. Every minute of every day some three billion cells in the body die and the same number are created to take their place. During any given moment in the life of any one of these cells, thousands of events are taking place, each one being precisely coordinated at the molecular level by countless triggers. The human body has more than a million million of them— a million in each square inch of skin, thirty billion in the brain, billions of red blood cells in the veins. Obviously such a complicated and unerring development of cells cannot possibly be the result of chance.[3]

The psalmist David knew nothing of the physiological phenomena presented by Mr. Tsiaras or Dr. Phillips—of molecular structures, of cells dividing and multiplying, or even of numbers large enough to describe the massive quantity of cells in the human body. And yet when it came to the bottom line, David knew what these men know. He understood that God's work in fashioning him was marvelous—as indeed it was.

Our Creator is an artist of infinite majesty—a craftsman of breathtaking detail. All He does is driven and guided by His infinite love for you and me.

Before You Were Born, God Knew Your Individuality

Your eyes saw my substance, being yet unformed.
And in Your book they all were written,
The days fashioned for me,
When as yet there were none of them.

—PSALM 139:16

Here David speaks of the unique individuality that was his from his first moments in the womb. From the very beginning, God knew David and ordained what his life was to be. David was not the first to contemplate God's role in the prenatal fashioning of his life. Consider this passage from Job:

Oh, that marvel of conception as you stirred together
semen and ovum—
What a miracle of skin and bone,
muscle and brain!
You gave me life itself, and incredible love.
You watched and guarded every breath I took.

—JOB 10:10–12 (THE MESSAGE)

A few chapters later Job affirms that God begins all human life within the womb: "Did not He who made me in the womb make them? Did not the same One fashion us in the womb?" (Job 31:15).

Writing several generations after David, the prophet Zechariah echoes the same theme, comparing the formation of the spirit within man with the creation of the universe: "Thus says the LORD, who stretches out the heavens, lays the foundation of the earth, and forms the spirit of man within him" (Zechariah 12:1b). The author of Psalm 119 also wrote about God's creative work within the womb: "Your hands have made me and fashioned me" (v. 73).

These biblical writers clearly understood that God initiated the creation of a human being in the womb—not at the moment of birth; not at the moment the baby takes its first breath. They are unambiguously affirming that human life begins not at birth, but at the time God begins to shape and mold the new person into the unique individual that he or she will become—the moment we know as conception.

In describing Mary's visit to her also pregnant cousin, the physician Luke provides a fascinating illustration that validates the full humanity of life in the womb:

> Now Mary arose in those days and went into the hill country with haste, to a city of Judah, and entered the house of Zacharias and greeted Elizabeth. And it happened, when Elizabeth heard the greeting of Mary, that the babe leaped in her womb; and Elizabeth was filled with the Holy Spirit. Then she spoke out with a loud voice and said, "Blessed are you among women, and blessed is the fruit of your womb! But why is this granted to me, that the mother of my Lord should come to me? For indeed, as soon as the voice of your greeting sounded in my ears, the babe leaped in my womb for joy."

—LUKE 1:39–44

Every mother has experienced similar activity within her womb—sometimes quite rambunctious—which leaves her with no doubt that a person is living inside her. The life in Elizabeth's womb already displayed the individuality God had infused into it. The baby's leap of joy reflected the unique future God had planned for this yet-to-be-born child. He was to be known as John the Baptist, whose mission and joy were to prepare the way for Christ.

Science, too, strongly supports the conviction that a child is fully human before birth as much as after. The facts are simply overwhelming.

Dr. Watson A. Bowes of the University of Colorado School of Medicine has stated, "The beginning of a single human life is, from a biological point of view, a simple and straightforward matter—the beginning is conception."[4] And after hearing expert testimony on when human life begins, a 1981 U.S. Senate judiciary subcommittee came to this conclusion: "Physicians, biologists, and other scientists agree that conception marks the beginning of the life of a human being—a being that is alive and is a member of the human species. There is overwhelming agreement on this point in countless medical, biological, and scientific writings."[5]

In his book *A Case for Life*, Scott Klussendorf summarizes these statements with these words: "In short, you didn't *come from* an embryo. You once *were* an embryo. At no point in your prenatal development did you undergo a substantial change or change of nature. You began as a human being and will remain so until death. Sure, you lacked maturity at that early stage of your life (as does any infant), but you were human nonetheless" (italics added).[6]

Both the conviction of mothers and the evidence from science are compelling. But once we consider the place of God in prenatal formation, the argument is settled with authority. God knew and loved you as a fully human person before He ever made you. He loved you as He prepared you for this world in the beauty of human pregnancy. And all along, He had a life and a purpose prepared for you, suited to your unique individuality.

Before You Were Born, God Knew Your Dignity

For by Him all things were created that are in heaven and that are on earth, visible and invisible, whether thrones or dominions or principalities or powers. All things were created through Him and for Him.

—COLOSSIANS 1:16

I would not have wanted to be president of the United States on February 3, 1994. Or vice president. Or a senator or congressman or any other high-ranking member of our government. Those jobs are challenging on any day, but on that day a tiny woman from India made the leaders of the most powerful government in the world feel much smaller. She didn't mean to. She didn't berate or criticize them. In fact, she spoke quite lovingly. She simply talked about how valuable human life is to God.

The late Mother Teresa, founder of the Missionaries of Charity, was invited to speak at the annual National Prayer Breakfast in Washington, D.C. Even standing on a platform, the tiny nun's head was barely visible over the top of the podium. But the room was so quiet that no one failed to hear her message, loud and clear.

Mother Teresa talked about the dignity and value of all life, the worthiness of all human life to be loved, something that everyone gathered at the prayer breakfast could agree with. But halfway through her talk she said,

> I feel that the greatest destroyer of peace today is abortion, because it is a war against the child, a direct killing of the innocent child, murder by the mother herself. And if we accept that a mother can kill even her own child, how can we tell other people not to kill one another?

And then, speaking directly into the room filled with some of the world's most powerful people, she pleaded,

> Please don't kill the child. I want the child. Please give me the child. I am willing to accept any child who would be aborted and to give that child to a married couple who will love the child and be loved by the child.
>
> From our children's home in Calcutta alone, we have saved over 3,000 children from abortion. These children have brought such love and joy to their adopting parents and have grown up so full of love and joy.
>
> If we remember that God loves us, and that we can love others as He loves us, then America can become a sign of peace for the world. From here [in Washington, D.C.], a sign of care for the weakest of the weak—the unborn child—must go out to the world. If you become

a burning light of justice and peace in the world, then really you will be true to what the founders of this country stood for. God bless you![7]

Mother Teresa spoke boldly to her elite audience that day, and they listened because she had earned the right to be bold. Everyone knew that Mother Teresa and her sister nuns walked their talk, caring for those the world has forgotten or chosen not to love. The point she made by both her words and her life is that *all* life has dignity and value in God's sight. The worm-infested beggar on an Indian street has value. The young mother carrying an unplanned baby has value. *And the unborn baby has value.*

In Colossians 1:16, the apostle Paul gives us one reason why God values all life, a reason we don't often consider: "For by [Christ] all things were created that are in heaven and that are on earth, visible and invisible, whether thrones or dominions or principalities or powers. *All things were created through Him and for Him*" (italics added).

I italicized that last sentence because it emphasizes Christ as the source of all life in creation. It all came into existence *through* Jesus Christ and *for* Jesus Christ. He blessed it as "very good" (Genesis 1:31), which means it is highly valuable to Him.

Now, here's where you and I enter the picture: Christ entrusted to us the high honor and responsibility of being stewards over everything He created on earth (Genesis 1:28). This means what is valuable to Him must be valuable to us. Therefore, we have a duty as stewards to ask of Him: "Am I honoring the dignity You infused into human life? Are the choices I make concerning the life You created pleasing to You?"

Can you imagine any possibility that Jesus Christ would answer, "Yes, your decision to end the life of millions of unborn children each year, children created through Me and for Me, is pleasing to Me"? No! This could never please Christ. I am convinced that He is deeply grieved every time we take an innocent life purposefully created in God's image.

While I am convinced that the answer to abortion is simple, I understand that it is a hard subject to talk about in today's social climate. Just as many government officials in Washington were uncomfortable with Mother Teresa's words in 1994, some who read these pages may be uncomfortable with my words as well.

You may be living with regret and remorse over a decision you made in the past. If so, I pray that you are not hearing the Father, Jesus, Mother Teresa, or myself condemning you for that decision. Abortion is not the unpardonable sin. Grace and mercy lie at the foot of the cross of Christ for all who have chosen other than God's best. I implore you to give yourself the advantage of seeing any wrong choice in life—including an abortion—as God sees it when it is confessed: as a choice that is forgiven through the blood of Christ.

Here is another word of hope and encouragement for those who have made this choice: If you accept Christ's offer of forgiveness and eternal life, I believe with all my heart that you will see your unborn baby again and rejoice with that child in a reunion of love that cannot be imagined. Based on a lifetime of seeking to understand the love and mercy of God—especially as applied to infants—I believe children whose lives were terminated before birth are now rejoicing in the presence of God, and will for all eternity.

Before You Were Born, God Knew Your Destiny

Before I formed you in the womb I knew you;
Before you were born I sanctified you;
I ordained you a prophet to the nations.

—JEREMIAH 1:5

In this passage God says four specific things to Jeremiah:

- I formed you.
- I knew you.
- I sanctified you.
- I ordained you.

When the Lord told Jeremiah he was ordained to be a prophet to the nations, he might have wondered if God had really thought this thing through! He began offering reasons why he wasn't qualified to fulfill the destiny God had for him: "Ah, Lord GOD! Behold, I cannot speak, for I am a youth" (Jeremiah 1:6).

But God knew exactly what He was doing. As the call itself indicates, He had thought it through quite thoroughly: "This is no spontaneous decision on My part, Jeremiah. Don't you realize that I knew everything about you while your mother was still carrying you? Don't you realize that I've had this destiny mapped out for you all along?"

God had planned for this moment; and with joy, He looked forward to the deep satisfaction of seeing His child put to use the gifts that were so lovingly reserved for him. When Jeremiah protested his youthful inexperience, God reassured him: "I am with you to deliver you" (v. 8). He put His hand on Jeremiah's lips and said, "Behold, I have put My words in your mouth" (v. 9).

Just as He did with Jeremiah, God treasures the moments in which He sees us growing into what He designed us to be and moving toward the destiny He has planned for us. The same is true in human relationships. John Ortberg explains: "If I love someone, it means I have certain hopes and intentions and wishes for them. I'm in their corner. I long for them to flourish and blossom. I want them to realize all their potential. I want them to become filled with virtue and moral beauty."[8]

The difference is that with God's love, these treasures exist before we do. He has reserved them for us from the very beginning. Paul speaks of this eternal knowledge and love of God when he writes to the Galatians about his own calling. He explains that God "separated me from my mother's womb and called me through His grace, to reveal His Son in me, that I might preach Him among the Gentiles" (Galatians 1:15–16a).

Just as God had a destiny for Jeremiah and for Paul, He also has a destiny for each of us—one that He designed before we were born.

Before You Were Born, God Knew Your Possibility

Then God said, "Let Us make man in Our image, according to Our likeness; let them have dominion over the fish of the sea, over the birds of the air, and over the cattle, over all the earth and over every creeping thing that creeps on the

*earth." So God created man in His own image; in the image
of God He created him; male and female He created them.*

—GENESIS 1:26–27

Warren Wiersbe has noted that "there is a divine conference among the members of the Godhead before man is created, something not seen at any other step of the Creation."[9] Out of this conference came God's determination to create man in His own image. Being in God's image doesn't mean that we are like God in every way. Our likeness consists of bearing His character and nature, even though those attributes have been diminished by the Fall.

We are created to be a special reflection of God's nature. In everything we do, we reveal a picture of God on a smaller canvas. Our work reflects God's work. Our love provides a hint of how He loves. He gives us dominion over this earth (Genesis 1:26) as He has dominion over all creation. Like Father, like son (and daughter).

Though we are physical creatures, we have a spiritual nature just as God does. This is why we feel guilt, love, and other complex emotions. Flawed though we are, we retain the image and glory of the Father.

To illustrate this concept, think of a proud new father waiting to hold his child for the first time. When the smiling nurse brings that red-faced, squinty-eyed little bundle over to him, the father smiles all over. His joy overflows, and he can't help but whisper a prayer of thanksgiving. This is his living, breathing child—bone of his bone and flesh of his flesh. This child is the special creation of himself and the person he loves more than any other—his wife. Already the father sees, with a rush of excitement, that the baby will have his eyes, his wife's lovely chin. This child bears his image!

This ecstatic experience of a new father reflects how God, looking through the window of time, feels about you and me. All of His creation is good—there are no exceptions. You are precious to Him beyond human imagination, and you have possibilities beyond your wildest dreams.

We have testimonies of countless lives in which those possibilities were almost snuffed out before birth. One such person is Tim Tebow. Here is his story, excerpted from the tract "Celebrate Life":

Perhaps you saw the "Celebrate family, celebrate life!" ad during Super Bowl XLIV, featuring Tim Tebow and his mother, Pam. Weeks before its airing, the ad had already stirred a wide range of intense emotions. Those "opposed" considered it offensive and demeaning. Those "in favor" rejoiced that its message would promote the value of life and family on the world's largest media stage. What caused such a stir? The simple story of a mother who chose to keep her unborn baby rather than abort him.

In the 1980s, Bob and Pam Tebow had moved to the Philippines with their young family. Months later, Pam became infected with a dangerous pathogenic amoeba and slipped into a coma. Strong medications turned her condition around, but during that extended treatment, Pam became pregnant. Her doctors, knowing the potent drugs could have already killed the embryo, recommended an abortion.

Pam chose instead to discontinue her treatments in hope of saving her baby. She and Bob asked God for help. The difficult time that followed ended with two final months of bed rest. Then, on August 14, 1987, a healthy (though somewhat malnourished) baby boy—Timothy Richard Tebow—was safely delivered.

If you've ever watched the six-foot-three-inch, 235-pound Tim Tebow play football, you know it's hard to imagine he was ever the outcome of a troubled pregnancy. But even if Tim had never played a single down of football, his story needs to be told in our day of cheap life and disposable pregnancies.[10]

A generation ago, everyone referred to an unborn child as a baby. And pregnant women had no doubt that what they were carrying was a baby—a human person. It is hard for anyone to think positively about killing a baby. So to get around the distastefulness of the idea, the word *baby* has been replaced by terms such as "fetus," "embryo," or even a "clump of tissue." These are impersonal, clinical terms easily associated with tumors or growths. These words, completely devoid of the tender emotions associated with *baby*, have allowed people to treat pregnancy as something like an unwanted disease instead of the exalted privilege it is—the privilege of creating beloved beings with eternal, God-given possibilities.

To make matters worse, a new term has emerged in the battle for human life: "after-birth abortion." Previously known as infanticide, after-birth abortion allows babies to be killed after they are born. According to a *World* magazine article by Marvin Olasky,

The core of the argument isn't new at universities like Princeton, where ethicist Peter Singer has long approved killing one-year-olds with physical or mental disabilities. But authors Alberto Giubilini and Francesca Minerva push the argument further by defending the killing of any humans incapable of "attributing any value to their own existence...Merely being human is not in itself a reason for ascribing someone a right to life."[11]

The possibility that this attitude could become accepted presents a peril of almost unmatched significance. One writer explains: "The so-called 'quality of life ethic' is deep down more dangerous than nuclear war, for it destroys the very soul of our civilization, not just bodies. It says a human person's value is not infinite and calculable, that it varies with health, intelligence, and social utility. That is exactly what Hitler believed."[12]

Amidst this frightening reality, perhaps it is time to reevaluate our strategies, refocus our message, and reallocate our resources to the places where the real battles are won and lost. For example, what if we began thinking of the abortion debate in terms of love? One author explains:

> What if we saw each pregnancy as a new opportunity for love, an irreplaceable gift that challenges us to love anew?...In the big picture, love is the far more powerful way of looking at the world. Love is the game-changer. People die for love; they stretch their energies and resources for love. They move to the farthest ends of the earth for love. They take on the greatest challenges for

love. They fast, tighten their belts, work extra jobs, and lose sleep for love. Love moves us to find a way. It is the most deeply human dimension of our lives, because it is at the same time the most deeply rooted in the divine. Every child must be special to us because each one is special to God.[13]

What if our strategies better reflected the selfless love of God? What if more Christians began to make sacrifices—big and small—to spread the love of God by either supporting or participating in ministries to the unborn?

One small way we have attempted to do this is by supporting the crisis pregnancy centers in our city. In the area surrounding Shadow Mountain Community Church in El Cajon, California, there are two crisis pregnancy centers that help young women make the right choices concerning their unborn children. In that same area, there are twelve Planned Parenthood centers to help young women make the wrong choices concerning their unborn children.

Early in 2012, we decided to partner with those two crisis pregnancy centers in a new way by helping to raise money for their ministries. They are, like many similar ministries across the country, funded almost entirely by pledges raised at an annual banquet.

These heroic centers save the lives of hundreds of innocent unborn, as well as the spiritual lives of their confused and guilt-ridden mothers. But unlike the well-funded and government-supported Planned Parenthood organization, there is no national network providing them with support. Most were started by local churches or groups of concerned Christians in the community. They are not sophisticated. They simply help young pregnant women make the right decision about their unborn children, arrange for good prenatal care and, in some cases, help the girls place their babies in Christian homes.

The crisis pregnancy centers are also equipped with ultrasound machines. These machines are perhaps responsible for saving the lives of more babies than anything being done today. Studies have indicated that when a mother actually sees the child she carries in her womb, the likelihood of her aborting that baby is reduced by 60 percent.[14] In many respects, the ultrasound machine is the modern equivalent of Psalm 139:13–16. It enables mothers to see exactly what David wrote so vividly and with such wonder about the unborn child.

In an attempt to support our two crisis pregnancy centers, our church launched a four-month fund-raising campaign. We bought more than five thousand baby bottles and distributed them to our entire congregation, from children through adults. We challenged our people to fill these bottles with their loose change and return them to our church by Mother's Day.

I cannot remember anything that has captured the enthusiasm and love of our people like this campaign. Each week our members return hundreds of bottles filled with change; and without exception, the donors want the bottle back so they can fill it again. At the pace we are on as I write this chapter, we will raise considerably more than one hundred thousand dollars to be divided between our two centers.

Our prayer is that many infant lives will be saved to fulfill the glorious possibilities God has reserved for them.

Before You Were Born, God Knew Your Legacy

For I know the thoughts that I think toward you, says the LORD, thoughts of peace and not of evil, to give you a future and a hope.

—JEREMIAH 29:11

The prophet Jeremiah wrote this verse to the Jewish exiles in Babylon to assure God's people that He had not forgotten them during their seventy years of captivity. But the verse certainly has application today: It assures us that we also have a future and a hope.

Yet the verse raises persistent questions about God's love: If before we were born, God knew everything about us (which He does), did He know about the difficult and painful things we would experience? If He knew about them but didn't prevent them, what does that say about His love? What future and hope can one have in the face of physical deformities, mental and congenital defects, and other disorders children are born with?

Though it is hard for many to imagine in a culture that judges value by "quality of life," even people bearing serious defects have a future and a hope. Many of them live in a state of joy that amazes the rest of us. One such person is Gianna Jessen, the inspiration behind the hit movie *October Baby*.

Gianna's seventeen-year-old mother was seven and one-half months pregnant when she decided to have an abortion by saline injection. In a saline abortion, the womb is injected with a saline solution and the mother is expected to deliver a dead baby within twenty-four hours. However, Gianna miraculously survived eighteen hours in the saline solution before being delivered alive. Upon delivery, EMS rushed the two-pound baby to the hospital, where after three-months of touch-and-go existence, she survived. At seventeen months, Gianna was diagnosed with cerebral palsy due to oxygen starvation caused by the attempted termination. The prognosis was grim: she would never be able to lift her head, sit up straight, or walk.

Many influenced by the common thinking of today's culture would think Gianna better off if her abortion had succeeded rather than leaving her to face such a diminished life. Surely she had no future and no hope.

But the love of a diligent foster mother proved these predictions wrong. After four surgeries, leg braces, and grueling physical therapy, Gianna not only walks; she has run in several marathons. She has written and recorded several songs and has become an effective advocate for life, speaking against abortion before state legislatures, parliaments of nations, and even the U.S. Congress.[15]

Even before Gianna Jessen's conception, God had a legacy planned for her—a future and a hope! He took what others meant for evil and used it for good. Gianna's life is no accident, nor is her work.

Sadly, hundreds of millions of individuals will never fulfill their legacy this side of heaven. Consider:

The first babies aborted in 1973, when abortion became legal in the U.S. would have been thirty-nine in 2012—in the prime of their lives. We will never know what would have become of the 52 million American babies aborted since then. As newspaper writer Sally Jenkins says, "Abortion doesn't just involve serious issues of life, but of potential lives—Heisman trophy winners, scientists, doctors, artists, inventors. Little-Leaguers who would never come to be if their birth mothers had not wrestled with the stakes and chosen to carry those lives to term."[16]

For those 52 million aborted babies, the grand possibilities God had in store for them will never be realized.

If God sees all of time from beginning to end—and He does—then He sees what we cannot. He sees beyond our difficulties and limitations to the eternal impact we will have on others. Although our vision of the future is worse than hazy, we can cling to the illusion that we have life figured out. We tend to think it will be just like the past and the present, but it never is. Several events of recent years have taken the world by surprise, from the World Trade Center attacks and Hurricane Katrina to the economic collapse and Japan's tsunami.

Consider your own life. Hasn't much of it happened while you were making other plans? We never foresee the bends in the road ahead. But God anticipates all things, and He sees the complete lives of people yet unborn. He sees your children, your grandchildren, and all the generations that will follow. His unending love for you includes filling your life with eternal meaning. He knows the things He has yet to do through you—the legacy you will leave through the lives you will touch and the lives that will be touched by those lives.

The language of Psalm 139, describing life in the womb, is powerful and irrefutable. The term "skillfully wrought" literally means "embroidered." God has embroidered us. We are part of His intricately designed tapestry, the design in which He weaves all things together for the good of those who love Him and are called according to His purpose (Romans 8:28). It's the design by which His intentions are slowly but surely fulfilled.

You have a place in that design—a place far greater than you can imagine. As a single thread in the tapestry, you can see only the threads that you cross. But God sees the entire length of every strand. He knows exactly what He will accomplish through your life, exactly what good works He has set aside for you (Ephesians 2:10). The full scope of the legacy you will leave is beyond your ability to see. You must simply believe, on the basis of Scripture, that the thread of your life will extend through time, influencing those you have never met.

I began this chapter with a story about a fictional carnival barker, and I want to finish with a story about a real one— a woman named Norma McCorvey. Norma was twenty-one years old in 1969, unmarried, and the mother of two children—one in the custody of the child's grandmother and one given up for adoption. While working at whatever jobs she could find—including being a barker for a traveling carnival— she discovered she was pregnant for a third time. When she sought an abortion, she found they were illegal in Texas except in cases of rape or incest. So she lied and claimed rape, but the claim was dismissed due to lack of evidence.

Two attorneys used Norma's desire to have an abortion as a reason to file suit against the state of Texas. To protect Norma's privacy, they gave her the fictitious name of "Jane Roe," a name immortalized in the now-famous *Roe v. Wade* Supreme Court case ("Wade" was the local district attorney in Dallas County, Texas). In 1973, the Supreme Court ruled in Norma McCorvey's favor, and abortions on demand have been legal in

America ever since. (Norma's third child was born before the case was decided.)

But Norma McCorvey had a change of heart. In the early 1990s, she professed faith in Christ and has written two books affirming her pro-life position. In her second book, *Won by Love* (1998), she described her sudden awareness that the life in a mother's womb is a baby, a child whom God loves:

When my conversion [to Christ] became public knowledge, I spoke openly to reporters about still supporting legalized abortion in the first trimester. The media was quick to use this to downplay the seriousness of my conversion, saying I typified the "general ambivalence" of our culture over abortion. But a few weeks after my conversion, I was sitting in [Operation Rescue's] offices when I noticed a fetal development poster. The progression was so obvious, the eyes were so sweet. It hurt my heart, just looking at them.

I ran outside and finally, it dawned on me. *"Norma,"* I said to myself, *"they're right."* I had worked with pregnant women for years. I had been through three pregnancies and deliveries myself. I should have known. Yet something in that poster made me lose my breath. I kept seeing the picture of that tiny, 10-week-old embryo, and I said to myself, that's a baby! It's as if blinders just fell off my eyes and I suddenly understood the truth—that's a baby![17]

This chapter is not about abortion. Abortion is only the most visible symptom of a deeper disorder—the lost awareness that God loves life, including life in the womb. The point of this chapter is that God loved you as a truly human person even before you were born. Nothing but love can account for God's seeing us and caring for us even before we were conceived, born, or had committed any sin.

Maintaining that big picture is important. Those who don't believe they are "fearfully and wonderfully made" by a God who has loved them before the beginning of time will have a hard time trusting that God's love surrounds them when they face life's challenges.

But if you believe that before you were born God lovingly strung together the days of your life from conception through eternity, then you have *context* for believing your life is ordered even to the point of using adversity to your eternal advantage. And that context is love.

God loved you before you were born. He loves you today. And your legacy is that He will love you forever.

THREE

God Carved His Love in Stone

&

The LORD came from Sinai, ...
From His right hand
Came a fiery law for them.
Yes, He loves the people.
   —DEUTERONOMY 33:2–3

Perhaps Ted Turner captured it best—this attitude that the Ten Commandments were given with the sole purpose of taking the fun out of life.

Some years ago, the founder of CNN and other cable networks told the *Dallas Morning News* that Christianity was "a religion for losers."[1] He commented that he'd lived a bit of the wild life, and if that sentenced him to hell, then so be it.

Shortly after these statements, Turner stood before the American Humanist Association and proclaimed that it was time to update the Ten Commandments. They were grossly out of date, he said. It was time for his "Ten Voluntary Initiatives," which took a much more politically correct direction.

These included ecological guidelines, a vow of nonviolence, an effort to be friendlier, and the promise to have no more than two children (though again Turner was off to a poor start; he had five).[2]

Some scoffed at "the Mouth of the South," as he was known. But in some humanistic circles, Turner's Top Ten list is still admired and studied. It certainly tells many people what they already want to hear without making any demands of personal morality or, for that matter, any mention of God at all.

Over the years, I've heard echoes of Turner's take from ordinary people. I recall a young man who came to me in the midst of a number of problems in his life. I talked to him about Christ, about sin, and the need for forgiveness. He sighed, rolled his eyes, and said, "Christianity is no more than a list of silly rules that take all the joy out of life. I need to tell you, Dr. Jeremiah, I can't think of a single good reason to become a Christian."

Something in us really doesn't like rules. When you're late for an appointment, and you're slamming down the accelerator to get across town quickly, that stop sign seems like a real annoyance. And if no other cars are coming, it feels like another "silly rule."

On the other hand, if you move into that intersection and spot another speeding car coming at you and ignoring the sign—well, then the rules look a lot better. At that moment, you appreciate stop signs, and you understand how they were placed for your protection.

The Ten Commandments are stop signs at the prime intersections of life. They were given by a God who loves us and wants our best.

In his book *The Lost Message of Jesus*, Steve Chalke discusses the common misconception that these rules are simply restrictive hoops God expects us to jump through. People get the idea, he explains, that the commandments are requirements for a demanding God's approval. But the Bible says nothing of the kind. The Ten Commandments were given to Moses and the Israelites in the wilderness where God had already demonstrated His love and acceptance.

The people had been slaves in Egypt, cruelly treated. God liberated them and then cared for their needs during their escape. Having done that, He took them to Mount Sinai to make a statement: "Now that you trust Me, I want to help you with your life. Do as I say, and you'll find happiness; and the world will see and know you are My people."[3]

The late pastor and writer Ron Mehl says that these commandments are, in fact, expressions of love from a Father to His children, "a tender, heartfelt message from the very hand of God...It's all there. He doesn't leave anything out. These ten statements are all-encompassing, touching virtually every part of our lives. They are the parameters to live by—the truths He knows are going to provide blessing and strength, a future and a hope."[4]

Going back in history, I discovered others who saw in the Decalogue an expression of God's love. In one of his sermons, British preacher Charles Haddon Spurgeon said, "That law of the Ten Commandments is a gift of great kindness to the sons of men, for it tells us the wisest and the happiest way of living. It forbids us nothing but what would be to our injury and it withholds from us nothing which would be a real pleasure to us...God does not make laws denying us anything that would really be for our good...We ought to see the love of God in the gift of law."[5]

In the past, I have not always seen the Old Testament Law as an expression of love. I wondered how the Jewish people bore the burden of all those rules and regulations that seemed to hem them in on every side. But my understanding was incomplete. Christian philosopher Peter Kreeft helped bring the truth into focus for me:

> Law expresses and serves love. We do not usually understand that. That is why we do not usually understand the frequent exclamations of love and joy in the Psalms when the psalmist contemplates God's law. "His delight is in the law of the Lord and in His law he meditates day and night" (Ps 1:2). And again: "The ordinances of the Lord are true, and righteous altogether. More to be desired are they than gold, even much fine gold; sweeter also than honey and drippings of the honeycomb" (Ps 19:9–10).
>
> We do not understand this because we think of the law as a dead and as a threatening thing. But the psalmist thinks of the law as a living and loving thing. He recognizes it as the expression of the will of the living God, and His will to us is love.[6]

And while we're discussing common misconceptions, how about those who suggest that Jesus somehow made the commandments obsolete? That, since we now live under grace, we need not bother with the baggage of commandments and divine law?

Jesus made it clear that He honored the Ten Commandments and considered them to have eternal authority. He also said, "If you want to enter into life, keep the commandments" (Matthew 19:17). When asked to be specific, Jesus named several of the ten. And far from abolishing the commandments, He extended them to the heart, showing how hate is tantamount to murder, lust is adultery in God's eyes, and so on (Matthew 5:21–30).

Jesus said, "Do not think that I came to destroy the Law or the Prophets. I did not come to destroy but to fulfill" (Matthew 5:17). Therefore, Jesus does not represent a break with the Old Testament Law, but rather the Law's perfect expression.

Wise old Solomon, Israel's king, spent his days examining the meaning of life. He summarized his accumulated wisdom in this formula: "Let us hear the conclusion of the whole matter: Fear God and keep His commandments, for this is man's all" (Ecclesiastes 12:13).

In this chapter, I want to take a fresh walk through these ten immortal directives. We need to rediscover what they meant then and what they mean now. I can assure you we're going to find the love of God again and again in the Word of a Father eager to protect His children. We will come to realize that when God gave Moses the Law on Mount Sinai, He indeed carved His love in stone.

The First Commandment:
The Fundamental Rule

And God spoke all these words, saying: "I am the LORD your God, who brought you out of the land of Egypt, out of the house of bondage. You shall have no other gods before Me."

—EXODUS 20:1–3

The first commandment is like the hub of a wheel from which all the others are spokes. This isn't simply another commandment—it's the one that brings all of them together.

As you read the narrative leading up to the giving of the commandments, God's love is everywhere on display. For instance, when Moses arrives at the top of Mount Sinai to receive the commandments, God tells him to remind the people of His great love for them in the past and His careful watch over their lives throughout their redemption from Egypt: "And Moses went up to God, and the LORD called to him from the mountain, saying, 'Thus you shall say to the house of Jacob, and tell the children of Israel: "You have seen what I did to the Egyptians, and how I bore you on eagles' wings and brought you to Myself"'" (Exodus 19:3–4).

Later, as Moses returns to the mountain, bearing the second set of two stone tablets, God passes before His servant again and refers to Himself as "the LORD, the LORD God, merciful and gracious, longsuffering, and abounding in goodness and truth, keeping mercy for thousands, forgiving iniquity and transgression and sin" (Exodus 34:6–7).

Israel stands at a crossroads in its history: behind, the pagan gods of the Egyptians; ahead, the pagan gods of the Canaanites. The Israelites have been and will continue to be caught up in cultures of false gods. So the one true God now wants His people to know that He insists on an exclusive relationship with them. There are no others like Him, and they must not allow their spirits to wander after the false hopes of pagan gods.

"If you will have no other gods," God is saying, "it is only then that you can have Me." There is no middle ground here; the Lord God will not be one option among many.

It still holds true. Idolatry is no outdated sin but the same threat it has always been and will always be. The gods have changed their names, of course. They are no longer Baal and Ashtoreth, but now they call themselves wealth or power or comfort or appetite—or whatever it is that is controlling your heart today.

Counterfeit gods never die. They simply come up with new disguises and continue trying to lead us away from the only God who offers a relationship of love and care.

Martin Luther wrote, "That to which your heart clings and entrusts itself is . . . really your God."[7]

Recently I read about a series of religious services that were advertised in Scottish newspapers. The first part of the ad was printed on page 1, and simply directed readers to the last page of the paper. There, in larger print, was the question "Is this where you are putting God?"[8]

Many Christians today have pushed God to the back page. They have allowed other "gods" to clutter up their lives. God does not ask for a prominent place among all our other gods; He insists that there be no other gods, period. A half-forgotten God is no God at all. He demands page 1 of our lives.

Many in today's secular culture criticize this commandment

as arrogantly exclusive, self-absorbed, and intolerant. Why start this list with a narrow ultimatum?

He starts the list this way for the same reason we take a vow before God and witnesses to love and cherish only one spouse. Few of us would marry someone whose vows included: "For richer, for poorer, in sickness and in health, from this day forward until the next cute person catches my eye."

God wants an exclusive love relationship with you. That's not arrogance, but a proper understanding of reality—life doesn't work any other way. A wheel can have only one hub. Try to set it spinning around any other point, and you crash. In the same way, God is the hub of this universe, "the still point in the turning world," as T. S. Eliot put it.[9] No one else can be at the center.

It was the love of God that caused Him to limit the worship of His people to Himself alone. To tolerate worship of other gods would have turned the Israelites loose to explore a pantheon of lifeless idols utterly incapable of meeting their needs or bringing them happiness. "Worship any god you choose" would have been the most unloving thing God could have said to the infant nation of Israel—or to us today. It is God's love for us, not selfish love, that is behind His jealous desire to be worshipped.

The Second Commandment: The Focus Rule

You shall not make for yourself a carved image—any likeness of anything that is in heaven above, or that is in the earth beneath, or that is in the water under the earth; you shall not bow down to them nor serve them. For I, the LORD *your God, am a jealous God, visiting the iniquity of the fathers upon the children to the third and fourth generations of those who hate Me, but showing mercy to thousands, to those who love Me and keep My commandments.*

—EXODUS 20:4–6

If the first commandment is about *whom* we worship, the second is about *how.* We must worship the right God, and we must worship Him the right way. That comes by hearing rather than seeing.

Worship from the heart is elusive and demanding. People demand gods they can see and touch. The Israelites never stopped struggling with this concept. Even as Moses received this commandment at Sinai, the people were down in the valley, melting their gold rings to create a calf idol. They threw a great party afterward, pointed to the calf, and said, "This is your god, O Israel, that brought you out of the land of Egypt!" (Exodus 32:4).

What a terrible moment in the history of that nation! The people couldn't wait for Moses to return, so they decided to take a shortcut. But God is telling us that nothing must be used to attract the eyes and thus distract the soul from Him. Pastor and author Jerry Vines explains this prohibition: "An image of God is limited. God is unlimited. An image of God is local. God is universal. An image of God is temporal. God is eternal. An image of God is material. God is spiritual. When you make an image it distorts God."[10]

This explains why God provides no likeness of Himself. We are never invited to gaze upon God, but rather to listen to His voice. He has spoken. He has revealed Himself through words. He is heard but unseen. Idols, on the other hand, are seen but never heard. The prophet Isaiah mocked those who revered impotent idols:

> Then the wood-carver measures a block of wood
> and draws a pattern on it.
> He works with chisel and plane
> and carves it into a human figure.
> He gives it human beauty
> and puts it in a little shrine.
> He cuts down cedars;
> he selects the cypress and the oak;
> he plants the pine in the forest
> to be nourished by the rain.
> Then he uses part of the wood to make a fire.
> With it he warms himself and bakes his bread.
> Then—yes, it's true—he takes the rest of it
> and makes himself a god to worship!
> He makes an idol
> and bows down in front of it!
> He burns part of the tree to roast his meat
> and to keep himself warm.
> He says, "Ah, that fire feels good."
> Then he takes what's left
> and makes his god: a carved idol!
> He falls down in front of it,
> worshiping and praying to it.
> "Rescue me!" he says.
> "You are my god!"

Such stupidity and ignorance!
Their eyes are closed, and they cannot see.
Their minds are shut, and they cannot think.
The person who made the idol never stops to reflect,
"Why, it's just a block of wood!
I burned half of it for heat
and used it to bake my bread and roast my meat.
How can the rest of it be a god?
Should I bow down to worship a piece of wood?"
The poor, deluded fool feeds on ashes.
He trusts something that can't help him at all.
Yet he cannot bring himself to ask,
"Is this idol that I'm holding in my hand a lie?"

—ISAIAH 44:13–20 (NLT)

The second commandment comes with a warning: Disobedience will visit "the iniquity of the fathers upon the children to the third and fourth generations of those who hate me" (Exodus 20:5).

Is that unfair—punishing children for what their parents did? The meaning is actually that the children (generations) are punished *by* their parents' sin. Our failures leave a legacy. Alcoholic children often come from alcoholic parents. Materialistic parents nurture the same values in their children, intentional or not. Sin is contagious within families.

Ron Mehl adds: "God says to us, 'The reason I'm asking you not to place any object or enterprise or image ahead of Me is because I don't want you to wake up one day with a broken heart, as you watch your loved ones making the same mistakes you made, tripping over the same rocks you tripped over, and struggling with the same cynical attitudes that afflicted you.'"[11]

The good news is that we leave positive legacies, too. While preaching, I've often asked for a show of hands from those whose parents led them to Christ. Each time, more than 50 percent of our people indicate that they're en route to heaven because of the testimony of loving parents.

This commandment springs from God's perfect love. "For I, the LORD your God, am a jealous God," He says (Exodus 20:5). *Jealousy* is a word used by lovers—and God is a perfect Lover. He created us to be in relationship with Him, and He knows that any other way will destroy our lives, the lives of those around us, and the lives of our children and our grandchildren.

I'm grateful that He is a jealous God.

The Third Commandment: The "Frivolous" Rule

You shall not take the name of the LORD your God in vain, for the LORD will not hold him guiltless who takes His name in vain.

—EXODUS 20:7

People often read this commandment as a rule against profanity. That's part of the intention, but the third commandment goes far deeper than vulgar language. It tells us that His name must be spoken with heartfelt sincerity and reverence. We are never to use the Lord's name in a frivolous way.

When we use God's name frivolously, we cheapen a word and an association that should drive our hearts to reverence. The name of God is the only handle by which we can know and worship our Lord and Creator. Names carry meanings to us, and signal us to think in certain ways. God carried the name "I AM" to the people of Israel. It invoked the knowledge that He was eternal and transcendent. When people begin to think of the word *God* or the phrase *Oh my God* as a casual expression, what happens to the meaning of that name in their hearts?

Jesus taught His disciples to pray, "Hallowed be Your name" (Matthew 6:9). Prayer, He was saying, must begin with the "making holy" of His precious name—because as the mouth goes, so goes the mind.

Our current generation has reduced the name of God to a word with little meaning, and that's no coincidence. Words and thoughts are inextricably linked.

Perhaps the closest parallel to the intent of the third commandment is found in a modern courtroom. A witness places his hand on the Bible and swears to tell the truth "so help me God." Then, if the witness commits perjury, he has used God's name in vain. In other words, the oath he took was empty, meaningless, or frivolous.

So God's warning in the third commandment is, "Don't use Me as your backup, as your collateral in an oath if you have no intention of keeping your word. Don't involve Me in a lying scheme that will defame who I am."

The third commandment also forbids us to use God's name as an oath in an attempt to manipulate Him in our favor. We aren't to ask God merely to fight on our side; we're to seek how we can fight on His.

God loves us, and He knows we cannot experience His love when we devalue the name by which we intimately know Him. The names of your spouse, your parents, and your children—these are special to you, and you wouldn't be happy about hearing them abused. In an even greater way, the name of God must be kept holy, to nurture the love we share together.

The Fourth Commandment: The Frailty Rule

Remember the Sabbath day, to keep it holy. Six days you shall labor and do all your work, but the seventh day is the Sabbath of the LORD your God. In it you shall do no work: you, nor your son, nor your daughter, nor your male servant, nor your female servant, nor your cattle, nor your stranger who is within your gates. For in six days the LORD made the heavens and the earth, the sea, and all that is in them, and rested the seventh day. Therefore the LORD blessed the Sabbath day and hallowed it.

—EXODUS 20:8–11

My wife, Donna, and I began our ministry together in a Baptist church in New Jersey. We had just come from four years of seminary training in Dallas, and we were both avid Dallas Cowboy football fans. To our dismay, when we arrived at our first assignment, we were told that watching TV on Sunday was forbidden, and reading the Sunday newspaper was frowned upon. I am not sure I should be confessing this, but I remember closing the blinds of our apartment so that no one would see us watching the Cowboys.

A bit legalistic? Perhaps, but you should have known the Pharisees of Jesus' day. They actually crunched the numbers of legalism, and came up with 1,521 things you couldn't do on the Sabbath day. That sounds like the title of a book no one would want to read.

Among the 1,521: no rescuing of drowning people; no wearing of false teeth (reinserting them, should they slip, would be work); no looking in the mirror (plucking a white hair, also work). If your friend grew ill, you could do certain things to forestall the illness, but actually trying to cure him—too much like work. At the beginning of a famous revolt, many Jews stood and let themselves be killed rather than risking work by defending themselves (1 Maccabees 2:29–38).

Men made a bureaucratic nightmare out of Sabbath-keeping, but it wasn't what God wanted. This commandment shows a deep affection for us. The word *sabbath* means "rest." God knows we grow weary in the cycle of work, so He established a day for us to regularly disengage from toil and refresh ourselves. God cares about our labor and our leisure.

The Sabbath was also to be a day to turn from the material to the spiritual, to connect in a deeper way with God. Before Christ, people worked *toward* the Sabbath, resting on the last day of the week. Since the Resurrection, we work *from* the Sabbath, living in the power of the risen Christ.

The early Christians began to worship on the first day of the week because that was the day on which Jesus rose from the dead (Mark 16:9). By the time we get to Acts 20:7, we see the disciples coming together on "the first day of the week" to pray, break bread, and listen to the teaching of the Word of God. By the beginning of the second century, Christians universally understood that the Lord's Day was to be on Sunday, the day after the Jewish Sabbath. And in AD 321, the Roman emperor Constantine, by royal edict, proclaimed Sunday a special day of worship throughout the entire Roman world. It is remarkable to realize that every Sunday from the day of Christ's resurrection until today, somewhere in the world, the church of Jesus Christ has come together to worship.

When I was growing up, Sunday was a special day. We went to church as a family both in the morning and in the evening. Our youth groups always met at six o'clock, just before the evening service. Back then, even those who chose not to attend church still reserved a certain respect for Sunday and how the day should be treated.

We need to accept the wonderful gift of God's day. We can do this by recognizing its special purpose: to honor Him by resting and reflecting on His goodness. As we do that, we'll want to find ways to return the gift to Him with gratitude— through ministry, through worship, and through avoiding anything that makes Sunday just another day.

The two commands here are to *remember it* and to *keep it holy*.

The story goes that when Africa was first being explored, native guides were taking their visitors through the region. After six days of pushing through the jungle, the natives refused to walk. They explained, "We need a day to let our souls catch up with our bodies."[12]

God has given you a gift to get your soul back in alignment. Will you accept it?

The Fifth Commandment: The Family Rule

Honor your father and your mother, that your days may be long upon the land which the LORD your God is giving you.

—EXODUS 20:12

There are two sections of God's list for life. The first section is made up of four commands concerning how to love God. Jesus summarized the first section as "Love the LORD your God with all your heart, with all your soul, with all your mind, and with all your strength" (Mark 12:30).

The second section consists of six commandments about loving others. Jesus summarized this section as "You shall love your neighbor as yourself" (Mark 12:31).

The fifth commandment, then, is transitional. Like the first four, it deals with authority and respect. Like the final five, it deals with human relationships. Therefore, this commandment is set in exactly the perfect place.

Parent-child relationships are important in the New Testament. We think of Jesus on the cross, asking John to care for His mother (John 19:26–27). Paul includes being "disobedient to parents" as a sin that provokes God (Romans 1:30).

The most familiar passage on the subject, however, is found in Ephesians 6:1–3: "Children, obey your parents in the Lord, for this is right," Paul counsels, and then quotes the fifth commandment, along with its promise of living "long on the earth."

The commandment is a very straightforward one, but like the others, it has a deeper level. We quote it to little children, which is appropriate, but the most significant application is for adult children, caring for aging parents who can no longer care for themselves. This way it fits the accompanying promise: If we care for aging parents, they'll have longer and better lives, and so will we, as our children follow our example.

It's the only commandment with a promise attached, though a curious promise at first glance. Are we to believe that longevity is directly tied to benevolent treatment of our parents? Not exactly. This is a general principle that works in life. Respectful people live longer. They're wiser, more obedient to God, and they tend to be more respected by others. People who walk better paths have longer journeys. Turning away from those who raised us, however, is a leading indicator of a lack of wisdom.

Why is this a loving commandment? For one thing, God is telling us He wants us to have long and happy lives before He takes us home. But also, this commandment saves us from the grief we bring on ourselves through whatever bitterness we might have over how we were raised.

Many people have unfinished business concerning the way they were brought up. In fact, all of us have been failed by our parents in one way or another. But we double down on the pain when we give in to bitterness. Reconciliation and unconditional love say this: "Mom, Dad, we've had our rough times, but why should that continue? Let's put the past behind us and recall that God gave us one another, and enjoy the years we still have together."

God loves us, and He wants to set us free from every kind of slavery, including the slavery of unhealed emotions. The Lord is saying, "Will you love your parents the way I love you—with no demands, no conditions? If you do, it will increase the quantity and quality of your years."

This "family rule" is well illustrated in the story "The Old

Man and His Grandson," from the collection *Household Tales* by the Grimm brothers:

> There was once a very old man, whose eyes had become dim, his ears dull of hearing, his knees trembled, and when he sat at the table he could hardly hold the spoon, and spit the broth upon the table-cloth or let it run out of his mouth. His son and his son's wife were disgusted at this, so the old grandfather at last had to sit in the corner behind the stove, and they gave him his food in an earthenware bowl, and not even enough of it. And he used to look towards the table with his eyes full of tears. Once, too, his trembling hands could not hold the bowl, and it fell to the ground and broke. The young wife scolded him, but he said nothing and only sighed. Then they bought him a wooden bowl for a few half-pence, out of which he had to eat.
>
> They were once sitting thus when the little grandson of four years old began to gather together some bits of wood upon the ground. "What are you doing there?" asked the father. "I am making a little trough," answered the child, "for father and mother to eat out of when I am big."
>
> The man and his wife looked at each other for a while, and presently began to cry. Then they took the old grandfather to the table, and henceforth always let him eat with them, and likewise said nothing if he did spill a little of anything.[13]

The parents in the Grimm brothers' fairy tale recognized their own future when they saw their son preparing to treat them as they had been treating the grandfather, and it shocked them into making a change. Our love and honor for our parents should enable us to care for them without the need for such a shock. God loves us and wants us to care for one another, which underscores one of the primary purposes of the family—to ensure health and stability from generation to generation.

In the fifth commandment, God made the care of parents a priority for His covenant people, Israel. As the New Testament shows, the principle still applies. Adults who care for their aging parents set an example for their own children to imitate. God is loving. God is good. And this commandment, perhaps more than any other, reflects His tender care for people when they reach a vulnerable place in life.

The Sixth Commandment: The Felony Rule

You shall not murder.
—EXODUS 20:13

Murder is a common word, and it makes for another straightforward and simple commandment. In the Hebrew, it requires only two words.

We live under the illusion of becoming more "civilized," but we've succeeded only in shrinking the category of murder to exclude abortion, suicide, and euthanasia. But the Bible places each of these under the definition of murder. And the most recent statistics tell us a gruesome story. There are approximately 1,210,000 abortions, 35,000 suicides, and 15,000 murders each year in the United States.[14]

As Christians, we recognize that only God creates life. Nothing is more precious or sacred, because we are made in His image—to kill the image of God is to murder God in effigy. It's not simply an act against humanity, but against heaven. Therefore, we preserve life however possible, and to take it away without biblical warrant is to be in contempt of the heavenly court.

With this commandment, we can fall into a classic trap. We think, *I'm looking good on this one—I haven't murdered, and I don't plan to.* But Jesus taught how deep this commandment penetrates. Hatred is a crime of the heart, and a murder in the imagination is a murder from God's perspective. When anger flairs, we are "in danger of hell fire" (Matthew 5:21–22).

For all the damage physical murder has done in this world, how much more has pure hatred done? How many lives have been broken either by people despising or by people being despised? How many churches? How many neighborhoods, towns, families?

God loves us enough to seek to protect us from ourselves, and from the emotional sparks that can begin raging fires, that, even if they don't kill, can wound at a depth that is equally serious. John picks up the theme: "Whoever hates his brother is a murderer, and you know that no murderer has eternal life abiding in him" (1 John 3:15).

God is love, and God made you. So how can you sow hatred? How can you give refuge to bitterness? If eternal life is abiding in you, then it should well up into hope, encouragement, and kindness to all those around you.

The Seventh Commandment:
The Fidelity Rule

You shall not commit adultery.

—EXODUS 20:14

Amazing but true: In the 1631 edition of the King James Version of the Bible, the word *not* was omitted from the seventh commandment. The omission made the commandment read, "Thou shalt commit adultery." That edition became known as "the wicked Bible." Let's hear it for proofreaders!

Today an appalling number of Americans behave as if this rendering were not a mistake. Dependable statistics on how many married people commit adultery are notoriously elusive, but most surveys show a rate of 30 to 60 percent. Adultery, as defined by the Old Testament, is consensual sexual intercourse between a married woman with a man who is not her husband or a married man with a woman who is not his wife. It is therefore a crime against marriage.

Once again, Jesus makes a sobering extension of this commandment. He teaches that lust is adultery of the heart (Matthew 5:27–28). As with the preceding commandment about murder, we're put on notice. It's more difficult to avoid guilt than we thought.

The Bible makes a point to distinguish between sexual desire and lust. The first is no sin at all, but part of God's plan for humanity; lust, on the other hand, is twisted or misplaced desire. It exists because of human depravity. The seventh commandment recognizes that lust and adultery destroy people, their relationships with one another, and their fellowship with God.

Recreational, impulsive sex is considered the norm in our troubled culture. Defending the seventh commandment against the modern world singles one out as a pious puritan stuck in a lost century. However, when we strip sexuality of the restraints God gave it, we create chaos that tears at the very fabric of society. And we place an obstacle that blocks the fellowship God wants to have with us.

God gives us this commandment from love. He is saying, "My child, sexuality is My gift to you. I want you to know that when it's rightly used, it can bring you joy and intimacy with the spouse I give you, and it can create a legacy of children to replenish the earth.

"But when it's wrongly used, it can create absolute havoc. It will destroy you from the inside out, and it will injure people who love you. I love your children, and I don't want them to suffer because your marriage has failed. I don't want your friends and coworkers to lose their respect for you. I don't want you to spend the balance of your life in deep regret over the damage and heartbreak that was your return for the impulse of a moment.

"I love you, and I know what will make you happy. Sexual 'liberation' is really one more brand of enslavement. It advertises thrills but delivers grief. A long and faithful marriage to your spouse will bring you peace and delight that are beyond price—and you and I will be drawn ever closer."

The Eighth Commandment: The Fraud Rule

You shall not steal.

—EXODUS 20:15

I recently read a story about a Soviet factory worker who attempted to steal items from his workplace. Every day he filled a wheelbarrow with cylinders, iron ore, and tools—and every day as he left, he got caught and the stuff was taken away from him.

Finally he was fired, and on his last day the commissar waited for him to come out with the contraband. When he arrived at the door the commissar pulled back the cover from the wheelbarrow, and there was the usual stuff. He confiscated everything and said to the thief, "You are a fool! We caught you every single day. You got away with nothing!"

"Sir, Mr. Commissar," he answered, "you are the fool. I have been stealing wheelbarrows."

When you are the victim of theft, it's not quite that funny. My wife and I were at the San Diego airport, preparing for an overseas trip, when a man behind us spilled some lotion on Donna's bag. He apologized profusely as he wiped away the mess; meanwhile, with the other hand, he was tucking away her purse.

By the time Donna realized it was missing, the man was long gone. We were fortunate to have our passports in hand, and some friends brought us money to tide us over. We went on to Europe, but we had a hard time focusing. We felt violated and began to eye every other traveler with distrust. In the United States today, property theft occurs in some form every three seconds.[15] We are not alone.

There is such a thing as stealing because there is such a thing as ownership. God dignifies us as His children by giving us work to perform, property to maintain, and rights to uphold. These principles are well established in Genesis 1 and 2, which describe God's creation and intentions for us as His children.

God is the true owner of all things. He says, "All the earth is Mine" (Exodus 19:5). David writes, "The earth is the LORD's, and all its fullness, the world and those who dwell therein" (Psalm 24:1). We are the stewards of what He has entrusted to us; this is His way of helping us grow, proving our wisdom as we bear fruit with these resources.

Imagine a world in which people obeyed this commandment. How much simpler life would be. Instead, we only find new ways to steal through technology. Identity theft is now a serious billion-dollar crisis. The music and movie industries have been shaken by online pirating, the widespread theft of intellectual property.

There are only three ways to acquire property: to work for it, to receive it as a gift, or to steal it. In the apostle Paul's Letter to the Ephesians, he addresses all three in one verse: "Let him who stole steal no longer, but rather let him labor, working with his hands what is good, that he may have something to give him who has need" (4:28).

Stealing demonstrates contempt for others and contempt for God. But honest work does just the opposite. It shows respect for others and gratitude to God for the opportunity to use our gifts and skills. Giving goes even further. It shows love for others and faith in God's love—*He will provide.*

In this commandment, God is asking us, "Can you trust Me to provide for you? I will meet your every need, and I've given you a way to grow and find great satisfaction in acquiring your property through honest work. How will you feel about yourself if you get caught up in a cycle of seizing what isn't yours?

"I don't want that for you, and thus I have said, 'You shall not steal.'"

The Ninth Commandment: The False-Witness Rule

You shall not bear false witness against your neighbor.

—EXODUS 20:16

There can be no meaningful exchanges in life apart from honesty. When someone tells a lie by either proclamation, promise, or pretense, he steals the trust and honor of the person to whom he lies. And when the lie is found out, he forfeits any honor he may have had, any esteem in which others held him.

Truth is the currency of God's kingdom. If you expect to conduct meaningful spiritual business in that kingdom, it will happen only through the exchange of truth. Anyone who lies becomes, in that moment, an agent of darkness, doing Satan's work instead of God's. The devil is the "father of lies" (John 8:44 NLT).

Because God loves you He does not want you to suffer the consequences of being defrauded by a lie, or of defrauding others by a lie. He loves you so dearly that He sent the incarnation of truth into this world to die for you that you might be saved, and to pray for you that you might be sanctified by His Word, which is truth (John 17:17).

God gave us a commandment prohibiting lying because He wants you to be made holy—to be conformed into the image of the God of truth. And that can't happen if your life is built on lies.

The Tenth Commandment: The Final Rule

You shall not covet your neighbor's house; you shall not covet your neighbor's wife, nor his male servant, nor his female servant, nor his ox, nor his donkey, nor anything that is your neighbor's.

—EXODUS 20:17

When Tim Keller was preaching a sermon on the seven deadly sins, his wife made an interesting prediction. She said that on the week when he dealt with greed, the service would have its lowest attendance.

His wife was right. Church members packed the auditorium for the topics of lust, wrath, and even pride. But there was no interest in greed. Keller observes that people have come to him to confess nearly every sin imaginable, but no one ever comes and says, "My greedy lust for money is harming my family, my soul, and people around me." Greed, he concludes, is set in the blind spot of the soul, hidden from our own detection.[16]

Greed and coveting are nearly indistinguishable sins. They rise from a lack of contentment in what God has given us, and what we have worked to earn. Therefore, this is a commandment closely related to the one against stealing—in essence, the "gateway sin" that leads to theft.

Just as the fifth commandment is transitional between love of God and love of others, this tenth commandment is transitional between outer and inner obedience—in essence, between Moses and Jesus. For the other commandments in this group have been about behavior, while this commandment is about the heart. We've already seen how Jesus made this connection in the Sermon on the Mount. God looks inside us, so that even if we don't steal, we can displease Him by our own displeasure with what He has given us.

Coveting is really more than wanting; it's a form of lust, which is allowing the heart to fantasize about taking hold of something we're not meant to have.

Notice that this commandment offers seven examples of coveted objects: a neighbor's house, his wife, his male servant, his female servant, his ox, his donkey, or any other possessions. Clearly the intent is to paint with a broad brush, to show that anything imaginable can seduce our attention away from God.

The Bible is filled with stories of lives broken by coveting. So is history, for that matter. Jesus sized up the rich young ruler and got right to the point with him: "Take heed and beware of covetousness, for one's life does not consist in the abundance of the things he possesses" (Luke 12:15).

It comes down to this: Jesus came to give us an abundant life. Isn't that enough? We find contentment, as He told that young man, not in the abundance of things but in the fullness of God's goodness. "Godliness with contentment is great gain," Paul wrote to Timothy (1 Timothy 6:6). But it is the last chapter of the book of Hebrews that gives us the clearest reason for the command against coveting: "Let your conduct be without covetousness; be content with such things as you have. For He Himself has said, 'I will never leave you nor forsake you'" (13:5).

The secret to not coveting is to be content with the presence and provision of the Lord. As C. S. Lewis said, "He who has God and everything else has no more than he who has God only."[17] God looks at us and says, "Am I not enough for you? Would you spend your life in the pursuit of trinkets and baubles, when you are heirs to the kingdom of God? The things your heart pursues are like stale crumbs compared to the feast I've prepared for you. Coveting is one more path that leads to destruction, so I'm asking you to seek contentment in Me."

Laws of Love

Mystery writer Dorothy Sayers was a follower of Christ. She observed that there are two kinds of laws: the law of the stop sign and the law of the fire.

The law of the stop sign is upheld by the community and enforced with fines. The fine can be increased if too many people continue not to stop. The stop sign could also be taken down. It's simply up to the city council. You might run that stop sign with no worries, as long as no one is watching.

The law of the fire is a different matter. It says, "Touch me and you'll be burned." All the city councils, all the state legislatures and national congresses and the United Nations itself could respond to the dangers of fire by gathering to pass a new law that fire will no longer burn. Every person in the world could vote on this law.

And the first man or woman to put a hand in the fire afterward will still get burned.

God's moral laws are like the law of fire. It doesn't matter whether you voted for it or not. It doesn't matter who's watching. You won't break God's laws; you'll break yourself upon them. Nor is the penalty negotiable, because it's bound up in the law itself.[18]

As a bumper sticker put it more concisely, "Gravity is not just a good idea; it's the law."

God's commandments are not arbitrary or flexible. They are woven within the very fabric of creation so that they endure forever. God is not saying, "Here is a list of rules. If I catch you violating any of them, I'll have to punish you." Instead, He is saying, "Let Me tell you how My world works, because I designed it Myself. I made it to be beautiful, and to give you joy, to give you fellowship with people. But there are hazards you must avoid. If you ignore My design for your life, you will have brought punishment upon yourself."

Author and pastor John Killinger explains God's purpose in giving the Ten Commandments with a wonderful illustration from literature:

In her novel about Maine, *The Country of the Pointed Firs*, Sara Orne Jewett describes the ascent of a woman writer on the pathway leading to the home of a retired sea captain named Elijah Tilley. On the way, the woman notices a number of wooden stakes randomly scattered about the property, with no discernible order. Each is painted white and trimmed in yellow, like the captain's house.

Curious, she asks Captain Tilley what they mean. When he first plowed the ground, he says, his plow snagged on many large rocks just beneath the surface. So he set out stakes where the rocks lay in order to avoid them in the future.

In a sense, this is what God has done with the Ten Commandments. He has said, "These are the trouble spots in life. Avoid these, and you won't snag your plow."[19]

Our Lord is not like an arbitrary, capricious god who delights in catching us doing something wrong. Instead, He has given us instructions on how life in His creation works. In fact, He wants us to know how life works so we can be eminently successful at it. It's as if He has given us the answers to the test to ensure that we pass with flying colors. That's how the law of God reveals the love of God. It shows to all who will trust in Him that He wants only what is best for us.

Once again, in the Ten Commandments, we hear God saying: I love you; I always have—I always will.

FOUR

God's Love Never Quits

&

But you, O God, are both tender and kind,
not easily angered, immense in love,
and you never, never quit.
—PSALM 86:15 (THE MESSAGE)

In his book *With: Reimagining the Way You Relate to God*, Skye Jethani tells of his meetings with college students from the House of Despair, an "underground safehouse" for those struggling with the difficult issues of life and faith.

Around their Christian campus, these students were known for numbing their pain with alcohol, drugs, sex, and, most curiously, raw conversation. When they met with Jethani, he insisted that they recognize only three rules: be honest, be gracious, and be present. Their range of subjects had no limits. One week it might be the doctrine of hell; the next about the pressure to find a spouse.

One night the subject was destructive habits. One student told his story, which turned out to be typical of many: "My parents were students at a Christian college in the early '90s when a revival broke out...A bunch of grads that year became missionaries and pastors. They were on fire for God. And here I am consumed by sin day after day. I don't feel like I'm supposed to be here. I know I'm not who God wants me to be." Other students shared similar stories, often through tears, about how disappointed God must be with them.

After listening to these stories, Jethani asked, "How many of you were raised in a Christian home?"

They all raised their hands.

"How many of you grew up in a Bible-centered church?"

All hands stayed up.

"This is incredible!" Jethani said, shaking his head in disbelief. "You've all spent eighteen or twenty years in the church. You've been taught the Bible from the time you could crawl... but not one of you...said that in the midst of your sin God still loves you."

Jethani concluded: "I did not blame the students for this failure. Somewhere in their spiritual formation they were taught, either explicitly or implicitly, that what mattered was not God's love for them, but how much they could accomplish *for* him. That night I finally understood why they called it the House of Despair."[1]

The title of this book is *God Loves You: He Always Has—He Always Will.* All in favor of that proposition? I see every hand up. Any against? None. It's not a title designed to stir controversy. The real issue is this: How deeply do we believe it?

Life experience persuades me to believe that one of Satan's

most effective strategies is to undermine our understanding of the love of God. He knows that our confidence in God's love tends to be fragile, dependent on whether we think our lives are going poorly or well—that God loves us when we please Him and withholds love when we fail. Satan wants to keep it that way because, as soon as we stumble or encounter painful obstacles, he needs only to whisper a negative thought here, a half-truth there, and we find ourselves whittling the infinite love of God down to a poor substitute based on the assumption that the Lord of creation loves in the capricious way that humans do.

With this attitude, we begin to envision our loving Father as an impatient taskmaster, pushed to the edge by our missteps, ready to come down hard on us at any moment. Maybe once—possibly when we were children—we thought God could be affectionate. But much water has passed under the bridge since then. That was before we committed *this* wrong or made *that* mistake. We're not sure just how much we've drawn from God's love account, but we're bound to be reaching the bottom. We must find some way to earn our way back into His good graces.

That's how love might function with your friend or even with a spouse or parent. But it's never how love works with God. Before, during, and after your stumble, and through every stumble to follow, His love remains intact and perfect. If you could somehow chart the love of God, it would show as a straight line across the top of the graph, never dipping, never plunging, but remaining constant, with a value of infinity. Any variance is simply imaginary, the result of our ignorance or inability to feel His love.

As I write this book, the e-mails flow in from people in pain, people who believe that God had good reason to write them off long ago. Many of these people know their Bibles inside out, and they still manage to miss the Bible's central message: You cannot keep God from loving you. You can know this truth clearly with your mind and never have it penetrate your heart. While I firmly believe that Christianity is rational, I also believe it must involve our emotions. As the French mathematician Blaise Pascal said, "It is the heart which experiences God, not the reason."[2] We need to *feel* the deep and abiding love of God.

There are two circumstances in which we are prone to doubt the love of God: when we are the victims of evil and when we are the agents of evil. In both cases, the error is in thinking that the presence of evil means the absence of God's love.

He has never promised to keep all evil away from us. In fact, He reminds us constantly that evil is all around us. The point is that God is always more powerful than the worst the devil can throw at us (1 John 4:4).

But the question remains, since God hates evil, how can He love us when we do evil ourselves? There are consequences to our evil acts; we reap what we sow. But those consequences do not include the loss of God's love. Nor does His love increase when we do good things. Our performance in either direction is simply not part of the equation. He loves because it is His nature to love—nothing more, nothing less. Even when we are faithless, God remains faithful (2 Timothy 2:13)!

The great, complex love story of the Bible does not whitewash the missteps people make and the resulting consequences. Yet, again and again, we are assured that God has no intention of abandoning us. His love is forever. He promises, "I will never leave you nor forsake you" (Hebrews 13:5). What part of *never* do we fail to understand?

Time and again, the Bible shows us examples of God's loyal love for those who have been disloyal to Him:

• God did not stop loving Adam and Eve, even after they had violated His one restriction in the Garden of Eden. He punished them, but He never quit loving them.

• God did not stop loving Noah, even though he dishonored the grace God had shown in saving his family from the Flood by lying naked in a drunken stupor before his sons.

• God did not stop loving Abraham, even though he sought relief from famine in Egypt instead of trusting God to provide for him. Even though he tried to fulfill God's promise of a son through his own ingenuity. Even though, on two separate occasions, he lied about the identity of his wife.

• God did not stop loving Moses, even though he committed murder and later violated God's command by losing his temper and striking the rock of provision. God punished Moses by denying him entrance to the Promised Land. Later, He showed his love and mercy by allowing Moses to stand with Elijah in the presence of Jesus on the Mount of Transfiguration.

• God did not stop loving David, even though David committed adultery with Bathsheba, had her husband murdered, and later conducted an unauthorized, pride-motivated census of Israel. David suffered greatly for his sins, but when he cried out in sincere repentance, God forgave him and restored him to fellowship.

• God did not stop loving Jonah, even though he refused to take God's saving message to Nineveh. After his experience in the belly of the great fish, we read that the "word of the LORD came to Jonah the second time" (Jonah 3:1). God gave Jonah another chance to obey, and Jonah went on to preside over one of the greatest revivals in history.

• God did not stop loving Peter, even though he denied Jesus three times. The Lord restored Peter to fellowship by matching his threefold denial with a threefold recommissioning (John 21:15–17).

Hosea: The Story of God's Unrelenting Love

Now we come to one of the most vivid and direct examples of God's unrelenting love—and one of the most beautiful stories in the Bible. It involves an eighth-century Jewish prophet named Hosea and his wife, Gomer. Hosea was called to prophesy to the ten northern tribes of Israel just before the Assyrians took them into captivity in 722 BC.

As a background to Hosea's prophecy, we need to remember that God formed a covenant with Israel that took the form of a marriage. The vows were exchanged at Mount Sinai in Exodus 24, then renewed when Israel entered the Promised Land (Joshua 8:30–35), and again after Israel had settled into the land (Joshua 24:1–28). God's love was like that of a cherishing husband—deep, intimate, tender, provident, and protective.

When a man and a woman first fall in love, the feeling is intense and ecstatic. When that love leads to marriage, the couple experiences the closest, most intimate and devoted of all human relationships. That is how God felt about Israel.

God, the heavenly Groom, and Israel, His earthly bride, had pledged their fidelity three times, but the bride did not remain faithful. Even though the time in which Hosea prophesied was one of great prosperity, it was also a time of great wickedness.

The nation of Israel blatantly broke every commandment. Lying, thievery, bloodshed, oppression, perverted justice, and prostitution were rampant and openly practiced. Excessive luxury existed side by side with abject poverty. Adultery was even incorporated into their religion. In Jerusalem, male cultic prostitutes were actually being housed in the Jewish temple along with women who wove fabrics for the idols. As one writer summarized the conditions, "Those who were first in rank were first in excess... The idolatrous priest loved and shared in the sins of the people... Corruption had spread throughout the whole land... the knowledge of God was willfully rejected; the people hated rebuke."[3]

Finally, Israel's disloyalty reached a tipping point. And it was then that God sent His prophet Hosea to teach a lesson to the nation. He wanted them to see that even through their faithlessness, He remained loyal and loving. When God says *forever*, He means it. When He says *love*, He lives it. The nation that God took as a bride had played the harlot. The people had prostituted themselves, literally and spiritually, in their pursuit of pleasure. But God continued to pursue them. His love never quit.

In his prophecy, Hosea likens the nation of Israel to an adulterous wife: "The spirit of harlotry has caused them to stray, and they have played the harlot against their God" (Hosea 4:12).

Is there anything more hurtful to a spouse than disloyalty? When couples marry, they stand before God and witnesses and vow to be faithful and loyal to each other. When someone says "I do" and then breaches that promise, the violated partner experiences one of the deepest hurts a human can feel.

One prominent person of recent times who endured the heartbreak of marital infidelity was Elizabeth Edwards, who died in December 2010 of cancer. She was the wife of vice presidential candidate Senator John Edwards, who disgraced himself, his family, and especially his wife by having an affair and fathering a child by another woman. Elizabeth describes the agony she experienced when she learned of her husband's infidelities:

> After I cried and screamed, I went to the bathroom and threw up. And the next day John and I spoke. He wasn't coy, but it turned out he wasn't forthright either... I felt that the ground underneath me had been pulled away.
>
> I spent months learning to live with a single incidence of infidelity. And I would like to say that a single incidence is easy to overcome, but it is not. I am who I am. I am imperfect in a million ways, but I always thought I was the kind of woman, the kind of wife to whom a husband would be faithful. I had asked for fidelity, begged for it, really, when we married. I never need flowers or jewelry, I don't care about vacations or a nice car. But I need you to be faithful. Leave me, if you must, but be faithful to me if you are with me.[4]

Infidelity like that committed against Elizabeth Edwards causes such pain and heartbreak because it pierces the very heart of the marriage relationship. Loyalty is the cornerstone of all relationships. It is at the heart of the biblical idea of covenant. It matters not whether the covenant is between God and man or man and woman—loyalty is the indispensable foundation.

The durability, loyalty, and permanence of God's love are portrayed in the Old Testament by the continual reference to His "steadfast love." The Hebrew word is *hesed*, and it occurs 248 times in the Old Testament. It is particularly frequent in the Psalms, appearing twenty-six times in Psalm 136 alone.

Israel has forsaken the Lord. So through the prophet Hosea, they are about to learn just how things stand between them and God:"You have lost your way, and you've turned to other gods. There will be dark consequences for you; there always are. But that does not mean My love has changed one iota. I love you now; I will love you through the hard lessons you'll be learning; and I will love you when you come back to My waiting arms."

Hosea is charged to deliver this message in one of the strangest and most strikingly dramatic ways you can imagine. At the beginning of Hosea's book, God gives His prophet this shocking command: "Go, take yourself a wife of harlotry and children of harlotry, for the land has committed great harlotry by departing from the LORD" (1:2).

What would it have been like to be a fly on the wall and hear God saying, "Hosea, I have a job for you. I want you to marry a woman who will be unfaithful to you. Let her dishonor your name, and when she does, I want you to hold fast to your marriage vow."

"But, Lord..."

"Think of it as a living parable, Hosea."

"A parable?"

"It's like a play. You'll be playing My part; your wife will represent Israel. I need to do something really dramatic that will mirror the wickedness of the people so they can see their unfaithfulness to Me."

"But Lord, this is not really the kind of marriage I had envisioned."

"Believe Me, Hosea; I know from experience what you're getting into. But trust Me on this. When your wife keeps committing adultery and you don't throw her out on the curb—when you love the unlovable and keep taking her back—your faithfulness will be so counterintuitive that the people will have to confront a truth they've lost about My unwavering faithfulness and love for them."

In obedience to God, Hosea took the harlot Gomer to be his wife.

Was Gomer a harlot before her marriage to Hosea, or is she called a harlot because that is what she would become? Dr. Frederick A. Tatford believes that the effectiveness of the whole pageant depended upon the wife starting from a position of love and fidelity. Hosea's grief would not have been genuine had he married someone he didn't truly love and who didn't initially love him.[5]

This human drama would accurately tell the whole tragic story of God and Israel, from a joyous exalted relationship to the bitter ashes of repeated infidelity. It was to be a lesson the hearers would never forget.

Even so, God knew the message would not sink in. Hosea's words and personal story would go unheeded, and the consequences for violating the covenant would have to run their course. Yet it was important that God let His people know that His love would never fail. To this end, Hosea spoke of a future day when God's love would draw them back to Him again, just as Hosea would draw Gomer back to himself:

> *"And it shall be, in that day,"*
> *Says the LORD,*
> *"That you will call Me 'My Husband,'*
> *And no longer call Me 'My Master,'...*
> *In that day...I will betroth you to Me forever;*
> *Yes, I will betroth you to Me*
> *In righteousness and justice,*
> *In lovingkindness and mercy;*
> *I will betroth you to Me in faithfulness,*
> *And you shall know the LORD."*
>
> —HOSEA 2:16, 18–20

This is a love that doesn't follow human nature, doesn't return evil for evil. It's a love that makes sense only when we realize it comes from God. The Old Testament is a lengthy chronicle of this love, telling the story of a wandering, faithless people pursued by a constantly loving God.

To understand Hosea's book, we need to be conscious of the prophetic style. In these chapters, there are two speakers and one voice. When Hosea speaks as the prophet of God, his words thunder with angry judgment against rebellious Israel. But when he speaks as the mouthpiece of God, we hear positive words of love and compassion. The anger and the compassion are both components of God's character.

Much of our focus on the enduring nature of God's love will center on the eleventh chapter of Hosea, which vividly unfolds both the anger and the compassion of God. In this chapter we come to understand the personal grief of the prophet as he communicates God's heart toward Israel and their response to His love. In four steps, we will see:

- The **commitment** of God's love—His loyal love for His people Israel.
- The **contempt** of Israel for God in spite of His loyal love.
- The **compassion** of God toward His people in spite of their sin.
- The **consummation** of God's love—resolving the tension between God's holy standards and His love for those who violate those standards.

In the rest of this chapter, we will explore these points to learn all Hosea has to tell us about God's unrelenting love.

The Commitment of God's Love

One of the most revealing commentaries on the sad state of love in modern cultures is the growing omission of the phrase "till death do us part" in traditional marriage ceremonies.

Couples are hedging their bets, removing *forever* from their shared vocabulary. Of course, keeping that phrase in a ceremony doesn't make a marriage bulletproof. We're staring down alarming divorce statistics, no matter what words we use. But there's something very sad about the ancient and holy institution of marriage becoming as casual, nonbinding, and fleeting as the rice thrown at the couple.

British poet Stephen Turner sums up our current disregard for loyal love in his poem "Declaration of Intent":

> She said she'd love me for eternity,
> But managed to reduce it to 8 months for good behaviour.
> She said we fitted together like a hand in a glove,
> But then the hot weather came and such
> Accessories were not needed.
> She said the future was ours,
> But the house was made out in her name.
> She said I was the only one who understood her completely,
> And then she left me.
> She said she knew I'd understand completely.[6]

English author and minister Roy Clements quotes this poem and adds that this kind of infidelity is destroying families throughout Western culture. He observes that when human love takes such a hit, then the love of God is that much harder for people to understand.[7]

This is why I mourn the current state of marriage, not only for its own sake; I mourn it also for the implications it has on how we see the love of God. *Forever* is a God-word, and we are God-people, created to reflect His character. God gives us marriage so that we can experience and reflect the higher love we enjoy with Him.

Greek mythology gives us one powerful example of marital faithfulness. Odysseus, the hero of Homer's *The Odyssey*, was away from his wife, Penelope, for twenty years—ten years in the Trojan War, and another ten encountering formidable obstacles on his attempt to return home. Most of his subjects had given up on him, thinking he had died in the wars. Thus more than a hundred suitors lined up to marry Penelope, but she held to a stubborn hope for the return of her husband, the king of her heart.

Eventually she was forced to make her suitors a promise: When she finished weaving a burial shroud for Odysseus's elderly father, she would choose a new husband. But every night she unraveled part of the shroud so it was never finished—until her ruse was discovered. Finally, Odysseus returned to a doggedly faithful wife whose love had been tested by time.

People could look at Penelope's loyalty and say, "Yes—this kind of love is possible. But does it happen only in myths? Does anyone love like that today?" Present-day examples are becoming all too rare, but I am grateful that they still exist.

Chris Spielman's story is a direct counterpoint to the infidelity of Senator John Edwards, right down to the wife afflicted with cancer. Spielman was one of the NFL's better linebackers. He had starred at Ohio State in a career that put him in the College Football Hall of Fame. After going professional, he played on four Pro Bowl teams. Then, in 1998, at the top of his form, he sat out a year. The NFL and his fans were moved to the back burner because his wife was fighting breast cancer.

Stefanie Spielman and her doctors fought the cancer aggressively. When chemotherapy made her hair fall out, her husband shaved his own head as a gesture of solidarity. All that year he ran the household, took care of their children, and supported his wife. He returned to football in the 1999 season, only to retire before the season actually began. His heart was at home.

Stefanie battled her disease for more than a decade before passing away in 2009. After she died, Chris said, "She was my only girlfriend."[8]

When we see such steadfast, unrelenting loyalty, our hearts are touched with deep admiration. We know we are seeing something very good—someone choosing to stand in the gap rather than walk away; someone loving at a high cost; someone saying, like God Himself, "I will never leave you nor forsake you."

Every time I read of a couple celebrating their golden wedding anniversary, my heart glows: fifty years of tests passed; fifty years of promises kept. These stories tell me that there are still good models of committed love out there—models that reflect an exalted, heavenly love.

And I love hearing accounts of couples who fought for their marriage, who could have bailed out but hung in there because they knew that all things are possible with God. Nothing should be more stubborn than married love.

In Hosea 11, God presents the idea of steadfast love in high definition through the story of a man's unfailing love for a failing wife. Sixteen times in this chapter God uses "I" in a sustained revelation to show that He is the one who has loved and sustained His people through every step of their lives. He demonstrates the all-encompassing characteristics of His love by employing three illustrative analogies: He loves us as a father, as a husband, and as a shepherd.

He Loves as a Father

When Israel was a child, I loved him,
And out of Egypt I called My son...
I taught Ephraim to walk,
Taking them by their arms...

—HOSEA 11:1, 3

Here the Lord reminds His people of the tender care He gave them during their infancy as a nation. Because He loved Israel, God called them out of bondage in Egypt, delivered them from their taskmasters, and taught them to walk—to make their own choices and determine their own direction.

As they were learning to walk, He often held them in His arms to protect them from dangers they were not yet ready to face. For example, the shortest land route from Egypt to Canaan would have been along the coast of the Mediterranean Sea and then north to Beersheba through Philistia. But Israel was not yet ready to stand against the aggressive Philistine army, so God took care of His people by leading them along a circuitous route (Exodus 13:17–18). Each step of the way, God nurtured Israel and kept them from injury as they slowly matured as a nation of God.

Like a father, He carried them when they stumbled and fed them manna from heaven when they were hungry.

In Hosea's day, Israel knew the fatherly love of God—but only as a nation. The idea that each individual could have a personal relationship with a heavenly Father was yet years to come. It may surprise you to know that the Old Testament never refers to God as the personal father of individuals. Not until the coming of Jesus did any individual Jew ever think of God as his or her personal father, which was something they learned from Jesus, who continually called God "My Father."

He Loves as a Husband

I drew them with gentle cords,
With bands of love.

—HOSEA 11:4A

The husbandly dimension of God's love is the primary analogy in the book of Hosea. It's a dimension that Hosea learned firsthand, having become a living illustration of God's steadfast love. Just as he had drawn his unfaithful wife, Gomer, back with gentle cords of love, so God had entreated His people to come back to Him.

He Loves as a Shepherd

And I was to them as those who take the yoke from their neck.
I stooped and fed them.

—HOSEA 11:4B

The agricultural people of Hosea's time clearly understood the kind of love a shepherd shows to his flocks. We recognize the caring, provident nature of a shepherd's love from Psalm 23, and it's a theme that runs throughout the entire Bible. It is yet another way of looking at the singular love God has for us.

Old Testament professor Gary V. Smith explains Hosea's depiction of God as a shepherd: "[This verse] describes God's tender care and provisions for his people. He 'bent down' gently to feed them by graciously providing manna and quail for the forty years of wandering in the Sinai desert (see Exodus 16; Numbers 11)."[9]

The Contempt for God's Love

But the more I called Israel,
the further they went from me.
They sacrificed to the Baals
and they burned incense to images.
It was I who taught Ephraim to walk,
taking them by the arms;
but they did not realize
it was I who healed them.

—HOSEA 11:2–3 (NIV)

Even though God called out to His rebellious people through His prophets, they did not listen. Israel's heart had become so calloused that they had lost all memory of the Lord's miraculous works on their behalf. As a result, they began to drift:

My people are bent on backsliding from Me.
Though they call to the Most High,
None at all exalt Him.

—HOSEA 11:7

In spite of all God had done for them, the people of Israel were deliberate backsliders. This jarring juxtaposition of God's commitment to Israel and Israel's contempt for God runs throughout the entire book of Hosea. But it reaches its climax here in the eleventh chapter where the dissonant concepts of *commitment* and *contempt* meet head-on in the same verses— something that should be impossible. How could there be such a rebellious response to such a perfect love?

More important is the question: How does God respond to Israel's infidelity? How would you respond? At first God considers immediate judgment:

> *He shall not return to the land of Egypt;*
> *But the Assyrian shall be his king,*
> *Because they refused to repent.*
> *And the sword shall slash in his cities,*
> *Devour his districts,*
> *And consume them,*
> *Because of their own counsels.*
>
> —HOSEA 11:5–6

We can easily understand these expressions of wrath. It seems the natural response of a God who has been so good to an entire nation, only to receive every insult in return. The great preacher G. Campbell Morgan explains it this way:

> What is to be done? There is only one thing to do, by all the laws of human conduct, and all the laws that are only laws of righteousness and equity and justice. Give them up, abandon them...I declare that when I see the Lover, teaching to walk, nursing with a tender care, healing...and then watch these people definitely, persistently,

positively rebellious; I say there is only one thing to do with them: give them up.[10]

This reaction makes sense to us because it would be the typical human response. How many times have we dealt out some form of retaliation when we were wronged or betrayed by people close to us? When people do you wrong, you leave them. You divorce them. You sue them. At the very least, you turn your back on them until they have paid the price. It's as if we want to apply the law of physics to the law of love: for every action, we want to render an equal and opposite reaction.

Verses 5 and 6 display the kind of response to Israel's infidelity that we would naturally expect from someone who has been jilted. But Hosea goes on to show us that while the adulterous people must endure judgment—the natural consequence they have brought upon themselves—God does not pronounce final condemnation upon them. Deep and compelling love overrules any thought of putting Israel away from Him forever.

The Compassion of God's Love

How can I give you up, Ephraim?
How can I hand you over, Israel?
How can I make you like Admah?
How can I set you like Zeboiim?
My heart churns within Me;
My sympathy is stirred.
I will not execute the fierceness of My anger;
I will not again destroy Ephraim.

For I am God, and not man,
The Holy One in your midst;
And I will not come with terror.

—HOSEA 11:8–9

Here God expresses a moving wave of poignant love that reminds us of Jesus' lament over the city He most loved: "O Jerusalem, Jerusalem, the one who kills the prophets and stones those who are sent to her! How often I wanted to gather your children together, as a hen gathers her chicks under her wings, but you were not willing!" (Matthew 23:37).

Jesus' unshakable devotion to the city that rejected Him should not surprise us. It is consistent with the heart of His Father, a heart filled with compassion for the rebellious nation of Israel. Hosea gives us four questions that display His agonized feelings:

How can I give you up, Ephraim?
How can I hand you over, Israel?
How can I make you like Admah?
How can I set you like Zeboiim?

What do these questions mean? Before we can answer, we need to understand the meaning of the four names mentioned.

Ephraim was a powerful Israelite tribe of the north, but it was often used as a synonym for Israel itself. *Israel*, of course, is the name of the ten northern tribes that split off from the southern tribes of Judah and Benjamin. *Admah* and *Zeboiim* were the names of cities destroyed along with the wicked towns of Sodom and Gomorrah (Genesis 10:19).

Here God asks whether He can really give His people what

they truly deserve. He thinks of those times when the destruction of other wicked people was the only option, and His love cries out, "My heart churns within Me; My sympathy is stirred" (Hosea 11:8).

What can this mean? D. A. Carson explains:

The passage as a whole means that the promised impending judgment will not be the last word. Exile will be followed by return from exile. In the entire context, when God declares that his heart is changed within him and all his compassion is aroused, he does not mean that he has changed his mind and Israel will be spared the punishment he decreed a few verses earlier. Rather, it is that any long-term threat of permanent judgment must be set aside. God will bring them back from Egypt and Assyria.[11]

Has God gone soft on sin? Is He pampering where discipline is called for? Absolutely not! He will allow the consequences of rebellion and He will not restrain His hand when punishment is required. But there will be no ultimate destruction of Israel as there was for Sodom and Gomorrah. The people will live to find their way back to God, who will wait patiently and lovingly.

In a sermon he delivered on this passage, Roy Clements said:

Though [Hosea 11] is comparatively little known, I regard it as one of the jewels in the Bible, for in it we see portrayed in a remarkable and vivid way what the love of God means to God Himself.

So here Hosea is bold enough to open for us the mind of God, God's inner thoughts. Dare we say, God's feelings?

What do we find when we peep through that audacious window? Do we find the stern impartiality of an omniscient judge? Do we find the aloof dignity of an omnipotent sovereign? No. Astonishingly, in this passage the prophet tells us that what we find when we look through that window at the heart of God is a broken heart, the broken heart of a deserted parent.

Hosea insists that there is one very fundamental and important way in which God is like us. He loves, and loves in a way that we human beings can understand and experience. And because he loves, he feels. He can be hurt. He can suffer.[12]

Many historic Christian documents declare that God is "impassible." In other words, He is emotionless. The *Westminster Confession of Faith* asserts the same thing.[13] But is that assertion true? After reading these verses from Hosea, how can we believe it?

Does God feel pain? Does God actually suffer when we sin and show contempt for His love? Verse 8 seems to indicate that He does. Some say that this is simply God's way of helping us understand deity in the language of humanity—the only language we understand. Was that not one of the purposes of God's becoming a man? So that we might know God in a way we can understand? Certainly, at some level, we must concede that Jesus' life—a life filled with emotions, pain, and suffering—helps us understand who God is.

The longer I live, the greater appreciation I have for the

truth that man is created in God's image. That means if you or I feel hurt when someone abuses our love, it is because we are made in the image of God, who is also hurt when His love is abused. I realize that man's emotions are all too often displayed sinfully, whereas God's emotions never are. We allow indignation to swell into rage or hurt to morph into revenge. But if God can experience the joy of love fulfilled, why would He not also experience the pain of love rejected?

Many people are afraid to love for fear of the pain of rejection. And so they hold back. But true love, unconditional love, loyal love—*God's love*—is not fearful.

What if God had taken a fearful approach to loving Israel? Or David, Moses, Abraham, Noah, or Adam and Eve? What if God had said, "I think I'll back off from creating the world because if I fill it with creatures after My likeness—creatures with the freedom to choose—they may choose not to love Me."

God made an incredible decision to instill freedom into His children. And sure enough, it brought Him the grief endured by any parent who has had a rebellious child. But for God it has been worse: That grief has come repeatedly and in every variation in every corner of the world. Every human child but One has dishonored Him.

Since the Garden, we have chosen to break laws as fast as He could give them to us. We have chosen to greet the incomparable, everlasting love of our Creator with insult and derision. In doing so, we injure ourselves and cause Him sorrow. And somehow, through it all, God's love continues, never responding in kind, never giving up hope and folding up shop, never reacting, but always reaching out to rescue, to restore. The deeper our insult, the deeper His resolve to bring us home.

Yes, love can be painful, and that's the very reason it can overcome the world. God shows us that miracles come to pass when the one who loves receives bad for good yet keeps offering the good, keeps loving without return. The doorway between heaven and earth is cracked open and the light of God's love shines through.

We could strike back when we're hit, or we could simply go hide in a cave. But we are the children of an eternal God, and we were made for something better. We were made to experience *and dispense* the miracle of selfless, patient, stubborn, love—a love that does not quit; a love that does not demand return; a love that does not avoid pain but is compassionate beyond measure.

The Consummation of God's Love

I will not execute the fierceness of My anger;
I will not again destroy Ephraim.
For I am God, and not man,
The Holy One in your midst;
And I will not come with terror.

—HOSEA 11:9

How can God possibly spare Israel when they obviously deserve the ultimate punishment? If He is a righteous God, how can He justify allowing them to rebel without bringing down annihilation? Or, as the apostle Paul put it, how can God simultaneously be both "just and the justifier" (Romans 3:26)?

The answer is found in the middle of verse 9: He is God and

not man! He does not have to lower His high standard of perfection in order to show compassionate love toward us. As the next line says, He is "the Holy One in [our] midst." God's holiness is not diminished when His love is increased. God is God and God is holy, and He can do as He will and love whom He will.

But there's still a difficulty to be addressed before we can understand how a holy God can forgive unholy sinners. Perfect holiness cannot rightly tolerate the contamination of sin. One cannot allow rats, roaches, and termites to infest his house and yet be a good homeowner. His house will become contaminated and it will fall. God cannot allow the contamination that sinners would bring into heaven and at the same time be a holy God. Heaven would no longer be a paradise. So how can God allow Himself to love us, infested as we are with sin?

We find the answer in the very name the prophet's parents chose for him—*Hosea*. This name is given to two others in the Bible—one before the prophet and one after. The first was Joshua. "These are the names of the men whom Moses sent to spy out the land. And Moses called Hoshea the son of Nun, Joshua" (Numbers 13:16).

The second: "And she shall bring forth a Son, and you shall call His name JESUS, for He will save His people from their sins" (Matthew 1:21). Interestingly, Hoshea, Hosea, Joshua, and Jesus are all renderings of the same name, meaning "salvation." As G. Campbell Morgan says, "There came One in the fullness of time whose name was Jehovah and Hosea: His name was Jesus... and at last we find out how God can be just and the Justifier of the sinning soul."[14]

Having no sins of His own, Jesus volunteered to take our sins as if they were His. He died on the cross so He could remove those sins from us and take them into death. That left us legally free of sin and washed us pure with the blood of Jesus so that we could enter the presence of God's perfect holiness. Dr. Morgan continues, "Through Jesus, the claims of justice which are against my soul are all met. Through Him the glory of holiness is maintained. The redemption of the human soul is not a pity that agrees to ignore sin; but a power that cancels it and sets us free from its dominion."[15]

Psalm 85:10–11 prophetically explains the result of Jesus' sacrifice when it says, "Mercy and truth have met together; righteousness and peace have kissed. Truth shall spring out of the earth, and righteousness shall look down from heaven." In the first two lines, mercy and truth are reconciled. In the last two lines, heaven and earth are reconciled. Biblical expositor John Phillips explains:

God cannot administer mercy at the expense of truth. He cannot uphold truth at the expense of mercy. But they have met together now at Calvary. There righteousness and peace have kissed each other. God can now uphold both His mercy and His truth, both His righteousness and His peace. With the coming of His Son, He has found a way to give us both His peace and His righteousness. Therefore mercy and truth are no longer at odds.[16]

Understanding the lengths God went to in order to reconcile us to Himself makes it easy to see why so many Christians see John 3:16 as the most endearing verse in the Bible: "For God so loved the world that He gave His only begotten Son, that whoever believes in Him should not perish but have everlasting life." At the cross, justice and mercy, grace and truth, righteousness and peace, flow simultaneously from the love of God.

When Rachelle Friedman attended her bachelorette party just before her wedding, she was about to realize the fulfillment of a dream: walking down the aisle to marry her sweetheart, Chris Chapman. That marriage took place—a year later. But instead of walking, Rachelle rolled down the aisle in a wheelchair. A freak poolside accident at the party left Rachelle paralyzed from the waist down.

Rachelle and Chris postponed their wedding for a year, but not their love. Chris said that after the accident he never thought, "'What am *I* going to do?' It was, 'What are *we* going to do.'...It was one step at a time."[17] Their lives and love are going strong with no looking back. A tragic circumstance changed the *look* of their love—wheelchairs, an access van, lots of physical therapy—but not its *loyalty*.

That's how God's love is:

No matter what you have done...

No matter how far you have fallen...

No matter what you've heard the enemy whisper in your ear...

God's love never quits. He loves you. He always has. He always will.

FIVE

God Wrote His Love in Red

❧

For God so loved the world that He gave His only begotten Son,
that whoever believes in Him should not perish but have
everlasting life.

—JOHN 3:16

Many years ago, in the little English village of Brackenth-
waite, there lived a quiet and lonely man named William
Dixon. His wife had died years before, and later he had lost
his only son. Dixon often could be seen sitting by his window,
watching the world go by and smiling at the happy families on
the streets.

One day he looked out and saw a neighbor's home on fire.
Other neighbors were already gathering, scrambling for water
and shouting for help. Dixon ran out and joined them just as
an elderly woman was pulled from the flames.

"Who else is inside?" someone shouted above the commotion.

"My little grandson!" she gasped through smoke-filled lungs. "Upstairs—trapped!"

The people groaned, knowing the stairway was impassable. But William Dixon hurried to the front of the house and found an iron drainage pipe running up the wall. Taking hold of it, he pulled himself upward to the window and found the terrified boy. He scooped up the child and scrambled back to the ground.

A few days later, the grandmother succumbed to her injuries, leaving the little boy an orphan with no home, no guardian. The village held a hearing to determine his fate.

When the meeting was called to order, two volunteers came forward. One good citizen answered the standard questions, giving every assurance that he would provide a good home. The second volunteer was William Dixon, the rescuer. He said few words, but his hands spoke for him. They were bandaged. The hot iron pipe he'd been forced to climb had burned them severely.

When it came to a vote, the man with the scarred hands went home with the orphan, a father once more. His love, everyone agreed, was written on his hands.[1]

The love of our Lord was also written on His hands—the two hands stretched out and nailed to the cross, where they flowed with the blood that indelibly wrote His love for us for all eternity.

That is the message of the greatest verse in all Scripture—John 3:16. As Charitie Lees Bancroft's great hymn expresses it,

Before the throne of God above
I have a strong and perfect plea.

A great high Priest whose Name is Love
Who ever lives and pleads for me.
My name is graven on His hands,
My name is written in His heart.

The historian Pliny once said that he had seen the entire *Iliad* of Homer written in so small a character that it could be stuffed into a nutshell. In the mid-1500s, English penman Peter Bales found a way to write the entire Bible on a single sheet of paper that folded to fit within an egg-sized walnut shell—not that you or I could actually read the minuscule type, mind you. (I've yet to figure out the practical value of that project.) In a sense, John 3:16 is the entire Bible stuffed into a tiny nutshell.

John 3:16 has long been regarded as our greatest, most direct, and most concise statement of the Gospel. With almost miraculous precision, it places the good news of the love of God in the smallest of packages. When you say "John 3:16," even many unbelievers either know what it means or know the verse itself. It is the most famous book-chapter-verse reference in the entire Bible. You'll see it on a banner at a sporting event, emblazoned on a T-shirt, or scrawled in graffiti on an underpass. It's a shorthand way of saying, "God loves us all."

Tim Tebow famously placed the reference on his eye black (the tape strip beneath a football player's eyes) before a national championship game in college, and the broadcasters frequently identified it as his favorite verse. Immediately afterward, Google received more than ninety million hits from people looking up John 3:16. And that was only the beginning. Three years later, after leading the Denver Broncos to a rousing play-off victory over the Pittsburgh Steelers, someone noticed he had thrown for precisely 316 yards. The Associated Press reported that he also averaged 31.6 yards per completion. Those who didn't "get it" again went to the Internet, and by Monday afternoon, John 3:16 was once more the most searched item on the Internet.[2]

It's often been said that the Lord moves in mysterious ways. Some may think that finding significance in a quarterback's passing yardage borders on superstition, but it may show us that God will use almost any means to tell us how deeply He loves us. When was the last time any of our efforts succeeded in getting ninety million people to hurry to the Internet and look up the Gospel?

Throughout history, millions of words have been written about John 3:16. Yet none of them are necessary to grasp the meaning of the verse. God communicated the heart and meaning of the Gospel—the most profound, far-reaching message of all time—in only twenty-five simple words of English text. When translated into any language, this verse is supremely easy to understand.

All we need in life is packed into those twenty-five words. Your Bible is the essential library of life, and every verse is profitable for wise living. But if worse came to worst, and we could retain only one of its 31,103 verses, this would be the one we could not let slip from our grasp.

When I was growing up, I heard a sermon on John 3:16 that really grabbed hold of me. The evangelist pointed out that not only was the entire Gospel contained in the message of the verse, but the word *gospel* was embedded in the verse itself.

> For **God** so loved the world
>> that He gave His **Only**
>>> begotten **Son**, that whoever believes
>> in Him should not **Perish**
>>> but have **Everlasting**
>>>> **Life**.

How well I remember grabbing my pen and scratching that formula beneath the words in my Bible so I would never forget how thoroughly and essentially John 3:16 *is* the Gospel. This simple little device is just one more aid, helping us to see this sentence for what it is—a statement of the Gospel so simple that a child can understand it and so profound that a scholar could never fathom its depths. It needs to be inscribed permanently on every heart.

John 3:16 is preached, studied, and cited more often than any other biblical passage, yet it never becomes yesterday's news, never loses its majesty or its freshness, never loses one microvolt of emotional power. It is so inexhaustible that over a period of many years, one obsessive preacher compiled from it more than six hundred preaching outlines. Talk about a month of Sundays! That's enough sermons to keep a church fed for almost twelve years.

It's a truism among pastors that the young ones preach John 3:16 again and again because it's so simple, so preachable. Yet the older ones hesitate to preach it because they've come to see the profundity and mystery of the verse, and they feel inadequate to do it justice. G. Campbell Morgan was one of the giants of preaching, yet he placed himself in the second category. He said, "There is a text that I have never attempted to preach on, though I have gone around it and around it—John 3:16. It is too big. When I have read it, there is nothing else to say. If we only knew how to read it, so as to produce a sense of it in the ears of people, there would be nothing to preach about."[3]

I had been preaching fifteen years before I ever delivered one message from John 3:16. When I considered preaching it, I would read those words again and think, *What is left to say? It's simple; everybody knows it by heart. What could I possibly add?*

In time, however, I changed my mind. I realized that it wasn't my job to exclude from my preaching anything God had communicated in His Word, especially not this crucially important verse. It wasn't my job to decide what people knew so well they no longer needed to hear. Nor was it my job to come to the pulpit loaded with theological zingers to delight and astound. I was just the messenger, and God had entrusted to me the greatest message of all time. It was not about me or what I could bring—it was about God and what He had done; it was about the most urgent message humanity could ever hear. How could I possibly justify failing to deliver it?

My entire mission in life is to say to the world, "God loves you, and here's how much. Now what will you do about it?" It's your job, too; and this is the verse that, more than any other, lays out what we have to say.

How Did John 3:16 Come to Be?

You might think that since the message of John 3:16 is for the entire world, it would have been delivered to a large assembly, maybe in Jesus' Sermon on the Mount or in some of His discourses in the temple. Instead, it was spoken privately to a single person.[4] Nicodemus was a leading member of the ruling Jewish council, the Sanhedrin. Jesus had aroused the anger and opposition of these Jewish leaders because of His claims to be the Son of God and what they saw as His disregard for some of their laws.

But Nicodemus was not so sure. He had seen the miracles of Jesus, and he could not write Him off as easily as his peers. We must remember that Nicodemus, like all Jews, saw himself as one of God's chosen people in a highly exclusive sense. They belonged to God by virtue of their birth into His favored race. Their coming Messiah would destroy all Gentiles—especially the hated Romans who occupied Israel. Could Jesus be the man? Nicodemus wanted to find out. So to avoid the censure of the Sanhedrin, he sneaked out at night to see Jesus alone.

But the conversation did not go at all like Nicodemus expected. Jesus began confusing him with talk about being born again and how the Spirit of God is like the wind, blowing wherever it chooses. Jesus was telling him that the Spirit would soon move even outside the Jewish nation and enter the hearts of Gentiles all over the earth. Then, just in case Nicodemus was still confused, Jesus drove the message home in words no one could fail to understand: "For God so loved the world that He gave His only begotten Son, that whoever believes in Him should not perish but have everlasting life."

God loves the *world*, Nicodemus; not just the Jews, but the *whole world*! The door to God is open to all people. It's not a matter of birth; it's a matter of belief.

To this one open seeker, Jesus delivered the striking message that summarizes the whole Gospel. Here He laid the foundation for mankind's relationship with God. It's not a foundation of judgment or condemnation; it's a foundation of pure love. In John 3:16, Jesus told Nicodemus—and the rest of us as well—that God would do anything to save us. Even if He has to die to do it. He loves us that much.

Now that we've seen something of the impact and background of John 3:16, let's take a brief walk through the verse and explore seven life-changing realities about God's love.

God's Love Is Extravagant

For God so loved…

It's difficult for modern people to understand the cultural world before Christ. Even among the Jews in Nicodemus's time, the idea that "God is love" was counterintuitive. If you had played word association with a citizen of that day, when you said "God," the response would have been "fear." Among the Jews, God was a strict observer of man's follies and quick to disapprove and punish. Outside the Jewish community, God was considered an outright tyrant.

Even today, heathen religions are all about appeasing the wrath of a furious god. Medicine men and witch doctors cycle through desperate incantations, warding off death, disease, famine, and calamities inflicted by their gods. At the root of this fear is the fact that all people recognize in their hearts that they are unworthy sinners. Not knowing the good news of John 3:16, they are left to dodge the lightning from heaven, which they sense they have earned.

And then into that context Jesus drops these words: *God so loved*.

It turns religion topsy-turvy. It confounds Pharisees. It forces a full rewrite of one's idea of the Creator. No longer could the ancients think God to be aloof, simmering angrily on His throne, leaving us to figure some way to forestall His wrath. They had to radically shift their concept of Him from fear to love.

But if we think John 3:16 announced a change in God from wrathful to loving, we miss the point. William Barclay wrote, "Sometimes men present the Christian message in such a way that it sounds as if Jesus did something which changed the attitude of God to men from condemnation to forgiveness. But this text tells us that it all started with God. It was God who sent His Son, and He sent Him because He loved men. At the back of everything is the love of God."[5] God was never the wrathful deity of the ancients; He loved us from the beginning.

John 3:16 opens with a bang, starting not only with God, but with God *doing* something—God *loving*. Excuse me— God *so* loving. The most intense word in this verse is the smallest. Bound up in those two letters, *s-o*, are all the agonies of the Cross; all the sufferings of the Son as He walked among men; all the exertion of a God willing to leave heaven and take on flesh, not because He simply loved, but because He *so* loved. Hands that hold us are loving. Nail-scarred hands that hold us are *so* loving.

Years ago, Donna and I had the opportunity to visit some of the great churches in London, England. At the world famous St. Paul's Cathedral, we noticed in the annex a huge statue of Jesus Christ, writhing in anguish on the cross. You could see the pain in His face, the blood-sweat of His body. Beneath the statue, a plaque read "This is how God loved the world." He *so* loved the world.

So loved is what we say when love drives someone to action. It's what we feel when we see the message of God's devotion written in flowing red script with a pen dipped into His lifeblood—love at great cost, love clearly understood in every language.

This is extravagant love. God didn't simply say, "I love you." He said it in torn flesh, in agony, in bearing unearned, vicious punishment. "God demonstrates His own love toward us, in that while we were still sinners, Christ died for us" (Romans 5:8).

God's Love Is Extensive

...the world...

In the sixth word of John 3:16, we find the object of God's love: the world. It is doubly amazing for a Jew to write such words. As I noted when speaking of Nicodemus, it was basic to Hebrew culture that a Jew loved fellow Jews, and others not so much or not at all. He looked down with proud disdain on every Gentile, knowing that the Jews were God's chosen, the people with whom He had a special relationship.

Leon Morris writes, "The Jew was ready enough to think of God as loving Israel, but no passage appears to be cited in which any Jewish writer maintains that God loved the world. It is a distinctively Christian idea that God's love is wide enough to embrace all mankind. His love was not confined to any national group or any spiritual elite. It was a love which proceeds from the fact that He is love."[6]

Jews like Nicodemus would be aghast: God loves—*so* loves—the *world*? Surely not! God so loves the Romans, with their cruel tyranny? God so loves the Assyrians and the Babylonians, who carried the Jews into bondage?

Absolutely. The world was put on notice that God loves the lovable (whoever *they* may be); He loves the unlovable; He loves Jews and the haters of Jews. He loves all people, and all fall under the love of Christ. No one is too evil or too far away for His love.

We need to be aware that the term "world" is used in two different ways. John says here that God loved "the world." But in another place he says, "Do not love the world or the things in the world. If anyone loves the world, the love of the Father is not in him" (1 John 2:15). This seems contradictory: God loves the world, yet He tells us not to love the world if we want to be like God. How do we reconcile these two verses?

There is no contradiction. In 1 John, the reference is to the world *system* that rejects God—the world Satan invaded at man's fall and blighted with lust and pride and all other evils. Later John will say, "The whole world lies under the sway of the wicked one" (1 John 5:19). The Greek word for "world," *kosmos*, has different meanings in the Scriptures based on the context. In his Gospel, John is telling us that God loves all the *people* of the world, sinners though they are. In his Epistle, John is telling us that we must be careful not to fall in love with a wicked and godless world *system*, which would be a form of idolatry. His message is to love the world's people but not its program.

Just as *the world* carries shades of meaning, so does the word *love*. C. S. Lewis wrote of four different kinds of love: friendship, affection, erotic love, and sacrificial love.[7] And it's here that many people get confused. We know that God loves us, and we need to understand just what kind of love that is.

I happen to love the United States of America. I'm deeply thankful to be an American, and I can tell you sincerely that I love America with all my heart.

But I also happen to love my new grandson by the name of Levi. And my love for Levi is not at all the same kind of love I have for America. As much as I love the United States of America, my love for Levi is far deeper, far more emotional. I love him with all my heart—and then some. That may not make logical or mathematical sense, but I know what I mean.

God loves every individual in this world with the same profound devotion with which I love Levi. The whole truth is, God's love is far deeper and more profound than even my love for Levi simply because His love is perfect and infinite, as no human love is. No one loves you the way He does—not your spouse, not your mother, not your child. No one.

God's Love Is Expensive

...that He gave His only begotten Son...

Only begotten means "unique"—one and only.

James Montgomery Boice explains what Jesus' uniqueness means to us: "Jesus is the unique Son of God; there is no one like Him, no one who is His equal. Therefore, because

Jesus Christ is the very image of God, and because there is no one like Him, when God gave Jesus, He gave the best gift in the universe."[8]

Dr. Boice's observation is another demonstration of the value God places on us. He gave the most valuable and cherished gift in His possession. He sent His one and only Son into this world to show how much we mean to Him. He did this because it was the only way to rid us of our fatal addiction to sin so that He could have us with Him through all eternity.

The apostles John and Paul both attest that the preciousness of God's gift demonstrates the extreme depth of His love for us: "In this the love of God was manifested toward us, that God has sent His only begotten Son into the world, that we might live through Him" (1 John 4:9). "He who did not spare His own Son, but delivered Him up for us all, how shall He not with Him also freely give us all things?" (Romans 8:32).

Some years ago, before a Communion service, I showed a short film clip to illustrate the love of God. It told the story of a farmer and his ten-year-old son who were deeply devoted to each other. The two of them worked side by side on the farm, laughed and played, and spent almost all their time together.

The father also had the responsibility of switching the train that passed nearby. Each day he walked to the tracks and pulled the switch that redirected the approaching locomotive to another track.

One evening with their farm chores complete, the father and son were fishing in a stream that ran through the farm. When the father heard the distant whistle of the train, he left his son to take care of the track switch. As he walked toward the track, he did not realize that his son had decided to join him. The boy had taken a shortcut through the woods and was now walking along the tracks to meet his father.

The train approached the switching junction moving at high speed, trusting the farmer to switch it to the track that ran straight ahead. Suddenly the farmer saw his son on that track in a place where he could not possibly get off in time. The father's first impulse was to leave the train on its present track. But that track curved away, and the train was moving too fast to negotiate the turn. The father knew that if he switched the train, his boy would die. If he didn't, the train would derail, and many people would die.

In that moment, the father experienced the most terrible agony imaginable. He had to weigh the life of his son against a trainload of passengers he didn't even know. We sat on the edges of our seats as the film lingered on the father's hand as it gripped the switch. What would he do?

The question was not answered. The film concluded right there. But the message was clear: You and I were on that train, and God the Father was at the switch. We know the decision He made. He did not spare His only Son, but freely gave Him up that we all might be saved.

God also gave the best He had in another sense. As John tells us, Jesus is *with* God, He *is* God, and He is God's Son (John 1:1–3). Though a son, He is coeternal with the Father. Exactly how all those statements can be true must remain a mystery on this side of eternity. But here's what we can know: Jesus Christ is the very image of God, but that does not mean He is a creature made in the image of God as man is. He is God incarnate. Though a man, He is the eternal God Himself.

Consequently, when God gave Jesus, He gave Himself. He gave His own life—the most expensive gift in this vast universe.

With Paul, we must stand up and shout, "Thanks be to God for His indescribable gift!" (2 Corinthians 9:15).

God's Love Is Expansive

...that whoever...

Richard Baxter once wrote that he was glad that God put the word *whoever* in John 3:16. He would rather have that word in the verse than his own name. "I thank God," he said, "for the word 'whosoever.' If God had said that there was mercy for Richard Baxter, I am so vile a sinner that I would have thought he meant some other Richard Baxter; but when he says 'whosoever' I know that it includes me, the worst of all Richard Baxters."[9]

Whoever is what we call a "big tent." It can hold everyone who wants to find shelter beneath it. It's a wonderful, loving, inclusive word that reaches out to invite all hearers. Leave your résumé at home; your qualifications don't matter. If you live and breathe, if you are born into this human race, here's a place for you.

Mr. Klein, it is said, was a miserable old man. He had lived every which way but good, fought every battle but the good fight, and he knew it. He wasn't worthy of anyone's friendship, so he reached out to no one. He didn't go to church, because the back pew was too far forward for someone like him. He wasn't proud of his sin, but he was painfully aware of it.

And then one Sunday evening, he walked by the church. He heard the people singing and rejoicing, and he felt that old familiar pang of loneliness. For just a moment, he paused in his steps and listened. He had heard the melody before, and now he listened to the words of the hymn:

Saved by grace alone
This is all my plea,
Jesus died for Old Man Klein,
And Jesus died for me.

He was astounded! Jesus died for Old Man Klein? How could there be a hymn that identified him specifically? And why would these people be singing it? He couldn't resist slipping into the church and sliding secretly onto that back pew. He had a lump in his throat, knowing for the first time that the Gospel was for him. Then he picked up a hymnal and found that what he had really heard was "Jesus died for all mankind."

Or was it?

It didn't matter: Old Man Klein knew what his heart had heard, and after all, "all mankind" had to include him.

I try to help people understand that word *whoever*, one of the most breathtaking, outrageous words in all of Scripture—a word with implications that make the devil tremble. I want people to see that this word allows each person to plug his or her own name into the verse.

For God so loved David Jeremiah...
For God so loved John Jones...
For God so loved Mary Johnson...

... that if David Jeremiah believes in Him...
... that if John Jones believes in Him...
... that if Mary Johnson believes in Him...

Now would be a good time to put your own name in this verse. Go ahead—give it a try. Personalize John 3:16, write it down, speak it aloud, let it soak into your mind, and see how your day goes. I challenge you.

God's Love Is Exclusive

... believes in Him...

Now we come to what is in a crucial way the key word in John 3:16. I don't mean it's the most holy word, which would be *God*, or the most affecting word, which would be His *love*, or the most astounding words, which would be the gift of His *Son*. But the word *believes* is crucial because it is the hinge upon which the door to heaven turns.

To show you just how important this word is, notice that in three consecutive verses (16–18), Jesus uses variations of *believes* four times. If you were to speak three sentences, and you included one verb four times, I would get the feeling you were stressing a highly critical point. And indeed He was.

John 3:16 begins with God and His love, and it ends in heaven—all stable and unchangeable elements. But the one variable in the equation is this word *believes*. Will we believe? You might say the verse is shaped like the letter *Y*. God is at the base, the foundation. His love and sacrifice get us to the fork where the upper arms begin. At the tops of the two arms are "eternal life" and "perish." At the fork in the Y is where we find the word *believes*. And that's where you and I stand. Whether or not we believe will determine whether we choose to perish or accept the offer of eternal life.

God's love is infinitely deep, infinitely wide, and poured out for every single person who ever lived or ever will. And yet all of that is for naught if you or I choose not to believe in Christ. What a tragedy that God could love a person so deeply, only to have that love rejected!

Nicodemus thought God was in the business of condemning. But in the following two verses, Jesus told him that God doesn't exclude people; they exclude themselves: "He who *believes* in Him is not condemned; but he who does not *believe* is condemned already, because he has not *believed* in the name of the only begotten Son of God" (John 3:18; italics added). There's that word again—three times. John wants us to see the life-or-death urgency of our choice.

In terms of how we relate to the love of God, there are two kinds of people in the world: Those who believe in Jesus Christ and those who do not. Those who believe will receive the salvation of God and all it brings. Those who don't believe will miss out. As I have been stressing, God loves everyone, but in order to receive His love, we must believe.

God's love gave us Christ, who died giving us our only access to heaven. Therefore, salvation is not in question. It is there for the taking. The only thing in question is our response. Will we *believe*? J. C. Ryle puts it succinctly: "Salvation . . . does not turn on the point, 'Did Christ die for me?' but on the point, 'do I believe on Christ?'"[10]

God has done everything possible to rescue us. If we refuse to jump into the net, it's not because of anything He has failed to do; it's because we didn't offer the simple and natural response of the heart to the supreme act of love—we failed to believe.

God's Love Is Exceptional

...should not perish...

To perish does not necessarily mean to be annihilated—to cease to exist. The currently popular idea—annihilation of the soul or destruction of the individual—is not found in the Bible. What we do find is that every single human being has an eternal soul that will live somewhere forever.

John Phillips explains that we've all seen what the work of sin gradually does to a human life. Drugs, sexual promiscuity, and unhealthy living ravage both body and soul and, if unchecked, lead to death. When we reject God, we allow sin to continue its deadly work. The result may be the death of our bodies, but not the annihilation of our souls. That part of us is eternal and accountable to God. The final effect is that if we die unrepentant, we carry our ungodly passions into eternity with us—our cravings, lusts, hatred, and fear. In hell these passions continue to rule the soul. They never satisfied us here, nor will they satisfy us there. Phillips concludes, "The word *perished* notes the final condition of the soul, the awful state of those who are 'filthy still' under the eye of God."[11]

Phillips is alluding to this verse from John: "He who is

unjust, let him be unjust still; he who is filthy, let him be filthy still; he who is righteous, let him be righteous still; he who is holy, let him be holy still" (Revelation 22:11). Heaven will complete our sanctification, or hell will complete our damnation.

To perish, then, is to remain aware of but separated forever from the loving God. Yet the Bible promises that once we receive God's love, separation from Him will become impossible. As Paul gloriously put it, "For I am persuaded that neither death nor life, nor angels nor principalities nor powers, nor things present nor things to come, nor height nor depth, nor any other created thing, shall be able to separate us from the love of God which is in Christ Jesus our Lord" (Romans 8:38–39).

God's Love Is Eternal

...but have everlasting life.

I remember reading of the apocryphal engraving for Les Moore of Tombstone, Arizona (an appropriate place to have an epitaph, I would think). Apparently his departure was not overly mourned, for his epitaph reads,

Here Lies Les Moore
No Les, No More

The humor rings true, but the theology falls flat. Somewhere, more or less, Les Moore abides. If Les found the love of God in the gift of Jesus Christ, then Les is more. In God's eternity he is more alive, more himself, more abounding in every good blessing, and more fully in loving fellowship with his Lord.

If Les Moore is experiencing the ecstasy of eternity, you can be sure that it began to happen before he was laid in the ground under that tombstone. Eternity is more than a someday promise to be fulfilled on the other side of a funeral. "Eternal life is our present position. Eternal life is now," says Kent Hughes.[12] If this seems confusing, think of it this way: When we accept Christ and begin living in His love, heaven's door opens to us, letting a pure light into our lives that we never had before. We receive the life of God's Spirit and experience the joy of fellowship with Him. In a real sense, we begin to live in heaven before we actually get there. This foretaste of heaven sweetens our lives now; and with eternal life already in our grasp, "now" is suddenly a very good place to be. As Paul put it, "To live is Christ, and to die is gain" (Philippians 1:21). Either way, we win.

Someone told me about a little girl who misquoted John 3:16 as "whoever believes on Him should not perish but have *in*ternal life." This time the theology is as sound as the humor. Indeed, we have new life internally even before we arrive in heaven because of what Christ has done for us. Jesus offers us more than a life insurance policy, more than a stamped ticket to heaven. He came that we might have life, and that we might have it more abundantly (John 10:10). That's how much God loves you.

John 3:16 tells an amazing love story, doesn't it? It begins with God, who has no beginning, and concludes with life that has no ending. That's life with no limits, and it can begin now.

Think of it: no limits to joy, no limits to kingdom service, and no limits to how much we will come to resemble His Son as we grow more like Him every day.

The great playwright Arthur Miller was married to Marilyn Monroe during the 1950s. In his autobiography, he describes the misery of watching the troubled actress descend into the lowest regions of depression and despair. It seemed there was no way he or anyone else could make her happy. He knew that her very life was on the line—that this could go only so far before she succumbed to her various demons—loneliness, paranoia, addiction to barbiturates.

One evening there was yet another visit from the doctor, who talked Marilyn into taking a sedative that put her to sleep. Miller was pensive as he stood and watched his wife. "I found myself straining to imagine miracles," he writes. "What if she were to wake and I were able to say, 'God loves you, darling,' and she were able to believe it! How I wished I still had my religion and she hers."[13]

What if indeed! If only he had *believed*—that crucial word. If only he had owned the joy of knowing Christ. If only he had been capable of sharing that joy with his suffering wife, a soul God loved and longed to heal.

John 3:16 could have been their answer. It's the answer to every human need, to every prayer. In fact, it is even the answer to Paul's prayer in Ephesians 3, where he implores the Father to grant believers the ability to "comprehend...what is the *width* and *length* and *depth* and *height*—to know the love of Christ which passes knowledge" (Ephesians 3:18–19; italics added).

It's an elegant prayer, and Jesus offers the elegant answer in John 3:16, where we see:

- The *width* of God's love: "God so loved the whole world." His arms are stretched wide to include everyone.
- The *length* of God's love: "He gave His only Son." That is the length to which God went to save us.
- The *depth* of God's love: "That whoever believes in Him." God reaches down to the very depths of mankind.
- The *height* of God's love: "should not perish but have everlasting life." We will live in heaven with Him forever.

God's love is enormous in every dimension. The one thing it is not is coercive. We are left with the free option of how to respond. He loves you as intensely as it's possible to be loved, yet never in a way that undermines your freedom to choose. Forced love is not authentic love. It is a gift that accepts the possibility of rejection.

God offers you everything He has to offer. He gives you the perfection and purity of His Son to die for you as atonement, to speak for you at the judgment, to live for you in the present, and to love you for all eternity. I cannot imagine any sane, informed human being turning down such a gift.

I urge you to say yes to that gift. Open the door to Jesus, and you let in a life of eternal joy now, with eventual delights that the mind cannot presently conceive. Say yes, and you will let in a new kind of life today—one that sets you on the one truly great adventure this earth has to offer.

Nicodemus, the man who first heard this verse, said yes. Not that night, but as John tells us later, he was one of two men who prepared Jesus for His burial and laid Him in His tomb (John 19:38–42). And according to early Christian tradition, Nicodemus was martyred as a Christian in the first century.

Obviously, saying yes to God's invitation does not mean that troubles will cease—not yet—but the presence of your Savior will bear you up until you leave all trouble behind forever. You will let in the Holy Spirit, a loving teacher, guide, and companion. You will let in restored relationships with friends and family. You will let in peace, security, and contentment.

Why not open that door?

Shortly after I came to Shadow Mountain Community Church, the church I now serve as pastor, I became acquainted with a man whose marriage had been on the rocks for some time. The breakup that followed was terrible. The marriage ended in a courtroom with him on one side of the room, his wife and son on the other. Here were the two people he loved more than anyone else in the world, and he was locked in legal combat with them.

Praise God, during the divorce process someone loved him enough to talk with him about the power of God, and he received Jesus Christ as his Savior. He felt the hostility toward his wife and son evaporate like a fog in the summer sun. What had been so thick, so obscuring one moment, became miraculously clear the next. He was in a fever to make peace with the two he loved so deeply.

"It was too late to pick up the pieces of our home, I was sure of that," he said. "I just wanted them to know how much I loved them—that there was nothing left of anger or resentment in me at all."

So he went into the courtroom for the final proceedings. Afterward, he saw his son standing near the front. With a lump in his throat, he approached the boy. No words would come;

only tears. He reached out to hug his son, but the boy pushed his father roughly away. There would be no embrace.

"Pastor," he told me, "I've never felt pain like that in all my life."

I've thought many times about that story. I'm blessed with a wonderful marriage and loving relationships with my children. I just can't fathom what this rejected man must have felt. And then I think about our heavenly Father, reaching out to embrace us. What must He feel when we push Him away?

"Here is My gift," He says. "It's all I have to give you. I allowed My Son to die on your behalf so you can put your sin problem behind you forever. I want to bring you into My house to live as My child, to be with Me forever. I want to begin blessing you immediately in so many ways."

How can anyone possibly say no?

In 1912 the *Titanic*, the largest, most luxurious, and most advanced ship of its time, sank on its maiden voyage, taking the lives of 1,514 passengers. Though the disaster occurred one hundred years ago, several movies, documentaries, and books have kept the horror of that night alive in our minds. We've all heard of passengers such as "the unsinkable" Molly Brown and the entrepreneur John Jacob Astor IV. But one of the most astounding stories from the *Titanic* has received little press.

It's the story of Pastor John Harper, a widower who was traveling with his six-year-old daughter at the invitation of the great Moody Church in Chicago. Not only was he to preach there, he intended to accept the church's offer to become their next pastor. His hopes were high, and it seemed he had a brilliant future ahead.

After the ship hit the iceberg and it became apparent that it would sink, Harper got his daughter safely aboard a lifeboat. It's likely he could have joined her, being her only parent, but he chose to stay aboard the sinking ship because he knew that with this disaster, God had given him an urgent mission.

Harper immediately began to go from one person to another, telling them about Christ's love and urging them to accept Him. He shouted for Christians to let the unsaved fill the lifeboats so they would live to come to belief. When one angry man rejected the message, Harper removed his own life vest and gave it to him, saying, "You need this more than I do."

Harper was still actively pressing his urgent evangelism when the ship tipped upward, wrenched in half, and slipped beneath the frigid North Sea. Even then Harper did not stop. Seeing the many passengers struggling in the water with little chance of rescue, he swam to as many as he could, urging them to accept God's loving offer until hypothermia finally overcame him.

Four years later, at a *Titanic* survivors meeting in Ontario, one survivor told the story of his own encounter with John Harper. He was clinging to a piece of flotsam when Harper swam to him and urged him to "believe on the Lord Jesus Christ." The man rejected the offer and Harper swam away. But soon Harper came around again, and this time, knowing death to be only minutes away, the man gave his life to Christ. Moments afterward, he watched the near-freezing water finally take Harper's life just as a returning lifeboat approached to rescue him. At the conclusion of his story, he said simply, "I am the last convert of John Harper."

The *Titanic* left England with three classes of passengers

aboard. But when accounting for their fate, the White Star Line set up a board listing only two classes: KNOWN TO BE SAVED and KNOWN TO BE LOST. These categories provided a fitting analogy for what John Harper already knew. There are only two classes of people in this world: those who have chosen to accept Christ and will spend eternity with God in heaven, and those who have not chosen Him and will not.[14]

Which class are you in?

SIX

God Loves You Even When You Don't Love Him

∽

But God demonstrates His own love toward us,
in that while we were still sinners, Christ died for us.
—ROMANS 5:8

A defiant son, a heartbroken father.

A willful journey into the depths of depravity.

An arrival at the place where hope dies; the defiant now the destitute.

The journey home.

A moment of suspense, an uncertain reception.

Eyes watching; heart hoping; aged feet breaking into a run.

The embrace: a sea of joy overwhelming a desert of despair.

No wonder it's been called the crown and pearl of all parables. One writer said it is "the most divinely tender and most humanly touching story ever told on earth."¹ Charles Dickens described it as the finest short story ever written. Another has called it "the most winsome picture of God ever drawn on earth."[2]

This story requires no more than twenty-two brisk verses, yet holds the great themes of human existence. Its cast of characters represents all of us. Its plot captivates us, telling a narrative that, somewhere, sometime, we've all lived out. And finally, it redefines the happy ending, nurturing hope and demanding a response from all who hear the story.

While this story is usually referred to as the parable of the prodigal son, it turns out that the father, not the son, is the main character. He is mentioned no less than twelve times in the span of these verses. Entire books have been written on the two sons, but the father, who is the central figure in the story, has often been overlooked. It is the father who loves his prodigal son even when his son does not love him. It is the father who shows the deepest, most compelling emotion as he waits by that lonely road, longing for his son to return home. It is the father who initiates the process of forgiveness. It is the father who leaps to his feet and runs to greet a starving, life-torn son who has done nothing but insult him. And it is the father who never stops loving his oldest son, pleading with him to experience the joy of his brother's life restored. This story is about a human father and his sons, but it tells an even greater story about our heavenly Father's love for all lost sons and daughters wherever they may be found.

Only in Luke's Gospel do we find this, the longest of Jesus' parables. The parable is easily divided around the characters who appear in the story. The youngest son (the prodigal) is featured in Luke 15:12–19; the father comes to the fore in Luke 15:20–24; and the elder son has his close-up in Luke 15:25–32.

The word *prodigal* appears only once in the New King James Version of the Bible. We are told that the younger son "wasted his possessions with prodigal living" (Luke 15:13). From this verse, many have come to associate the word *prodigal* with the idea of licentiousness and rebellion. However, the word does not mean "wayward" but "recklessly spendthrift." It means to spend until you have nothing left.

Surprisingly, we can use that same word to describe the father. He not only gives the departing son everything he asks for, but showers him with gifts when he returns. And to the older son he says, "All that I have is yours" (Luke 15:31). The father's treatment of his two sons is literally reckless. He keeps back nothing, but pours everything out for his two boys. There is, of course, an enormous difference in the prodigality of the father and the son. The son's is wayward and self-centered. The father's is loving and selfless.

It helps to understand the context of this story. In Luke 15, Jesus tells three parables that make a single point: God loves the lost. We find lost sheep, a lost silver coin, and finally a lost son— a trilogy of increasing preciousness of value. The lost sheep is one of a hundred, the lost coin is one of ten, and the lost son is one of two. In the first story, Jesus is the good shepherd. In the second, He is the good woman. In the third, He is the father who seeks his lost sons. Yes, sons—plural. While only one son is called the prodigal, as we will see, both sons were lost. One was lost in a distant land and the other at home.

As we move through these verses and retell this riveting

story, don't forget why it was told. Don't miss the picture of God's prodigal, pursuing love as seen in the heart of the father.

God Loves You When You're Wounding His Heart

Then He said: "A certain man had two sons. And the younger of them said to his father, 'Father, give me the portion of goods that falls to me.' So he divided to them his livelihood."

—LUKE 15:11–12

As Jesus' story begins, the younger son grows impatient to get out from under authority at home. Kenneth Bailey, an authority on Middle Eastern customs, spent years talking to people from all walks of life, "from Morocco to India, and from Turkey to the Sudan," about what it would mean for a son to ask for his inheritance from a living father. Everywhere he went, he heard the same:

"Has anyone ever made such a request in your village?"
"Never!"
"Could anyone ever make such a request?"
"Impossible!"
"If anyone ever did, what would happen?"
"His father would beat him, of course!"
"Why?"
"This request means—he wants his father to die!"[3]

Here in essence is what the young boy was saying: "Dad, I wish you were dead. You are in the way of my plans. You are a barrier. I want my freedom. I want my fulfillment. And I want out of this family now. I have other plans that don't involve you; they don't involve this family; they don't involve this estate; they don't even involve this village. I want nothing to do with any of you. Give me my inheritance now, and I am out of here."[4]

While such behavior on the part of a son toward his father would be egregious in our culture, it was one hundred times more insulting for a Jewish family. The fact that after his son left, the father referred to him as "dead," is mentioned twice in Luke's account (15:24, 32).

The Jewish laws of inheritance worked this way: When a father died with two sons, the estate would be divided between them, with two-thirds going to the oldest son and one-third to the youngest.

In order for the prodigal to receive his inheritance, the portion of the father's property and holdings equal to the son's share would have had to be liquidated—turned into cash. While it was common for a Jewish father to divide the family inheritance as he approached the end of his life, Jewish law did not permit the inherited land to be sold until after his death. But the prodigal wanted what he wanted, and he wanted it now. It could not have been easy for the father to accommodate his son's request, but he found some way to do it and gave his rebellious boy what he asked for.

While it is not stated explicitly in the text, we know that this father was a wealthy man. He had hired servants, fatted calves and goats, and the capacity to hire musicians and dancers and throw a huge banquet at a moment's notice. So this is a high-profile family, and the father is a well-connected and respected man in the community.

In the village life of that day, there were no secrets. Everyone knew everyone else's business. With the sale of real estate, the private rift in the father's household went public. The entire family was subjected to shame and embarrassment. There was no time for damage control, for the text says that the prodigal left "not many days after" (Luke 15:13).

In leaving home, the prodigal was taking an enormous risk. If a Jewish boy squandered his inheritance and dared to come home, Bailey tells us, the entire community would greet him by breaking a large pot and crying out that this young man was "cut off from his people." After that, the boy was an outcast, invisible to everyone. This was the risk the younger son was taking; if he lost his money, he lost his name. There were no second chances.[5]

Surely, the prodigal knows this as he bundles his money together and hits the road. He's doubling down on a risky future, burning the only bridge he has ever crossed. But he does just that. He takes his portion of the family wealth and walks away.

The father lets him go; there's no hint of pleading, of retaliation, of angry shouting, though any or all of these things were to be expected. The father might simply have refused the insulting request: "I'm going to pretend this conversation never happened, and hope that you come to your senses." Instead, the father absorbs the pain of his son's rejection. His father-heart is broken, but he loves his son. He always has and he always will.

The English evangelical philanthropist Hannah Moore, a friend of William Wilberforce, wrote, "Love never reasons, but profusely gives; gives, like a thoughtless prodigal, its all, and trembles then lest it has done too little."[6]

Just as the prodigal's father was wounded by his son's rebellion, our heavenly Father is wounded by our sin and rejection of Him. You may think you have sinned away your place in God's heart, but that cannot happen. Like the father of the prodigal, He will never stop loving you.

God Loves You When You're Walking Away from Him

And not many days after, the younger son gathered all together, [and] journeyed to a far country . . .

—LUKE 15:13

It was just a few days after making his outrageous request that the prodigal pulled up stakes and left. Luke says that he "gathered all together" (15:13). In other words, he took what his father had given him, liquidated it into cash, and left. More than a few commentators have suggested that, because he was in such a hurry to leave, he was probably forced to sell what was his for a price way below its value.

The people of the community—the neighbors, farmhands, and servants—were probably shaking their heads in disbelief. "How can this father allow his son to disgrace him and bring such reproach upon his family? He just gave him everything he asked for and watched him walk out the door! He should have rebuked him publicly. Instead, he played the fool and granted his request."

In his book *The Return of the Prodigal Son*, Henri Nouwen shows that the prodigal was turning his back on more than just home. He was arrogantly dismissing all that was good:

> The son's "leaving" is...a much more offensive act than it seems at first reading. It is a heartless rejection of the home in which the son was born and nurtured and a break with the most precious tradition carefully upheld by the community of which he was a part. When Luke writes, "and left for the distant country," he indicates much more than the desire of a young man to see more of the world. He speaks about a drastic cutting loose from the way of living, thinking, and acting that has been handed down to him from generation to generation as a sacred legacy. More than disrespect, it is a betrayal of the treasured values of family and community. The "distant country" is the world in which everything considered holy at home is disregarded.[7]

How difficult is it to restrain our hands when we see the inevitability of suffering approaching a loved one? The father knows that one day his son will regret his behavior. He knows that his son is headed for disappointment and failure. But in spite of his own personal agony and rejected love, he allows the boy to leave.

Just as this father is willing to endure pain rather than disown his son, so our heavenly Father sometimes releases us to reject His love and pursue our own self-will. Sometimes nothing will bring us around as effectively as experiencing the head-on consequences of our own sinful choices. The father could have tried to describe to his son the pain he was about to experience, but he would not have listened. The boy's mind was made up. So his father let him go.

Could God not stop us from making that painful journey away from Him? Surely He knows the suffering that awaits us! Yes, He could force us to stay home, but He wants us to stay because we love Him of our own free will, not because He forces us. He allows us to experience the far country so that when we finally return, we are fully prepared to appreciate and receive His love.

God Loves You When You're Wasting Your Life

...and there wasted his possessions with prodigal living. But when he had spent all...

—LUKE 15:13–14

Luke tells us that the prodigal gathered his things together and took off for the "far country" (15:13). This is more than a geographical reference; the "far country" also represents moral and spiritual separation from God.

Twice in this text we are told of the prodigal's conduct while on his wild journey. In verse 30, the older brother tells his father that the prodigal "has devoured your livelihood with harlots." In verse 13, Jesus tells us that the younger son spent his substance in "riotous living" (KJV).

Here is this young boy with bags full of money, determined to live it up in a faraway city. Within hours, surrounded by "friends" eager to help him spend his fortune, he is buying drinks and women for everyone. For days he pursues this lifestyle of immorality and drunkenness, throwing his money to the wind with no accountability to anyone. It is hard to imagine a more graphic picture of unrestrained sinfulness. The prodigal was wasting his life.

And then one day, he dips into those generous, licentious pockets and comes up with nothing but lint. The text says, "when he had spent all" (Luke 15:14). He had come to town with his pockets full and now they are empty. Suddenly his "friends" are nowhere to be found. He is bankrupt. His life's inheritance is gone, and he has no way to recover it. He had sown to the flesh and reaped corruption (Galatians 6:8). Or, as the prophet Hosea put it, he had sowed the wind and reaped the whirlwind (Hosea 8:7).

Yet his father, far away as he is, loves the boy even when he is squandering everything he has given him.

God Loves You When You're Wallowing in Sin

There arose a severe famine in that land, and he began to be in want. Then he went and joined himself to a citizen of that country, and he sent him into his fields to feed swine. And he would gladly have filled his stomach with the pods that the swine ate, and no one gave him anything.

—LUKE 15:14–16

Wallowing is a good word; it suggests the image of a pig wallowing in its pen. With his money gone and his friends nowhere to be found, the prodigal probably thought he was as low as he could go. How could things get any worse? Well, they did; life has a way of making that happen when we've been foolish.

Jesus tells us that at that precise moment, a famine hits the land. The prodigal now finds himself without funds, without friends, and without food.

I believe it is at this moment that the prodigal begins to think about home. But he cannot go home. He has squandered his inheritance among the Gentiles, and, as we have already learned, that was an unforgivable sin to the Jews.

And then he has a thought. He could work—it wasn't in the original plan, but desperate times call for desperate measures. He could work, and then he could *earn* the right to go home. Though we may shake our heads at his naïveté—did he really think he could earn back the amount of money he had lost?—we can give him credit for wanting to work. It's a hopeless option, but he thinks it's the only one he has.

Jesus says that the prodigal finds a *citizen* (a word that suggests wealth), and to that citizen he "joined himself" (Luke 15:15). In other words, he finds someone who is rich and "glues" himself to that person. The picture is surely one of desperation. But apparently the wealthy citizen wants nothing to do with such a broken-down specimen of humanity so, to get this young profligate off his back, he gives him the lowliest of jobs: feeding pigs.

Jesus doesn't spare us the sordid details. The boy was so famished that "he would gladly have filled his stomach with the pods that the swine ate, and no one gave him anything" (Luke 15:16).

This is the lowest point in the prodigal's story. Here he is, the son of a wealthy Jewish landowner, living among what were, for a Jew, the most ceremonially unclean and despised animals on the face of the earth. Now he is wallowing, if not in mud, certainly in shame and abject poverty. He is hungry enough to eat the pods that the pigs were eating! We can't help but wonder what the Pharisees were thinking at this point as they listened to Jesus' story.

As I was writing this chapter, I watched an interview of Leigh Steinberg, the famous sports agent who was once the most successful and sought-after agent in football. He represented almost every major quarterback in the NFL, and it was his life that inspired the film *Jerry Maguire*. As I watched, I could not help but think of Jesus' story. Steinberg talked about his fame and how it destroyed his family and drove him to alcoholism. After losing everything and walking away from every rehab opportunity, he said, "I ended up in Hoag Hospital in a diaper, not knowing where I was."[8]

It's not hard to see the sad parallels between Steinberg and the prodigal son: both were lost, unclean, defiled, broken—"having no hope and without God in the world" (Ephesians 2:12). But I can assure you that even then God loved Steinberg just as the father in Jesus' story loved his prodigal son.

God Loves You When You're Working to Come Back

But when he came to himself, he said, "How many of my father's hired servants have bread enough and to spare, and I perish with hunger! I will arise and go to my father, and will say to him, 'Father, I have sinned against heaven and before you, and I am no longer worthy to be called your son. Make me like one of your hired servants.'"

—LUKE 15:17–19

I've always seen this as the turning point of the story. Jesus says that at the moment of his greatest misery, when he is broke and hungry and eating with the pigs, the prodigal "came to himself" (Luke 15:17). This expression means, as we would commonly say it today, "He came to his senses." These are amazing words, words that are a prerequisite for turning to God. Henri Nouwen writes:

> When the younger son was no longer considered a human being by the people around him, he felt the profundity of his isolation, the deepest loneliness one can experience. He was truly lost, and it was this complete lostness that brought him to his senses. He was shocked into the awareness of his utter alienation and suddenly understood that he had embarked on the road to death. He had become so disconnected from what gives life—family, friends, community, acquaintances, and even food—that he realized that death would be the natural next step. All at once he saw clearly the path he had chosen and where it would lead him; he understood his own death choice; and he knew that one more step in the direction he was going would take him to self-destruction.[9]

There are a lot of misconceptions about this moment. I have heard numerous messages on this parable and preached several myself. In most of the messages I've heard, this moment in the story is seen as the point where the prodigal realizes what he has done and repents. He gets on his knees before God to confess his sin.

But is that what happens here? Is there anything in the text that says the prodigal is sorry for what he has done? Does he even once acknowledge that he has broken the heart of his father and humiliated him in front of the community? Is there one shred of evidence in this story that the prodigal repented while in the far country? Not that I can find.

What he does express is a need to find a way out of the mess he has gotten himself into. At least a job as his father's servant will lead to more-palatable meals and a place to rest at night. Quite pragmatically, he draws a comparison between his lifestyle now and what it might be at his father's house. It's his mind that is in motion, not his heart. There has to be some way for him to benefit from his father's riches without facing his failures. He makes a turnaround, but it's mostly a practical one.

I wonder how many of us today hit rock bottom, then try to wrench ourselves up into the arms of God by sheer effort and calculation, rather than facing our sins flat out, bringing our brokenness to God, and asking for forgiveness. This is the pattern of so many today—Christians and non-Christians alike. But this approach to a relationship with God does not represent the Gospel, which tells us that God's love and acceptance rest on His grace and not on our effort.

The prodigal decides he will go back home and work as a hired servant for his father. He believes he cannot go home as a son, that he would not be welcomed even as one of the household servants. But he holds out hope that his father will allow him to sign on as a hired slave or, as we would say today, a per diem laborer. We can only wonder if he is thinking, "As a hired servant, I can still keep my distance, still revolt, reject, strike, run away, or complain about my pay."[10]

At this point in Jesus' story, the prodigal is executing his own plan. As hard as it is for us to comprehend, he still has not come to the end of himself. He is still lost. Please understand: If he were to find his way back into the good graces of his father as a result of his own ingenuity, the whole point of the parable is lost. The sheep did not seek its shepherd, nor the coin its owner. Likewise, the prodigal did not seek his father. He was simply looking for a paycheck. In Jesus' three parables it's clear that the shepherd, the woman, and the father are the seekers.

Even the prodigal's words to his father at the edge of the village fall short of repentance. "I have sinned against heaven and in your sight" (Luke 15:21) is usually understood as a statement of repentance and regret, but according to Kenneth Bailey, Jewish culture viewed it differently:

> Jesus' audience…is composed of Pharisees who know the Scriptures well. They recognize that confession as a quotation from the pharaoh when he tries to manipulate Moses into lifting the plagues. After the [ninth] plague, Pharaoh finally agrees to meet Moses, and when Moses appears, Pharaoh gives this same speech. Everyone knows that Pharaoh is not repenting. He is simply trying to bend Moses to his will.[11]

So the prodigal is not really repenting any more than Pharaoh was. He still carries the illusion of control. He is still trying to manipulate his own way back into the family. His attempt to make things better in the far country has failed. Perhaps his new plan will work and he can get on with his life. He will save himself.

God Loves You When You're Wrapped in His Arms of Forgiveness

And he arose and came to his father. But when he was still a great way off, his father saw him and had compassion, and ran and fell on his neck and kissed him. And the son said to him, "Father, I have sinned against heaven and in your sight, and am no longer worthy to be called your son."

—LUKE 15:20–21

With no place else to go and starvation staring him in the face, the prodigal is coming home. How different this trip is from the last time he journeyed down this road. He left home with a full stomach and a full wallet. He returns with nothing but rags on his back. He is broken and alone, perhaps thin beyond recognition to anyone but a loving parent. His inheritance has been lost, his eyes are hollow, his stomach is empty.

The famous painting by the Dutch artist Rembrandt titled *The Return of the Prodigal Son* (ca. 1669) graphically shows the sorry state of the prodigal on his return. He is clothed in what appears to be a ragged undergarment stained with the colors, and likely the odors, of the pigsty. His sandals are falling apart, and his hair and head are filthy with grime.

As he nears the village and his father's house, his father recognizes him. Perhaps there is something in the way he walks, in the way he moves, that reveals his identity. It is significant that the father recognizes his son when he is "still a great way off" (Luke 15:20). The Greek text puts the emphasis on the words "a great way off," indicating that the father did not remain in his house waiting for his son. Instead, he seems to have been scanning the horizon for the possibility of his return. In my imagination I can see him going up to one of the towers that protected his farmland and, shading his eyes with his hands, looking for his son, wondering if this might be the day that he would come home.

The Bible says that when his father saw him, he "had compassion, and ran and fell on his neck and kissed him" (Luke 15:20). Literally, "he raced to meet his son." Bailey points out that this would be somewhat embarrassing for a Mediterranean man of means; he would be expected to walk slowly and with dignity. But now he grabs up his robe so his feet can fly—thus exposing his legs, also an unbecoming gesture. Pride and dignity mean nothing to this father at this moment. Compassion and love push him at full run. "He knows what his son will face in the village. He takes upon himself the shame and humiliation due the prodigal."[12]

When the running father reaches his son, he pours out his love upon the boy, showering him with kisses. You might be surprised to find that the father doesn't wait for an apology. He doesn't seem interested in such a thing—only embraces and kisses and party-plans. He has lived with a sorrow that is now eclipsed by pure joy.

When the son is finally able to speak, in a moment of genuine repentance, he accepts his father's love.

Where does the father find the son? He finds him at the edge of the village. The prodigal was still lost when he got to the outskirts of town. There is no break in the imagery of Jesus' three stories about lost objects. In all three, something that has been lost is found. The lost thing does not find itself; it is found by another. This father loves his son so much that he is eager to forgive whatever he has done. This is surely one of the most beautiful pictures of our heavenly Father's lavish love for us in all the Bible.

God Loves You When You're Welcomed Back Home

But the father said to his servants, "Bring out the best robe and put it on him, and put a ring on his hand and sandals on his feet. And bring the fatted calf here and kill it, and let us eat and be merry; for this my son was dead and is alive again; he was lost and is found." And they began to be merry.

—LUKE 15:22–24

The father turns to the servants who have accompanied him to the outskirts of the village and he gives them instructions: "Go get the best robe we have and bring it here." The best robe would have been a beautifully crafted piece of formal wear, usually belonging to the patriarch of the family.

He turns to the servant and says, "Get the ring." The ring in a Jewish estate was a very important piece of jewelry. It not only adorned the hand, but it was used for the purpose of transacting family business, and it signified that the authority of the family had been granted to the son.

Then the father says, "Get him a pair of sandals." Sandals were worn by sons, but never by servants. The father wants to make it clear that this is his son, not his servant.

The robe, the ring, and the sandals provide answers to the speech that the prodigal has made to his father: "Father, I have sinned against heaven and before you, and I am no longer worthy to be called your son. Make me like one of your hired servants" (Luke 15:18–19).

The robe answers the statement "Father, I have sinned." The father's robe isn't put on over filthy garments. There is no doubt a cleansing that precedes the robing of the son, a cleansing that symbolizes the forgiveness of sin.

The ring answers "I am no longer worthy to be called your son." The ring was the sign of sonship. He is given the sign of family authority.

The sandals answer "Make me as one of your hired servants." Servants don't wear shoes. That's reserved for sons.

With his robe, his ring, and his shoes, the prodigal is now ready for the celebration. The servants are instructed to get the fatted calf and prepare a banquet. The prodigal is not headed for the servants' quarters but for the banquet hall. His mind must be in a haze. Somehow he has stumbled from hell to the threshold of heaven.

Rejoicing returns to the father's household. The one who was lost has been found. The one whom the father feared was dead is alive! A sinner has come home and the only proper response is to throw a party. As if to make sure we understand this point, Jesus also emphasized the joy of recovering the lost as He told the stories of the lost sheep and the lost coin: "There is joy in the presence of the angels of God over one sinner who repents" (Luke 15:10; also see v. 7).

John MacArthur reminds us of the significance of the prodigal son's extravagant welcome home: "This is a picture of God's lavish grace, which triumphs over every imaginable kind of sin. God saves sinners—including the very worst of sinners. And when He does, He instantly elevates the newly reborn sinner to a position of privilege and blessing that is exceedingly and abundantly beyond anything we could ever ask or think."[13]

God Loves You When You Won't Love Him

Now his older son was in the field. And as he came and drew near to the house, he heard music and dancing. So he called one of the servants and asked what these things meant. And he said to him, "Your brother has come, and because he has received him safe and sound, your father has killed the fatted calf." But he was angry and would not go in. Therefore his father came out and pleaded with him. So he answered and said to his father, "Lo, these many years I have been serving you; I never transgressed your commandment at any time; and yet you never gave me a young goat, that I might make merry with my friends. But as soon as this son of yours came, who has devoured your livelihood with harlots, you killed the fatted calf for him." And he said to him, "Son, you are always with me, and all that I have is yours. It was right that we should make merry and be glad, for your brother was dead and is alive again, and was lost and is found."

—LUKE 15:25–32

Out in the field, diligently supervising his father's business, is the older son. He does not witness his brother's return. But as he comes home at the end of the day, he hears the music coming from the house and questions one of the servants.

The servant reports, "Your brother has come, and because he has received him safe and sound, your father has killed the fatted calf" (Luke 15:27). They are having a party! But the older brother bristles with resentment and anger and refuses to attend (v. 28). He even refuses to call his younger brother a brother. In speaking with his father, he refers to his brother as "this son of yours" (v. 30). I remember reading somewhere that once you meet the older son, it is easier to understand why the younger son wanted to leave home. For all his good works, he doesn't come across as someone we'd enjoy knowing.

It's easy to think this older boy was treated unfairly. I used to think that myself—that the older brother was angry because the younger brother got his inheritance, and he didn't get his. But go back to verse 12, and you will see that the father divided his inheritance to both sons. So the older brother was the owner of two-thirds of his father's substance. No wonder his father said, "All that I have is yours" (Luke 15:31). It really was!

In verse 29 the older son reveals his heart with these words: "Lo, these many years I have been serving you; I never transgressed your commandment at any time." You can almost see the fire in his eyes and hear the indignation in his voice as he compares his perfect behavior to the irresponsibility of his brother. "Dad, I've been a perfect son. I've done everything you've told me to do." With every bitter word he reveals what a proud, self-righteous man he is.

It is now we realize that there are two lost sons, and only one has been found. All along, the older brother was as lost as the younger! As the younger son returns home from the far country of rebellion and licentiousness, the older son remains in the far country of smug self-satisfaction and resentment. Jesus said that the older brother would not even go into the house to join in the celebration.

The lostness of the older son is much harder to identify than that of the younger. After all, he does all the right things. He is obedient, dutiful, law-abiding, and hardworking. People respect him, admire him, praise him, and likely consider him a model son. Outwardly, the older son is faultless. But when confronted by his father's joy at the return of his younger brother, a dark power erupts in him and boils to the surface. Suddenly there emerges a resentful, proud, unkind, selfish person. The older son is lost because he has based his relationship with his brother and father on his own obedience rather than his father's love. As a result, he is alienated from both.

Remarkably, the father responds tenderly and with deep sympathy for the older son. He reassures him of his love, reminds him of the treasures he possesses, and even begs him to join the party for his brother! We would understand if the father threw up his hands in disgust and resignation. Is there anything more frustrating than a proud, pouting, self-righteous soul? But he doesn't. Instead, he continues to love his son even when his son won't love him.

As far as we know, the older son never responds to the father's love. By all appearances, his heart remains as hard as stone.

One Last Question

And there we have it—the greatest short story ever told, a story that people never tire of hearing. I certainly never tire of preaching it. It gives so many answers—and yet it leaves us with one last question.

Jesus, who spoke in short parables and quick, galvanizing truths, surely had something on His mind when He told the stories of the lost sheep, the lost coin, and the lost son. What was it? What stirred the heart of God's Son to deliver this masterpiece?

It's worth taking one more look at this passage to find out.

Luke, we find, gives us no more than a two-verse introduction to the telling of this tale. But those two verses suggest all we need to know: "Then all the tax collectors and the sinners drew near to Him to hear Him. And the Pharisees and scribes complained, saying, 'This Man receives sinners and eats with them'" (Luke 15:1–2).

Jesus was surrounded by people with great needs, people hungry physically and spiritually; people eager to hear His teaching. But He could also look up to the fringe of the crowd, and His eyes would fall on a separate group. The Pharisees and scribes watched impassively and disapprovingly, eager to find fault.

They didn't like what Jesus said. But more than that, they

didn't like what He did—and with whom. To their minds, Jesus threw Himself away on *lost* people like tax collectors who cheated their own neighbors. These were low and immoral types who should be shunned according to the Law.

But Jesus even had a tax collector for a disciple. Matthew was the man's name. Matthew went on to write a Gospel that tells a story similar to the one here in Luke, with the Pharisees asking, "Why does your Teacher eat with tax collectors and sinners?" (Matthew 9:11). On that occasion, Jesus told them that doctors were for sick people, that He "did not come to call the righteous, but sinners, to repentance" (v. 13). In other words, Jesus came to seek and to save the lost (Luke 19:10).

In Luke 18 Jesus tells another story of a tax collector and a Pharisee. The Pharisee, like the older brother, was very moral and upright and also very arrogant and proud. The tax collector was a dishonest man—a moral failure. But just as in our story, the tax collector (youngest son) repented. Jesus gives His final evaluation: "I tell you, this man went down to his house justified rather than the other; for everyone who exalts himself will be humbled, and he who humbles himself will be exalted" (Luke 18:14).

Clearly, Jesus' view of the lost was quite different from the Pharisee's view. The Pharisees knew all about lost and found. As they saw it, they themselves were the found, and the lost? Well, let them be. They had only themselves to blame. Yet, rather than blaming them, Jesus welcomed and loved them. He spent time in their homes and even ate with them. It was all shocking to the Pharisees.

I believe one day Jesus looked up at those crowds, His heart filled with love, as always. Then He looked a little farther and locked eyes with the Pharisees. He read their faces, their disapproval. And suddenly, He told three stories that answered the question: Who is a lost person?

He told a simple story about a sheep. He told another one about a coin. And then he told this story of a father and two sons, with a genuine, jaw-dropping twist at the end—*it turns out that both sons are lost.*

The "sinners" in the crowd saw themselves in the story. They sat in suspense as the haggard figure stumbled home, and they wept when the father took the prodigal into his arms.

The Pharisees, caught up in the tale despite themselves, suddenly realized they were represented, too. They were the older son, and Jesus was suggesting some serious propositions:

First, that those who seemed lost could be forgiven.

Second, that "found" people might actually be lost.

Third, and most important of all—that God loved both. God forgave both, whether for dirty hands or for a haughty heart. Forgave? Why, He pursued! Here came God, weeping for joy, coming after a son—or sons.

The Pharisees could see in the eyes of Jesus an invitation to come to the party and be restored to that forgotten Father, the Father whose greatest law turned out to be love. Were these teachers going to lay down their pride and join the feast? Or would they continue to lurk at the fringes, finding fault and promoting misery?

That question, my friend, is left open. Because Jesus looks up one more time, even past the Pharisees, to another set of eyes. He looks down through time to this very moment and His eyes meet yours. He wants you to know that whichever son represents you in this story, the result is the same.

God loves you, even when you don't love Him.

God is *after* you. It doesn't matter how far you have wandered, or what you have done. It doesn't matter if you attend church every night of the week and obey every rule you can find. All that does matter is that God loves you with a deep and abiding passion—that on your road of life, He is gaining on you. He won't stop until you are enveloped in His great, prodigally affectionate arms.

Now He is inviting you to that party, a sheer celebration of the lost being found, of love being restored. Will you accept? He is waiting for your answer.

SEVEN

God Loves You When He's Correcting You

◈

Whom the LORD loves He corrects,
Just as a father the son in whom he delights.
—PROVERBS 3:12

The train chugged its way through Indiana at twenty-four miles per hour. That doesn't seem like a frightful speed. That is, until you take into account how long it takes to stop a 6,200-ton train...and what lay upon the tracks ahead.

"That's a baby!" yelled Robert Mohr, the attentive conductor.

The engineer, Rodney Lindley, had thought it was a small dog, but the thatch of blonde hair and the colorful clothes made it all clear.

Emily Marshall, a child of nineteen months, was playing

on the rails. She had strayed from safety as her mother picked flowers in the garden.

It was all chaos and shouting at the controls of the train. The engineer hit the brakes, but there was no way the train could stop short of disaster. Mohr, forty-nine and a Vietnam vet, had to think quickly.

He threw open the door, moved along a catwalk to the very front of the engine, and leaned precariously forward, steadying himself with one arm as Lindley continued to pull frantically at the brake. The train slowed to about ten miles per hour—still much too fast. Lindley said, "It felt like we were just eating up the rail, going faster and faster."

As the great locomotive approached, Emily heard the noise and sensed danger. "She sat up and watched us for what seemed like an eternity," said Lindley. Then she began to crawl off the rails, but not fast enough. Just as the train was about to go over her, Mohr, at the leading edge of the locomotive, stretched out one leg as far as he could and, like a field-goal kicker, booted the baby over the edge and down the soft embankment. Then he leaped down, picked up the crying child, and comforted her.

Emily came out of the near fatal experience with cuts on her head, a chipped tooth, and a swollen lip.[1]

We know how deeply grateful the mother was—remorseful, too, I'm sure. But I wonder if that little child truly comprehended how blessed she was that a stranger with a big foot kicked her down a hill. She was trying to play, there was a lot of noise, and suddenly something jarred her and sent her tumbling like Jack and Jill. It hurt!

Perspective makes a difference. What seems hurtful from one vantage point can, when seen in full perspective, turn out to be an act of compassion. That's how it is with discipline and correction. Sometimes we have to hurt a little now so we won't hurt a lot later. Some lessons come only through tears. We know this as parents; we also need to know it as children of God.

C. S. Lewis had a lot to say about the pain of discipline. He noted that some of us have a shallow view of God's correcting love:

> We want, in fact, not so much a Father in Heaven as a grandfather in heaven...whose plan for the universe was simply that it might be truly said at the end of each day, "a good time was had by all."...I should very much like to live in a universe which was governed on such lines. But since its abundantly clear that I don't, and since I have reason to believe, nevertheless, that God is Love, I conclude that my conception of love needs correction.
>
> As Scripture points out...it is for people whom we care nothing about that we demand happiness on any terms: with our friends, our lovers, our children, we are exacting and would rather see them suffer much than be happy in contemptible and estranging modes.[2]

What brand of love would keep that conductor from rescuing a happily playing child on the grounds that a good boot is rude and painful? What brand of love would have kept your parents from scolding you for not doing your homework, since scolding would have put a damper on a pleasant dinner? As Lewis points out, the willingness to administer pain to prevent a greater harm is a mark of true love.

Charles Ryrie writes, "Love consists of affection and correction. Babies are cuddled and corrected, and both are true expressions of parental love. Furthermore, both are done by parents in the belief that they are doing the best thing for the child at the time. Love seeks good for the object loved. What is good? In God it is the perfection of holiness and all that that concept implies."[3]

I have always enjoyed the following verse about training toward perfection:

I must not interfere with any child, I have been told,
To bend his will to mine, or to shape him through some
*   mold of thought.*
Naturally, as a flower, he must unfold.
Yet flowers have the discipline of wind and rain,
And though I know it gives the gardener much pain,
I've seen him use his pruning shears to gain
More strength and beauty for some blossoms bright.
And he would do whatever he thought right.
I do not know, yet it seems to me
That only weeds unfold naturally.[4]

No one wants to be a weed, yet we resist the painful pruning required to make flowers of us. There isn't one of us who hasn't asked that ageless question about why people suffer. Why can't God simply make all the bad things go away? We've heard all the well-reasoned answers. Yet when we get a flat tire or some calamity befalls us, we hear ourselves praying, "God, how can You? Surely this wasn't Your plan for me. Can't You fix it?"

However, when the deepest conviction of our hearts is that

God loves us, our questions will turn to prayers. Instead of accusing God, we will begin to pray prayers like, "Father, help me to trust You." "Lord, what are You teaching me and how do You want me to change?" "How is this trial evidence of Your love for me?"

The Reasons for God's Discipline

To help answer these questions, let's begin by cutting through some of the confusion that exists about God's discipline. Much of the confusion exists because we fail to distinguish between the different reasons for God's discipline. As we shall now see, not all discipline is the same. In fact, there are at least three categories of discipline. By examining all three, we will learn much about why and how the discipline of God comes to us.

God Disciplines to Punish Us

> *If his sons forsake My law*
> *And do not walk in My judgments,*
> *If they break My statutes*
> *And do not keep My commandments,*
> *Then I will punish their transgression with the rod,*
> *And their iniquity with stripes.*
>
> —PSALM 89:30–32

The need for punishment is a hard but necessary truth. God is not Lewis's laid-back grandfather; He loves us too much to be so lax. He is determined that we will learn our lesson.

When King David committed his appalling double sin, Nathan the prophet confronted him: "Why have you despised the commandment of the LORD, to do evil in His sight? You have killed Uriah the Hittite with the sword; you have taken his wife to be your wife...Now therefore, the sword shall never depart from your house, because you have despised Me" (2 Samuel 12:9–10).

David had used the sword to destroy the house of Uriah, and now the sword would wreak havoc on his own house. The infant son he fathered by Uriah's wife died. Another son was killed in a war of rebellion against David. Another raped his own sister and was murdered by his vengeful brother. Another was assassinated as a rival to the son who succeeded David.

Sometimes, God will mercifully withhold the punishment of His child, even relieving him of the consequences of his sin. At other times, even if the believer repents and God forgives him, the discipline of punishment must be gracefully administered. It will hurt, but the hurt is meant to help. In fact, God's discipline never involves His wrath; His wrath is reserved for the unbeliever.

Old Testament scholar Theodore Laetsch makes this point very clear: "His plans concerning His people are always thoughts of good, of blessing. Even if He is obliged to use the rod, it is the rod not of wrath, but the Father's rod of chastisement for their temporal and eternal welfare. There is not a single item of evil in His plans for his people, neither in their motive, nor in their conception, nor in their revelation, nor in their consummation."[5]

God Disciplines to Protect Us

And lest I should be exalted above measure by the abundance of the revelations, a thorn in the flesh was given to me, a messenger of Satan to buffet me, lest I be exalted above measure.

—2 CORINTHIANS 12:7

The speaker in this verse, the apostle Paul, indicates that he did not suffer because he had committed the sin of pride; rather, his suffering was to keep him from becoming proud, or "exalted above measure." It was protective discipline meant to prevent a soul-destroying problem. While we do not know what Paul's "thorn in the flesh" was, we do know that he suffered greatly because of it. Three times he asked God to remove the thorn, and three times the Lord denied his request.

Instead, God gave His apostle the grace to endure the pain. God's preventive discipline greatly increased Paul's effectiveness. He wrote that his weakness had actually made him stronger (2 Corinthians 12:8–10). It forced him to depend on God's strength instead of his own.

Sometimes God disciplines us to "kick us away" from trouble, as did the conductor for the little girl. But if He fails to get our attention, He may collapse our lives into rubble, forcing us to wake up to the danger. As C. S. Lewis wrote, God "shouts in our pain: it is His megaphone to rouse a deaf world."[6]

Jack Abramoff, a political lobbyist who was at the center of a 2006 political scandal, recognized this truth as well. After his house of cards came tumbling down, he ruefully observed, "God sent me one thousand hints that he didn't want me to keep doing what I was doing. But I didn't listen, so he set off a nuclear bomb."[7]

God Disciplines to Purify Us

He [chastens us] for our profit, that we may be partakers of His holiness.

—HEBREWS 12:10

Hebrews 12:5–11 is the key passage in the New Testament for understanding God's correcting love. The key word in these verses is *chastening*, a translation of the Greek word *paideia*, which appears nine times in various forms in these seven verses.

Paideia comes from the word *pais*, which means "child," and it denotes the training of a child. It is a broad term that can mean anything parents and teachers do to train, correct, cultivate, and educate children. The goal of this discipline is always to help the child grow into a mature adult.

We are born contaminated with an inherently sinful nature—or "the flesh," depending on your Bible translation (Romans 7:18, 25). One day that contamination will be completely eradicated. But in the meantime, God often uses the tools of suffering and affliction to sanctify us. These trials function like a fire that burns off every impurity impeding our progress toward holiness.

Malcolm Muggeridge, in his book *Jesus Rediscovered*, wrote, "Suppose you eliminated suffering, what a dreadful place the world would be... The world would be the most ghastly place because everything that corrects the tendency of this unspeakable little creature, man, to feel over-important and ever-pleased with himself would disappear. He's bad enough now, but he would be absolutely intolerable if he never suffered."[8]

To ask God to do less is to ask Him to love us less—to leave us infected with sin that will not only defile our earthly lives, but also destroy us eternally.

The Reality of God's Discipline

> For whom the LORD loves He chastens, and scourges every son whom He receives.
>
> —HEBREWS 12:6

Instead of wondering why God disciplines us, we might do better to wonder why He doesn't. The author of Hebrews makes it clear that discipline is a sign of God's love, and conversely that the lack of discipline means that God does not count you as His. That should thoroughly stifle our envy of those who live in reckless opposition to God yet never seem to experience trouble or pain.

The Presence of God's Discipline Proves That We Are His Sons

> If you endure chastening, God deals with you as with sons; for what son is there whom a father does not chasten?
>
> —HEBREWS 12:7

"Sons" is the English translation of the Greek word *huios*, which we find five times in Hebrews 12:5–8. In the New

Testament, *huios* never means "small children"; it always designates an adult son—the kind who is an heir.

Why is this important? The use of *huios* implies that the discipline verse 7 speaks of isn't simply for beginner Christians. Even mature believers need chastening. "Behold, happy is the man whom God corrects; therefore do not despise the chastening of the Almighty" (Job 5:17).

Though children may dislike discipline on the surface, somewhere deep inside they appreciate the sense of security it gives them. The very fact that they are being chastened proves that they are sons who have a loving father who cares about their future. All men are subject to God's punishment, but only His children receive His discipline.

The Absence of God's Discipline Proves That We Are Not His Sons

> *But if you are without chastening, of which all have become partakers, then you are illegitimate and not sons.*
>
> —HEBREWS 12:8

You might think you would love to go through life without ever enduring an ounce of discipline. But wouldn't you have second thoughts if you knew it meant you were an illegitimate child?

In New Testament times, there could be no more serious charge than to question one's legitimacy. Imagine three boys playing in the courtyard of a wealthy man's estate. They get into some kind of mischief, and their father comes out, his face beet-red, fire in his eyes, and he drags away two of his sons by the ear. The other boy, who is also his son by a female servant, stands and watches, totally ignored. He has misbehaved, too. He even lives on the same estate. But his father doesn't care what he does because he doesn't consider him a true son.

How that would have stung! The rejected boy would have learned that a father's indifference is far worse than the momentary pain of chastening.

The message of Hebrews 12 is that discipline is the mark of the beloved child. It saddens me to know that an ever-increasing number of today's children are growing up without that mark. The old spiritual "Sometimes I Feel Like a Fatherless Child" describes one out of three of our precious children in America. They live in homes without their biological fathers. Some of these children live in homes with an admirable stepfather who has taken them in, loved them, and claimed them for his own. But the rest simply don't have a father of any kind at home; millions more have a poor excuse for one. The results are tragic.

There is a wealth of evidence that demonstrates the harmful effects of a father's absence from his post: higher rates of incarceration, teenage pregnancy, mental illness, and drug use. We need our fathers. Most any man can help make a child; that's easy. But it takes love to be a father to that child. And part of that love is discipline.

The writer of Hebrews does not whitewash discipline: "Now no chastening seems to be joyful for the present, but painful" (12:11). This has to be one of the most obvious statements in the Bible. If chastening were pleasant, it wouldn't be chastening. It is painful! It hurts! It's never easy to appreciate discipline at the point of impact, and no one chooses to go through it. I've never risen in the morning, greeted the sunshine, and prayed, "Lord, I know that trials bring wisdom, so hit me with one today! I can't wait to see how I grow."

Here the Bible freely admits that if you enjoy the process of discipline, something is wrong with you. On the other hand, if you don't appreciate the result of discipline, something is wrong with your commitment. Within every son or daughter of God, there must be a tough, hardened core of determination that says, "I'm not going to like it, but I'm going to take it. It's for God's glory, and it's for my best, so why fight the rain that makes flowers grow?"

Pastor John Piper was asked this peculiar question: Should a true Christian pray for more trouble in his or her life? He replied that when he gets on his knees and reflects on the rough spots in his character that need to be smoothed out, his prayer is, *Lord, whatever it takes.*

He admits he isn't about to ask for a car wreck or more pain—"that seems presumptuous." But he readies his spirit to be submissive to God for any chastening he may need that day.[9]

We should cherish our chastening because it is God's way of saying, "You belong to Me, and I love you." His discipline may anger us at times, but it will protect us, teach us, and prepare us. This is why the early church theologian Jerome is reported to have said, "The greatest danger of all is when God is no longer angry with us."

Our Reaction to God's Discipline

And you have forgotten the exhortation which speaks to you as to sons: "My son, do not despise the chastening of the LORD, nor be discouraged when you are rebuked by Him."

—HEBREWS 12:5

The first-century audience for the book of Hebrews knew Proverbs 3:11–12, which is quoted in the verse above. The writer probably included it because he thought hearing it again would encourage them. It was a time of severe hardship for the early church, and they needed to understand that even followers of Jesus Christ have to endure painful discipline.

These early believers may have expected severe discipline to cease once they became Christians. It's easy for us to adopt a similar outlook. We may think becoming one with Christ should mean that God has accomplished His goal with us, and therefore His discipline should ease up. But as we have just noted, when we become God's children, those lessons are not likely to ease up, but rather to intensify. How we react is up to us. Here are four possibilities:

We Can Be Indifferent to God's Discipline

My son, do not despise the chastening of the LORD.

—HEBREWS 12:5

The Greek word for "despise" means "to think lightly of," or "to make light of." We despise God's discipline when we grit our teeth and endure it without letting the hard truth of it soak in. After the trying time is over, we breathe a sigh of relief and go on our way without reflecting on why we experienced it. To make us stop and reflect may have been God's very reason for the exercise. He has something for us to learn that will make us wiser or save us from some worse pain in the future. Or it may be a door-opener, unlocking new possibilities in our lives.

In the Old Testament, Jonah learned the hard way not to despise the chastening of the Lord. When God first sent him to preach salvation to the Ninevites, Jonah was angry. He hated Nineveh because it was the capital of Assyria, the cruel historic enemy of Jonah's homeland, Israel. So he boarded a ship headed in the opposite direction. When God sent a great fish to swallow him and spit him back in the right direction, Jonah gave in and trudged reluctantly to Nineveh.

The Ninevites heard God's message, repented, and the city was spared. The angry Jonah stomped off to sit and sulk. God quickly grew a shading plant to shelter him from the sun. But on the next day He sent a worm to kill the plant, exposing Jonah to the blistering heat. That was the last straw: Jonah wanted to die.

Now that Jonah was broken and ready to hear what he needed to learn, God zoomed in on his shamefully inverted priorities. He had wanted the shading plant to live while wanting a city of 120,000 people to perish. He had no love for people whom God loved, but God still loved him.

If we are honest, our response to God's call on our lives is often similar to Jonah's. We, too, can become angry, indifferent, and stubborn. But God's discipline will always prevail. Why not embrace it, knowing that every trial, whether light or severe, has something in it for our benefit (see Romans 8:28)?

We Can Be Intimidated by God's Discipline

Nor be discouraged when you are rebuked by Him.

—HEBREWS 12:5

It is not unusual for Christians to be overwhelmed or fearful of God's rebuke and correction—to grow "weary and discouraged in [their] souls" (Hebrews 12:3). In these times it helps to understand that chastisement is not God's judgment; it is His correction, protection, or prevention. Though at times it may be severe, it will not kill us. No painful experience touches the Christian without the permissive and loving will of the Father in heaven.

Intimidation was the first reaction of the psalmist in Psalm 42:11, but as you can see, his hope in God banished his fear:

Why are you cast down, O my soul?
And why are you disquieted within me?
Hope in God;
For I shall yet praise Him,
The help of my countenance and my God.

God disciplines to help us—to build us up, not to tear us down. In her book *Hope Has Its Reasons*, Rebecca Manley Pippert makes this point in a story about dealing with loved ones who have substance abuse problems. She describes the frustration of watching a close friend destroy her life. She was disgusted and furious—not because she hated her friend, but because she loved her. "Love detests what destroys the beloved," she writes. "Real love stands against the deception, the lie, the sin that destroys."[10]

Pippert concludes that we wouldn't want a God who didn't become angry over our self-destruction. Such a God wouldn't be good or loving. "Anger isn't the opposite of love. Hate is, and the final form of hate is indifference."[11]

Jesus was not indifferent when He saw swindlers using the temple to cheat poor worshippers who had walked many miles to experience God in Jerusalem. He was angry! He toppled tables, scattered money, and shouted at the offenders, emphatically expressing His wrath against anything that stands between God and His children (John 2:13–17).

Would you want a dispassionate Jesus who is indifferent to the things that hurt us, one who merely shrugs over the terrible fallenness of this world, who occasionally tidies things up without ever getting particularly personal about it?

I don't want a dispassionate doctor. I want one who listens and cares, who relates to me not just medically but also personally. As much as my doctor cares, he sometimes comes down hard on me when I ignore his advice and eat the wrong foods or become lax in my exercise. I want the same from God. It strengthens me to know that He rages over the sin in my life, whether it is inflicted on me or I inflict it on myself. I'm not intimidated by the anger that erupts in God's discipline, because I know it is controlled by His love for me.

We Can Be Ignorant of God's Discipline

The most common response to discipline is to fail to see it as discipline. The world tells us that all events just happen randomly, without rhyme or reason. The Bible teaches otherwise; it tells us that God is sovereign and that in all things He is working. Thus we should never see any obstacle as "bad luck" or "just the breaks" or merely a random event. We serve a God who "does great things past finding out, yes, wonders without number" (Job 9:10).

Eugene Peterson writes:

> Suffering is not evidence of God's absence, but of God's presence, and it is in our experience of being broken that God does His surest and most characteristic salvation work.
>
> There is a way to accept, embrace, and deal with suffering that results in a better life, not a worse one, and more of the experience of God, not less. God is working out his salvation in our lives the way He has always worked it out at the place of brokenness, at the cross of Jesus, and at the very place where we take up our cross.[12]

As God's beloved children we must carefully examine our unpleasant experiences, looking to see God's faithful hand in them. Don't allow ignorance to deprive you of the blessing of having God root out of your life some obstacle to your spiritual maturity.

We Can Be Instructed by God's Discipline

Before I was afflicted I went astray,
But now I keep Your word…
It is good for me that I have been afflicted,
That I may learn Your statutes.

—PSALM 119:67, 71

As fallen humans, our natural rebellion against God makes it hard for us to learn God's lessons the easy way. I'm reminded of the joke about the farmer who bragged about his extremely obedient mule. His skeptical neighbor insisted on a demonstration. The farmer hitched the mule to a wagon, then picked up a two-by-four and walloped the animal on the head.

The neighbor was appalled. "Why did you do that?" he said. "I thought your mule was the model of obedience."

"It is," the farmer replied. "But first you've got to get its attention."

God knows that we don't learn His ways or grow unless He gets our attention. Growth requires concentration and determination. It's a fight to move forward, with every inch of ground contested. The more relaxed we become in our relationship to the world, the more we buy into the illusion that we can pursue God at an easy jog, without any bumps in the road, without any looming rainstorms, without any stumbles.

Malcolm Muggeridge recalled what he once said to William Buckley regarding how he had come to learn the most meaningful lessons in life: "As an old man, Bill, looking back on one's life, it's one of the things that strikes you most forcibly— that the only thing that's taught one anything is suffering. Not success, not happiness, not anything like that. The only thing that teaches one what life is about—the joy of understanding, the joy of coming in contact with what life really signifies—is suffering, affliction."[13]

God doesn't love chastising us, but He loves what He sees at the end of the process: children who are "perfect and complete, lacking nothing" (James 1:4). So He administers His tough love, and He does it with all the gentleness possible in order to drive home instructions vital to our spiritual growth. Consider the words of the prophet Jeremiah:

> *Though He causes grief,*
> *Yet He will show compassion*
> *According to the multitude of His mercies.*
> *For He does not afflict willingly,*
> *Nor grieve the children of men.*
>
> —LAMENTATIONS 3:32–33

The Bible overflows with instructions telling us what we should be. But without discipline, we tend to follow those instructions at our own comfortable pace. We're like a novice swimmer inching into the pool to avoid the shock of cold water. God pushes us into the deep water, forcing us to endure the shock, because He knows we'll never learn to swim on our own terms.

The book of Proverbs is liberally salted with passages showing how discipline is a necessary component of instruction. Many are directed at parents, stressing the necessity of discipline in teaching and molding their children into godly beings. Yet as you read the verses, it's easy to see how this need for discipline also applies to adult believers. Here are five typical passages:

> *He who spares his rod hates his son,*
> *But he who loves him disciplines him promptly.*
>
> —PROVERBS 13:24

Chasten your son while there is hope,
And do not set your heart on his destruction.

—PROVERBS 19:18

Foolishness is bound up in the heart of a child;
The rod of correction will drive it far from him.

—PROVERBS 22:15

Do not withhold correction from a child,
For if you beat him with a rod, he will not die.

—PROVERBS 23:13

The rod and rebuke give wisdom,
But a child left to himself brings shame to his mother.

—PROVERBS 29:15

My generation was brought up on these principles. I think we all know that the succeeding generation or two have loosened the reins a bit. Parents today are told never to rebuke, challenge, or punish their children, because "correction," as described in the Bible, is cruel. Thus many parents have rejected the value of parental discipline because they are afraid of offending their children. Discipline requires pain, and pain does not seem loving. So parents adopt the attitude of the grandfather in Lewis's illustration and allow their children to do just about whatever they want as long as it makes them happy. The result is that more and more children are exhibiting disrespect, self-centeredness, rudeness, irresponsibility, and resentment toward authority. Fewer parents today are forming their children into what they ought to be—loving and responsible humans.

Recently, I read a disturbing article in the *New York Times* titled "For Some Parents, Shouting Is the New Spanking." The author, Hilary Stout, points out that parents are "friending" their children—using the terminology of the Facebook generation—rather than guiding and leading them. We cheer for our children in team sports; we congratulate their every tiny achievement; and we shout rather than spank. Quoting a prominent parenting expert, Stout shows how this approach generates an endless cycle of frustration:

> "I've worked with thousands of parents and I can tell you, without question, that screaming is the new spanking," said Amy McCready, the founder of Positive Parenting Solutions, which teaches parenting skills in classes, individual coaching sessions and an online course. "This is so the issue right now. As parents understand that it's not socially acceptable to spank children, they are at a loss for what they can do. They resort to reminding, nagging, time-out, counting 1-2-3 and quickly realize that those strategies don't work to change behavior. In the absence of tools that really work, they feel frustrated and angry and raise their voice. They feel guilty afterward, and the whole cycle begins again."[14]

In the Bible there is no absence of "tools that really work." Discipline, offered with abiding love, builds children into strong adults. God's principles are universal. If we can lovingly chasten our children in order to instruct them, He can lovingly chasten us for the same reason.

The Rationale for God's Discipline

*Furthermore, we have had human fathers who corrected us,
and we paid them respect. Shall we not much more readily be in subjection to the Father of spirits and live? For
they indeed for a few days chastened us as seemed best to
them, but He for our profit, that we may be partakers of His
holiness.*

—HEBREWS 12:9–10

Here the writer of Hebrews uses an analogy from everyday
life to illustrate how we should respond to God's discipline.
Our human fathers disciplined us imperfectly, yet we respected
them because we knew it was for our own good. How much
more should we yield to God's perfect discipline and hold Him
in awe?

These verses display a contrast between our human fathers
(more accurately translated *fathers of our flesh*) and our heavenly
Father (rendered here as *Father of spirits*). Here the writer sets
down the basic rationale for accepting God's discipline: God is
perfect; human fathers are not.

Our Human Fathers Disciplined Us as It Seemed Best to Them; Our Heavenly Father Disciplines Us as It Is Best for Us

Even with all the best intentions in the world, good human
fathers make mistakes. They under-discipline; over-discipline;
fail to discipline at all; or discipline from the wrong motives, in
the wrong way, or at the wrong time.

The discipline of God never misses the mark. It is perfect in its timing, its application, and its intensity. He always disciplines in fairness and firmness to achieve His perfect purposes. The superiority of God's discipline gives us good reason to subject ourselves to it with patience, humility, and gratitude.

Our Human Fathers Disciplined Us for Earthly Reasons; Our Heavenly Father Disciplines Us for Heavenly Reasons

A father on earth disciplines to teach and shape his child into a responsible adult who functions well in society. He focuses mainly on practical realities the child will face in everyday life. This, of course, is good and necessary.

The discipline of God also shapes us into responsible citizens, but ultimately His focus is much higher. He takes the longer view. He knows that our time on earth is but a droplet in the vast sea of eternity, so eternity is where he directs His attention. Just as an earthbound caterpillar has no clue that its destiny is to fly, we have no clue as to precisely how we fit into God's eternal purpose. It's because we see it all with caterpillar minds. Our earthly father does his best to train us to be good caterpillars, whereas our heavenly Father, who knows our eternal destiny, trains us to soar. God designed us for heaven and eternal fellowship with Him, and He is determined to shape us into heavenly creatures.

This is why God's discipline doesn't always make sense to us—why accepting it requires faith and trust as we pray: *Lord, You know Your plan for me and I do not. You know every part of me that needs work. Please do whatever it takes to get me there.*

The Results of God's Discipline

Now we come to the best part. The results of God's work can never be anything other than wonderful and majestic. His purposes are perfect. Although we can't always know the particulars in advance or trace the direction of His hand, we can trust His heart. He gives us good reason for that trust by revealing the broad outlines of His ultimate goal for us:

He Wants Us to Receive Holiness

That we may be partakers of His holiness.
—HEBREWS 12:10

Our loving Father's ultimate goal for us is that we share in His holiness. This is not just *holiness*, mind you; this is *God's* holiness. The Lord wants us to "be holy, for I am holy" (1 Peter 1:16). As the apostle Paul said, "For God did not call us to uncleanness, but in holiness" (1 Thessalonians 4:7).

To be holy means to be set aside for a special purpose. The story goes that Renaissance sculptor Michelangelo chose a block of marble and set it aside to sculpt an angel from it. His hammer and chisel pounded and scraped away until out of that dull cube of rock emerged a beautiful angel for the tomb of the pope. "My task," he told his admirers, "is to look at a block of stone and see an angel. Then I carve away everything that is not the angel."

That's what God does with us. Since we are not insentient stone, the hammering and chiseling may hurt. But we are in the hands of the Master Artist, and we are His masterpiece. If we submit to His sculpting, we will see holiness emerge from the dullness of ordinary living as we are transformed chip by chip into the image of Christ.

For fallen creatures bent on going their own way, hardship and holiness are inextricably linked. There are no shortcuts; it's a slow and painful process. God chips and chips until an unworthy attitude crumbles away. He scrapes incessantly until a bad habit disappears. All the while He sees beyond these imperfections to the beauty He intends for us.

Not only do we see the old, sorry attributes falling away, we begin to know God as only discipline can reveal Him. Sculpting is a close, detailed, intimate process through which we develop a fellowship with Him that makes any conceivable discomfort more than worth it.

He Wants Us to Reflect Righteousness

Afterward it yields the peaceable fruit of righteousness.
—HEBREWS 12:11

Although we can never know all of God's purposes in our lives, at times He gives us the perspective to look back at the blow we endured and see the good that came from it.

Joni Eareckson Tada was a college-bound seventeen-year-old with grand plans for her life when a dive into a shallow swimming hole left her permanently paralyzed. Unable to move her arms or legs and facing years of rehab, she went into deep depression. She was angry with God and despairing of life. She even wanted her friends to help her commit suicide.

Eventually Joni came through her despair with a strong faith in God and a desire to glorify Him with her life. She became a highly effective Christian writer, artist, singer, and speaker, and she also founded an organization to aid others struggling with disabilities.

Looking back, Joni can see how her severe trial moved her from self-sufficiency to complete dependence on God. In a recent interview she said, "Sometimes healing doesn't come, and you've got to live with it, and when you do you really do learn who you are. God uses suffering. He lobs it like a hand grenade and blows to smithereens these notions we have about our self and who we think we are. Blows it to smithereens until we are left raw, naked, and we have to let suffering do its work."[15]

Just as Joni could look back and see how God's discipline enabled righteousness to flower in her, we can look back and see how His discipline planted the seeds of righteousness within us. I'm not speaking here of the *imputed* righteousness of God (2 Corinthians 5:21), but of a daily life of practical righteousness: an active, visible goodness that becomes a model to the watching world. This righteousness is a manner of living—a wide set of disciplines developed in the laboratory of life as we learn to live and act in ways that reflect God's glory. The Scriptures symbolically describe such righteousness as "fine linen, clean and white...the righteousness of saints" (Revelation 19:8 KJV).

He Wants Us to Radiate Peace

It yields the peaceable fruit of righteousness.

—HEBREWS 12:11

You may wonder just how the pursuit of peace fits with the acceptance of God's discipline. It would seem that struggling through the pain and affliction of discipline would drive away all possibility of peace. Very unpeaceful questions would trouble our minds: *Why is God doing this to me? When will it be over? Am I going to survive it? If I do, will I ever recover?*

Accepting discipline produces peace in two ways: First, there is a peace that "surpasses all understanding" (Philippians 4:7). It's a peace that works like a ship's gyroscope, keeping us upright and stable in a storm. No matter what kinds of turmoil threaten, you have an inner calm that banishes all anxiety because your spirit is steadied by the knowledge that you are in God's hands.

Second, the discipline you endure now instills peace in you about your future, just as surgery to remove a tumor frees the patient from anxiety. When we endure the discipline that achieves righteousness, the peace that comes from a closer relationship with God follows in its wake.

In Hebrews 12:14 we are challenged to "pursue peace." Just remember that you cannot achieve peace by pursuing it for its own sake. Peace comes when you acquire the character traits that produce it: righteousness and holiness. Pursuing these godlike attributes brings God into that God-shaped vacuum in our hearts, giving us the peace of knowing we are one with Him.

The work of righteousness will be peace,
And the effect of righteousness,
quietness and assurance forever.

—ISAIAH 32:17

Will You Let God Do Whatever It Takes?

Psychologist Jonathon Haidt suggests a hypothetical exercise that vividly illustrates the hard choices God must make when administering discipline. Imagine that you are a soon-to-be parent, and you receive an advance script for the life of your child. You are also given an eraser and told that you can freely edit the script.

So you read with eager eyes, and your heart begins to sink. Your child will have a learning disability in grade school, making it difficult for him to read. In high school he will lose a close friend to cancer. Good things also happen in this script: Your child gets into the college of his choice, but he loses a leg in an automobile accident and experiences depression. He will get jobs and lose them. He will get married and separated.

You look up from the script with tears in your eyes. You had dreamed of nothing but sunshine ahead—a future president, the next Billy Graham, a Nobel Prize winner.

So what do you erase?

Your immediate reaction is to edit out the pain and obstacles. But there's that rule of unintended consequences: If you erase the bad stuff, what else might you be inadvertently erasing with it? What lessons might God be teaching with the bad stuff that are critical to your child's eternal salvation? What eternal values may be undermined by the use of your well-intentioned eraser?

John Ortberg, quoting the scenario above, asks, "Is it possible that in some way people actually need adversity, setbacks, maybe even something like trauma to reach the fullest level of development and growth?"[16]

Ask Abraham, who waited decades for the son God promised him. Ask Job, who had to lose almost every earthly possession to gain heavenly wisdom. Ask Christ, who had to drink from the cup God gave Him and march courageously to the cross. Ask Paul, who had to embrace his "thorn in the flesh" as a gift of grace.

Ask yourself. Is it possible you need a little adversity? Could it be that it's going on right now, and that God is doing something wonderful in you even as you fight it off? Could it be that you should accept your present pain as a beloved friend and not a despised enemy?

A certain tribe of Native Americans had a special rite of passage for training young braves. On one boy's thirteenth birthday he was blindfolded and taken deep into the forest, where he was left to fend off the terrors of the night.

The young man had never been apart from his family until now. He had learned of all the dangerous creatures and of the danger of becoming lost forever in the labyrinth of untamed vegetation. But now it was his role to show his courage.

When he took off his blindfold, he found himself alone under the moon and the stars. The darkness and solitude magnified every sound, infusing every snap of a twig with foreboding possibilities. Could a wolf be stealthily drawing near? Or maybe a poisonous snake, coiling itself in the branches above? He wondered if the privileges of adulthood were worth such a trial.

After a moonlit eternity, the first rays of sunshine broke through the thick green canopy above him. He began to see flowers, trees, and finally a forest pathway. Looking a bit farther, he was jolted by the sight of a fierce warrior only a few feet away, bow and arrow at the ready. It was his father. He had silently kept watch through the night.[17]

Life can bring us to dark and foreboding places—lonely places in which we feel isolated and desolate. Yet there is always Someone keeping watch. Why doesn't He speak? Why doesn't He disclose His presence so that we might relax? He keeps His silence because otherwise we would not learn to be courageous. We would not build trust.

The trials that bring us into maturity are often terrifying or painful. But who wants to remain a child forever? Not me! I want to be a fully grown, mature disciple of the Lord. I want the traits He wishes to instill in me through His perfect love— traits that will be evident only if I trust Him, even when I can neither see Him nor feel His loving hand.

EIGHT

God's Love Will Never Let You Go

∽

I give them eternal life, and they shall never perish; neither shall anyone snatch them out of My hand.

—JOHN 10:28

Something in a man needs a mountain to climb, a challenge to meet. And what challenge is greater than the ultimate peak, the highest of mountains—Mount Everest? More than three thousand climbers have made it to the top. But, several thousand have failed, and more than 220 have died in the attempt.

One place where they commonly fail is the trek from the South Summit to Hillary Step. Here climbers face a knife-edge ridge made of ice, snow, and fragmented shale—10,000 feet straight down into Tibet on one side, 7,000 feet down into Nepal on the other. The ridge must be crossed with tiny, cautious steps and a good ice ax. Erik Weihenmayer, who made it all the way to the top, knows of the unnerving sound of rock chipping off, plunging into the void.

Erik would have heard this sound more crisply than nearly any other climber, for he was the first blind man to reach the summit of Everest. That isn't Erik's only achievement. On August 20, 2008, he reached the top of Carstensz Pyramid in Indonesia, the tallest mountain in Australasia. This completed his goal of reaching the Seven Summits, a group of imposing peaks, one from each of the world's seven continents. Totally blind since the age of thirteen, Erik has overcome one mountain-sized challenge after another.[1]

It all started with Alaska's Mount McKinley. A friend challenged Erik to climb the peak with him. Given Erik's impediment, the idea seemed crazy. Since the mountain is filled with massive, man-swallowing crevices, climbers who take it on must be tightly fastened to a rope. As Erik recalled later, "Even when the wind was howling and I wouldn't be able to hear footsteps crunching in front of me, I'd have the direction of the rope to follow."[2]

I love stories like Erik's. In my mind's eye I can see myself on that mountain: the wind howling, icy dust filling my lungs, massive crevasses yawning before me—and I confess that my knees get a little weak. At that point my cozy chair in the family room feels awfully good to me.

But I can't help but think about the rope. How important is that piece of equipment to mountain climbers? Vitally important. It's the difference between death and glory. The rope is a lifeline bonding a half-dozen adventurers who must have utter faith in its strength.

The rope is even more important to a blind man such as Erik. All his information comes through his elevated senses of hearing and touch. He and his friends are all tethered to the rope, and he feels the tension of their movement as they climb upward. When someone slips, his hands instantly clutch the line, and through it he knows what is happening and sets himself for danger. The rope is his guide in the midst of a perilous journey, the one thing that will not fail him when he is uncertain of his next step.

The Rope of God's Love

In one significant way, we are all just as blind as Erik Weihenmayer. We cannot see the future ahead of us any more than he can see his next step. We cannot know what lies five weeks or five minutes or five seconds into the future. Sometimes it may turn out to be a walk in the park, other times a steep ascent across a sheet of ice in howling winds. Either way, we have a rope. God's love is the unbreakable line that tethers us to truth and to one another, and keeps us on the path as we ascend toward heaven. That rope is our sure and steady lifeline, whether it's so stormy that we can hardly push ahead or so calm that we tend to wander.

Here is the Bible's description of the unbreakable rope that binds us to God:

Who shall separate us from the love of Christ? Shall tribulation, or distress, or persecution, or famine, or nakedness, or peril, or sword? As it is written:

"For Your sake we are killed all day long;
We are accounted as sheep for the slaughter."

Yet in all these things we are more than conquerors through Him who loved us. For I am persuaded that neither death nor life, nor angels nor principalities nor powers, nor things present nor things to come, nor height nor depth, nor any other created thing, shall be able to separate us from the love of God which is in Christ Jesus our Lord.

—ROMANS 8:35–39

In these verses the apostle gives us, if you will, a sales demonstration of God's love. It's a bit like an old commercial for superglue in which a car was suspended in midair, held to the cable by nothing but a dab or two of that incredible adhesive. The test was intended to convince people that this glue would do any job needed. If it could hold that car, surely it would patch up your broken vase.

Twice Paul emphatically asserts that nothing can separate us from the love of God found in Christ Jesus (vv. 35, 39). Surely few would disagree that this is the greatest message of the Bible—that nothing in the entire universe can stop God from loving us. It simply cannot and will not happen.

Please notice that Paul doesn't say *we* must hang on to God's love; he says that God's love hangs on to us. Think again of the climber, bound by a powerful line to his fellows and the mountain. His hands are free to work with tools, to interact with the surface, to get his canteen. The rope is wrapped around him, and it's not going to break. He can slip, he can fall, or he can even faint, and the rope will bear him up.

God's love doesn't depend on how well we love Him back. It doesn't depend upon whether or not we let go. We don't earn it, deserve it, or maintain it. Yet His love is wrapped around us, reinforced by His promises. It holds us perfectly and permanently. We may slip and fall, but we are not lost. As Paul wrote to Timothy, "If we are faithless, He remains faithful; He cannot deny Himself" (2 Timothy 2:13). Whatever happens, the rope holds fast. Nothing can separate us from His love.

The apostle Paul, writing from the inspired insight of the Holy Spirit, knows us pretty well. He understands that we struggle with this concept of the durability of God's love. Why? One reason is that what we know of love we learn from other people. People stop "loving" one another for just about every selfish or faulty reason imaginable. Marriage vows are signed with vanishing ink. Friends fall out. Even parents and children become irreconcilable. Most human love is conditional and limited. Fail to meet the conditions, and the "love" is withdrawn.

Another reason we have trouble believing in the tenacity of God's love is the sense of our own sin. We can't quite believe we are lovable. How could God love us after what we've done? We know that we are not worthy of His love, and it's hard to believe that God will not give up on us.

These human impediments to love do not affect God one iota. With Him, the cord of love is unbreakable. Unlike human love, it has no conditions and no limits. Yet think of the mental energy people needlessly expend in anxiety over messing up and somehow losing His love. If we think some sin in our past has caused Him to fold His arms and turn away, Romans 8 should banish that idea forever. We must listen to what Paul tells us: Nothing can separate us from God's love. What part of "nothing" don't we understand?

In Romans 8:35–39, Paul confronts one final reason why we might be tempted to doubt God's love: suffering. In these verses, the apostle tests the sticking power of God's love against life's heaviest burdens. He mentions seven of these—tribulation, distress, persecution, famine, nakedness, peril, and sword (the threat of death). He is countering the false assumption that if we find ourselves in any of these traumatic situations, then the love of God must not have held. That assumption misses the point: God's love is not a "trouble-be-gone" spray to fend off pain and trouble; it's a glue to keep us bonded to Him when trouble comes. A glue that holds no matter what.

"But Paul," you may counter, "you don't know the depths of the suffering I've been through. If you had suffered as I have, you wouldn't be so quick to say that God's love has remained intact." Well, let's see just what Paul knew of suffering. He offers a résumé of his misfortunes in 2 Corinthians 11. He endured tribulations, various kinds of dire needs, five beatings with thirty-nine lashes (three with rods), frequent imprisonment, tumult, hard labor, sleeplessness, fasting, dishonor, lies, deceit, chastening, sorrow, poverty, stoning, three shipwrecks, twenty-four hours adrift in the sea, travel dangers, robbers, persecution by Jews, persecution by Gentiles, trials in the cities, trials in the wilderness, hunger, thirst, cold, and nakedness—all of this on top of the daily stress of guiding and directing new churches across the Roman Empire.

Paul's final suffering, which naturally he could not list, was his martyrdom at the hands of the Roman emperor around AD 67–68.

I believe we can safely say that Paul knew something about suffering. And all it did was increase his appreciation for the extent of God's tenacious grip of love. He believed himself to be profoundly blessed.

Paul's point in Romans 8 is that our difficult or painful circumstances are no reflection on the love of God. In verse 36, he appeals to a passage from the Old Testament to emphasize the point: "Yet for Your sake we are killed all day long; we are accounted as sheep for the slaughter" (Psalm 44:22). He is simply telling us that bad things happen to people, and it's nothing new. Bad things also happened to the ancient Jews. Sin brought evil into the world, and death comes with the territory.

Paul's quote from Psalm 44 reflects a historical period when Israel's enemies were cruelly dominating the nation, inflicting tribulation, distress, persecution, peril, and death by the sword. The people saw themselves as sheep lined up for slaughter.

How did they feel about God during their oppression? We can answer this question by looking at the part of the psalm that Paul didn't quote:

> *Awake! Why do You sleep, O Lord?*
> *Arise! Do not cast us off forever.*
> *Why do You hide Your face,*
> *And forget our affliction and our oppression?*
> *For our soul is bowed down to the dust;*
> *Our body clings to the ground.*
> *Arise for our help,*
> *And redeem us for Your mercies' sake.*
>
> —PSALM 44:23–26

I love the honesty of the Scriptures. Here we see that those ancient Israelites thought just the way we do now. The troubles people face may vary in different epochs, but the people never change. They always seem to believe they are entitled to smooth sailing. When high winds and waves lash at them, they look to the heavens and cry, "God, why won't You remove this tribulation?" Yet God understands our emotions and allows our complaints and misunderstandings to be part of our honest prayers to Him.

The enemies came, the Israelites suffered, and it seemed as if God had abandoned His chosen people. They were like Erik Weihenmayer on Mount Everest—blind travelers going through a terrible storm and unable to see what lay ahead. Yet they were still held firmly by the unbreakable rope.

Where do we get the idea that God has promised us an easy ride through life? Not from Scripture; it's not there. Loving parents never promise their children a problem-free life. Instead, they say, "We will always be here for you, we will always offer all we have to help you, and we will always love you—even if you disappoint us, even if you walk away from us, even if you don't return our love." Such is the love of God.

John Stott writes, "Christian people are not guaranteed immunity to temptation, tribulation or tragedy, but we are promised victory over them. God's pledge is not that suffering will never afflict us, but that it will never separate us from his love."[3]

What Can Separate Us from God's Love?

In Romans 8:35, Paul emphatically affirmed that none of the personal crises he had experienced affected the constancy of God's love. But Paul doesn't stop there. He continues on, showing us that the personal troubles we all encounter are just the tip of the iceberg. In verses 38–39 he gives us a second list that opens the window to another level of obstacles, many of them great, cosmic, universal powers so enormous that Christians could easily fear them as threats to God's love.

In addressing this second list, Paul expresses his complete confidence in the love of God in one of the most profound and eloquent statements of faith in the entire Bible:

> *For I am persuaded that neither death nor life, nor angels nor principalities nor powers, nor things present nor things to come, nor height nor depth, nor any other created thing, shall be able to separate us from the love of God which is in Christ Jesus our Lord.*
>
> —ROMANS 8:38–39

What a grand, powerful, lofty, and moving passage! It can give you a chill to read it. We sense that Paul is challenging the limits of his vocabulary, his educated philosophy, and his considerable powers of literary expression to show us that no threat, regardless of how great and imposing, is greater than the love of God.

Paul gives us five pairs of contrasting forces that may challenge us. The big idea is that you can go from one end of any spectrum to the other—from life to death, from things present to things to come—without going beyond the scope of God's love.

Here Paul uses a rhetorical device known as a *merism*, which involves stating a pair of contrasting words to represent the full range of everything in between. We use a merism when we say, "He knows his subject from A to Z." When the psalmist declares that God has removed our sins from us "as far as the east is from the west" (Psalm 103:12), he is using a merism to explain that God has removed our sins in totality.

Let's explore these weighty pairs in greater detail in order to confirm the answer to Paul's rhetorical question: What can separate us from the love of God?

Not the Crisis of Death or the Calamities of Life

Neither death nor life...

We can imagine no greater natural wall of separation than death. To lose a loved one is to face the hard fact that never again in this life will we encounter this person. Death is so absolute, so uncompromising, that it forces us to mourn and grieve as we endure a terrible emotional adjustment.

I suspect that most Christians have uncertain feelings about their own death. We don't look forward to separation from our loved ones, and we have some natural apprehension about entering this unknown realm. Death separates us from everything familiar; can we really be sure it won't also separate us from God? Will He be there to receive us when we are thrust into that unknown void?

Here is where Paul's supreme confidence gives us great reassurance. He, too, loved many people in this world, and he didn't want to leave any of them. But, as we have already seen, the executioner's sword didn't worry him a bit. Christ, he knew, had conquered death forever, and a tomb stood empty in Jerusalem attesting to the fact. He cried triumphantly, "O Death, where is your sting? O Hades, where is your victory?"

(1 Corinthians 15:55). He wrote to Timothy, saying, "Jesus Christ...has abolished death and brought life and immortality to light through the gospel" (2 Timothy 1:10). Because Paul knew these facts to be true, he actually anticipated death (Philippians 1:21–24).

The writer of Hebrews explains how Jesus, through His death, destroyed the devil who held the power of death, and released those who were captive to the fear of death (Hebrews 2:14–15).

Death, then, is not a wall that separates us from God. Dr. James Montgomery Boice points out that it's much the opposite. Far from tearing us away from God, death ushers us into the full glory of His presence. "The separator becomes the uniter."[4]

If death cannot separate us, what about life? Life can afflict us with terrible crises that, for some, are harder to face than death. Deep grief, despair, depression, serious physical challenges, the loss of one's child—we sometimes call blows like these "a fate worse than death." Think of the worst calamity you can imagine. If that event occurred, could you still love God? Would you still believe that He is in control? That He loves you?

I've seen people overcome those worst imaginable crises too many times to count. These people proved to be overcomers— ordinary people who trusted in an extraordinary God. These modern-day heroes of faith have moved me and deepened my own faith as I have watched them walk with God through the valley of the shadow of death. The darker their days, the brighter God shone in their lives, because they came to a deeper understanding that there is no place so terrible that the love of God cannot reach into it.

A fourth-century Archbishop of Constantinople was such an eloquent preacher that, after his death, the Greek word *chrysostomos* ("golden mouthed") was added to his given name, John. History has since known him as John Chrysostom. He did not hesitate to point out abuses of power wherever he found them, and his outspoken oratory got him in trouble with both the church and the Roman Empire. On one such occasion, he was brought before the Roman emperor. Tradition tells us that the emperor fixed Chrysostom with a glare and said: "I will banish you if you do not give up your faith."

"You can't banish me," Chrysostom replied, "for the whole world is my Father's house."

"But I will put you to death."

"No, you can't. My life is hid with Christ in God."

"Then I will take away all your material possessions."

"No, you can't. My treasure is in heaven along with my heart."

"But I can drive you away from man. You will have no friends left."

"No, you can't make me friendless. I have a Friend in heaven from whom you can't separate me. I defy all your attempts to silence me. There is nothing you can do to hurt me."[5]

This brave and bold man had a firm grasp on the power behind true courage, the power behind clear resolution, the power behind unshakable faith. He believed without wavering that the love of God held him firmly and would never leave him, no matter how severe the adversity he faced.

How different would your life be if you found the same security in God's love? How much more freedom would you feel? How bold would you be? How much more peace and contentment would you have? The same power that motivated John Chrysostom is within your grasp—the overcoming power that comes from realizing how tenaciously God loves you.

Not the Intervention of Angels or the Intrusion of Demons

... nor angels nor principalities ...

On this earth we contend with more than just the evils that can be inflicted by nature, accidents, or other people. Paul tells us that we have even greater enemies: "For we do not wrestle against flesh and blood, but against principalities, against powers, against the rulers of the darkness of this age, against spiritual hosts of wickedness in the heavenly places" (Ephesians 6:12). Powerful invisible beings in the spirit world are waging a mighty war for our eternal destiny. How can we contend with these supernatural beings who possess supernatural powers? It seems like fending off a nuclear missile with a BB gun.

Scholars have argued that the term "angels" here refers only to evil angels. Given the context, that makes sense. Why would we need God's protection from good angels who serve Him faithfully? Yet, since this is a passage of contrasting opposites, it makes literary sense to think that these must be good angels in order to contrast with their demonic opposites.

While it is not clear just how God's faithful angels could hurt us, it is abundantly clear that Satan's demonic hosts can. In their hatred of God and His creation, they would do anything to get their hands on us, either to inflict serious trauma or to destroy us completely. No doubt much of the evil we endure is inflicted by these demonic beings. But they cannot destroy us, and they cannot hurt us in our inner spirits where we are firmly tethered to God's love.

From archangel Gabriel to archdemon Lucifer and the full range and ranks of forces in between, there is no power sufficient to break the hold of God's love upon His children. By His death and resurrection, Jesus Christ "disarmed principalities and powers" (Colossians 2:15; 1 Peter 3:21–22). They cannot destroy us because His love protects us fully. This is why the devil must flee when we resist him in the name and power of Christ (James 4:7). In spite of his formidable powers, Satan is helpless in the approaching shadow of God's love.

Not the Cares of Today or the Concerns of Tomorrow

. . . nor things present nor things to come . . .

In every era people have been under some kind of attack that threatened their physical lives, their financial lives, or their spiritual lives—if not all the above. In my early childhood, the threat was World War II. At the time, I was too young to be aware of all that was going on, but I knew that nobody could predict who would win the war. It threatened both our present and our future.

Prosperity came after the war, but with prosperity came the beginnings of rampant materialism, another kind of threat to the present. Would the temptation of wealth erode our dependence on God? Today, it seems as if our daily worries are only magnified as the Western world veers sharply away from God and a declining economy causes widespread losses of homes and jobs.

We also face uncertainty about what is to come. Will the economy collapse? Will the inner cities become war zones that breed rampant disorder? Will rogue nations develop an atomic bomb? Are terrorists about to wage another major attack on us? Will government rulings keep backing Christians into corners where we must either defy the law or go underground to avoid persecution?

At every moment in all the history of our fallen race, people have faced threats from both the present and the future, on both a personal and a cosmic level. And each time Christians have asked, "Is God still with me through all this?"

If ever a young man had the right to ask this question, it would seem that George Matheson did. Born in nineteenth-century Scotland, George became a brilliant student in theology at the University of Glasgow, where he earned a graduate degree. While at school, he fell in love and was soon engaged to be married. Meanwhile, his eyesight began to fade rapidly. When he became totally blind at age twenty, his fiancée broke off the engagement, explaining that she was not cut out to be the wife of a blind man.

Matheson was devastated. The pain of her abandonment stayed with him in his blindness. He never married, yet he went on to become a highly successful pastor at a large church in Edinburgh where he preached to fifteen hundred members every Sunday.

Many men enduring such blows might have struck out at God, thinking He had abandoned him. Many would have thought: *I've dedicated my life to You, God. Yet You allowed me to fall in love, and then You snatched away my fiancée and my eyesight. You must not really love me after all.*

But Matheson knew better. Though his beloved fiancée

had left him, he knew that God would not. Out of his pain emerged the classic hymn "O Love That Will Not Let Me Go." His first verse is a ringing affirmation of the love of God, reaching across the chasm of his sadness:

> *O Love that will not let me go,*
> *I rest my weary soul in Thee;*
> *I give Thee back the life I owe,*
> *That in Thine ocean depths its flow*
> *May richer, fuller be.*

Though George Matheson was physically blind, his spiritual vision was 20/20. Those who trust in the ways and purposes of God will be strengthened in the present and prepared to face whatever the future holds. Suffering is inevitable; it comes to everyone. But only those who live in the certainty that God's love will never let them go are able to accept with confidence and assurance both the troubles of the present and the troubles that may come tomorrow.

Not the Pinnacle of Heaven or the Pit of Hell

... nor height nor depth ...

Here Paul uses the terms "height" and "depth" to describe the unlimited scope of God's love. What does this mean? Imagine traveling multimillions of light-years straight up into deep space until you reach the outer edge of the Milky Way galaxy. It's impossible that the suns or nebulae or novas you would see out there would pose any threat to God's love for you. Neither would you find such a threat if you turned around and drilled downward to the hot core at the center of the earth.

Although it's unclear, whether or not this *merism* refers to physical space or to a specific reality, that does not mean it is any less true. In fact, it may mean it is so true—or true in so many ways—that Paul uses the nonspecific terms "height" and "depth" to allow the truth to be applied to many circumstances.

There are heights and depths in every life that could affect one's awareness of God's love. A person who inherits ten million dollars would likely reach a height of self-sufficiency that could easily drive out all thoughts of God. Or he could suddenly go bankrupt and be convinced that God does not love him. Another could achieve positions or accomplishments that would lift his pride to the heights. Or he could have failures that would plunge him into the depths of despair. A successful athlete's physical prowess could put him at the height of his profession, or a serious injury could lower him to the depths of perpetual disability. We find potential threats to our confidence in God's love in both our highs and our lows.

In all such cases, the love of God is intact at the heights, even though the person's attention may be far from God. And His love is intact at the depths, when the person believes God must have abandoned him.

As Psalm 139 tells us, there's nowhere we can go to get beyond God's love. Or, in the words of heavyweight champion Joe Louis, we can run, but we can't hide. God has every inch of the universe covered. He made it, He is the landlord of it, and His love is deeper and wider than all dimensions of His creation.

Not Anything Mighty or Anything Made

...nor powers...nor any other created thing...

The Greeks of Paul's time used the word translated as *powers* to refer either to mighty deeds such as miracles or to people in positions of authority. Authority is a good and necessary thing to maintain order, enforce law, and to manage activities and organizations efficiently. But anywhere you have authority, you have the potential for tyranny, whether it's in the workplace, in government, or, sadly, even in the church. Lord Acton's truism, "Power tends to corrupt," is continually operative in this fallen world.

I suspect that almost everyone has experienced these abuses of authority—managers who take credit for their employees' ideas or squelch promotions in order to keep productive employees in their own departments. Much worse, we're aware of heads of governments who rule capriciously, forcing citizens into labor camps, dictating the size of their families, or inflicting brutal punishment without trials. People enduring such afflictions may question whether God has abandoned them. Rest assured, He has not. There is no power in this world or in this universe that can prevent the flow of God's love.

Paul ends his list of things that cannot stop God from loving us with a handy catch-all phrase, "nor any other created thing." This closes off any possible loophole in the list. Here Paul tells us not to bother racking our minds to uncover some possible obstacle that could block God's love. Such a thing does not and cannot exist. In fact, Paul's list is so inclusive that it encompasses all of God's created reality. So the bottom line is this: There is *nothing* in all His creation that can separate us from the love of God that is in Christ Jesus our Lord.

It's easy to believe God's love is intact when all is going well, but when bad things happen even Christians sometimes begin to conclude, *If He really loved me, He wouldn't have allowed this thing to happen.* When we entertain this thought, we slip into the error of thinking that God's love means protection from serious trouble.

The answer to this age-old problem of suffering is really quite simple; but when we're in the throes of sorrow or deep trouble, emotion overpowers our knowledge and it's easy to doubt. Because of this human tendency, it's worthwhile to remind you again of what I've already noted in this chapter: We all must travel through valleys of pain and despair. But even when we walk through the deepest valley, God's love remains intact. He is there with us at every step. You won't be aware of Him unless you train your eyes of faith. Even then you may not understand why you must suffer. But if you remember His promise in Romans 8, you can rest assured that God is loving you even in the deepest valley. He will protect you from spiritual harm and see you through the darkness.

If you are in a place where you cannot realize this, it's time to get on your knees and do a faith-check. Maybe in your pain you have torn yourself from His arms. But let me tell you this: Even then, the rope holds. God's love remains intact in spite of your anger. Spiritual maturity is arriving at the point of unwavering certainty that God will never fail us in this life or the next. It is a certainty for all seasons—one that stands firm regardless of the circumstances.

Paul had that certainty. Martin Lloyd Jones, in his study

of Romans, says that when Paul makes these assertions about God's love, he is not persuading himself, guessing, or engaging in gut feelings or hunches. He is speaking from cool, hardened certainty. He says, "I am persuaded," which carries the meaning "I have worked through a process of persuasion to a settled conclusion." He is saying that beyond any shadow of a doubt, he knows that there is nothing that can separate us from the love of God.[6]

More Than Conquerors

Paul goes on to say one more thing about God's love that should help us to rest in His love and also to love Him even in the worst of traumas. He tells us that not only is God's love constant and unfailing, it is also triumphant. Not only will it endure all circumstances, it will overcome all circumstances: "Yet in all these things we are more than conquerors through Him who loved us" (Romans 8:37). We are not merely conquerors; we are more than conquerors. What can this mean?

The Greek word for "conquer" is *hypernikao*, a compound word made up of *hyper* ("more, above, beyond") and *nikao* ("to conquer or prevail"). The term is a unique one, occurring nowhere in the Bible but this particular verse. It has no single-word counterpart in English, so we must cobble together two or three words to get the sense of what it means. Scholars have tried such phrases as "overwhelmingly conquerors" and "beyond conquering," but the favorite by far is "more than conquerors." Many of our contemporary translations contain that familiar phrase.

But let's try another one: "hyper-conquerors." It has a modern ring to it and suggests the idea of a new league of superheroes—"The Hyper-Conquerors"! I think I like it. Let's try it out on what Paul is telling us:

In the midst of all these things that try to bring us down (tribulation, distress, persecution, you name it), we are hyper-conquerors.

When facing any problem that life can dish out—you are a hyper-conqueror.

In struggling with that problem you're worrying about this very day, which is _____ (fill in the blank), you are a hyper-conqueror.

The very term lifts our spirits and seems to infuse us with a ray of hope. But there's more to being a hyper-conqueror than just emotional hype. William Hendricksen says that if we were merely conquerors, we would have nothing to complain about. We would neutralize the forces that opposed us. We would prevail. But as *more than* conquerors, whatever comes against us actually ends up working in our favor. Every difficulty that challenges us finally serves to prove the love of God, from which nothing can separate us.[7] When those evils lie in chaotic rubble, God's love stands high and unfazed like an immovable monolith.

How does this work in real life? Here's a story that gives us the answer. During his reign of terror, Italian dictator Benito Mussolini turned his war machine on Ethiopia and expelled all the Christian missionaries there. Christians everywhere began praying immediately. The answer came in two waves: first, in the protection of the expelled missionaries; and second, in reopening the doors of Ethiopia to the Gospel after the military pride of Italy lay broken in the dust and Mussolini was executed by his own countrymen.

But during the missionaries' absence, the Word of God multiplied in Ethiopia, and the returning missionaries found a larger, stronger church than the one they left. One group, the United Presbyterian Mission, had only sixty believers when the missionaries were expelled. On their return, the sixty had grown to thirty churches with a membership of sixteen hundred! These believers were more than conquerors.[8]

With God's love holding us when evils attack, we don't merely prevail; we turn every traumatic event to our advantage. We feed on adversity and grow stronger. The greater the problem, the more we gain in wisdom, spiritual power, and maturity. That's what it means to be a hyper-conqueror.

At the roaring approach of a towering wave, the beginning surfer lets it pass in fear. The advanced surfer sees the same wave, musters up his strength, and paddles into it. He knows the dangerous power of the wave, but he turns that power to his advantage. By skillfully cutting across the face of the wave he allows it to propel him into a thrilling adventure.

Like the inexperienced surfer, the nonbeliever encounters a looming problem and eventually gives in to despair. Life's problems, in his worldview, are random and meaningless. They simply happen, and they have no significance beyond the damage they do. The believer encounters the same problem, but he summons up the courage to face it because he knows that within every seemingly random event, God injects a purpose. Though he may not immediately understand the purpose, he rides the wave and struggles to keep his balance because he knows that when the wave has passed, it will leave him stronger and more adept at riding greater waves in the future.

Nothing is meaningless in the world of the believer. Everything has a purpose; and in a world ruled by a loving God, the purpose is always to use every encounter to shape us into the perfect image of our Lord. Every difficulty will be turned to our favor and help us to become "perfect and complete, lacking nothing" (James 1:4). Or, in Paul's words, to become more than conquerors.

Making the Vital Choice

Paul expressed the unwavering constancy of God's love through pairs of dynamic opposites: death or life, things present or things to come, height or depth. I want to close by expressing, in the same way, your choice of how to live in the face of difficulty. I will offer you two stories, each expressing an opposite end of the spectrum. You must decide which one expresses true reality.

The Romanian Elie Wiesel, winner of the 1986 Nobel Peace Prize, was not a stranger to suffering. He endured four German prison camps during World War II—Birkenau, Auschwitz, and Buna—before finally being liberated from Buchenwald in 1945.

Wiesel and his father were placed in Birkenau, while the rest of his family was sent to the gas chambers. Wiesel watched his father deteriorate until, finally, he was beaten to death by the guards. Other prisoners often beat Wiesel himself simply to steal his meager food ration.

On being liberated, he left prison shaken to the very core and would not talk about his ordeal for ten years. At the end of that time, he wrote a grim little memoir called *Night*, in which he offered the following account of his first night in camp and what it did to his soul:

> Never shall I forget that night, the first night in the camp, which has turned my life into one long night, seven times cursed and seven times sealed. Never shall I forget that smoke. Never shall I forget the little faces of the children, whose bodies I saw turned into wreaths of smoke beneath a silent blue sky.
>
> Never shall I forget those flames which consumed my faith forever.
>
> Never shall I forget that nocturnal silence which deprived me, for all eternity, of the desire to live. Never shall I forget those moments which murdered my God and my soul and turned my dreams to dust. Never shall I forget these things, even if I am condemned to live as long as God Himself. Never.[9]

As Elie Wiesel was suffering his dark night of the soul, a Dutch woman named Corrie ten Boom had also descended into the same hell on earth. She and her family had sheltered Jews in their home, protecting them from being spirited away to the German camps. An informant turned them in, and soon the ten Booms themselves were on a truck.

Corrie never saw her beloved father again; he died only ten days after the arrest. She and her sister were sent to Ravensbruck, a women's camp north of Berlin. Every morning, roll call came at 4:30. Mornings were bitterly cold, and the women would often have to stand for hours on end without moving a muscle. As the chill permeated their bones, they stood at attention, hearing only the noises from the punishment barracks: fists upon flesh in rhythm, screams for mercy, the taunting of the torturers.

Corrie and her sister, Betsie, somehow kept a Bible near at hand. It was their rock, their fortress. Whenever they were sure it was safe, they would gather the women, conjure up a modest fire, and read the precious, encouraging words of Romans 8: "Who shall separate us from the love of Christ?" Then they would read that list describing everything these women were experiencing: tribulation, distress, persecution, famine, nakedness, peril, and sword. After that, a quotation through which the Old Testament seemed to peer right into the twentieth century, right into Ravensbruck:

> *For Your sake we are killed all day long;*
> *We are accounted as sheep for the slaughter.*

Then they read those glorious words about being "more than conquerors through Him who loved us." Even to be conquerors, not to mention *more* than conquers, seemed incredible in the light of their suffering. Yet power came through those words as surely as heat from the fire reached their cold bones.

As Corrie listened to Betsie read the words, firelight danced upon the haggard features of those huddled around the fire. *More than conquerors,* she thought, stated not as desperate hope but as ironclad fact. And it was really true—the words gave strength that pulled them through the horrors of one day after another.

"Life in Ravensbruck," she later wrote, "took place on two separate levels, mutually impossible. One, the observable, external life, grew every day more horrible. The other, the life we lived with God, grew daily better, truth upon truth, glory upon glory."[10]

Earlier in this chapter we met two blind men—men who knew how to move past the limits of human sight. George Matheson knew that God's love would never let him go. Erik Weihenmayer understood the simple wisdom of trusting the rope, which enabled him to ascend peaks that sighted people could only dream about.

Life on earth will inevitably have its pits and snares, its crevasses and howling winds. It will have lonely times, when we must make the climb in solitude. It will have confusing days, when we simply can't understand the logic of what is happening.

In all of these times, we must choose. We can believe that God has died, as Wiesel did, and that the presence of evil has extinguished faith forever. Or we can see, as Corrie ten Boom once said, that no pit is so deep that God's love isn't deeper still. We can try climbing out of the dark pit by our own efforts and exhaust our meager reserves of strength. Or we can depend upon the rope, letting the rope do its work; letting it bear us up toward the light.

Which will you choose?

I'm here to tell you that there is marvelous power, astounding power, supernatural power that comes when we cease our striving and simply begin to trust the rope—the infinite love of God. You need never let go of your hope, because God will never let go of His love for you.

NINE

God Loves You and Wants You with Him Forever

❧

And if I go and prepare a place for you,
I will come again and receive you to Myself;
that where I am, there you may be also.
—JOHN 14:3

One of the most enchanting concepts in the human experience is the idea of home. The word *home* evokes memories of rest, security, and the presence of those we love most.

As I look back over my life, I have a mental picture of every house or apartment that I have lived in. Beginning with the house my parents lived in when I was born in Toledo, Ohio, to my present residence in El Cajon, California, I can picture them all. Altogether I have lived in fifteen different homes and can recall something special about each one. But two of the fifteen I remember with greater clarity than the others: the home in Cedarville, Ohio, where I grew up with my parents, my brother, and two sisters; and the home in El Cajon, where Donna and I brought up our four children.

These two homes were more than mere dwelling places. They were centers of activity and personal interaction, not only between family members but also with many friends who have spent hours with us. The people I have always loved and wanted to be with lived in those houses, and for that reason those places are sacred to me.

When my siblings and I became adults and began our own journeys in life, we moved out of our parents' house, but we never stopped wanting to go back. At Christmas and during vacation days in the summer, we always found our way back home.

On several occasions when I was a student at Dallas Seminary, my wife and I would drive home to Ohio just for the weekend—1,051 miles if I remember correctly. We would have only a few hours to be home before we would have to turn around and drive back to Dallas so as not to miss classes or work on Monday. Truly, home was like a magnet to us. When my parents decided to downsize and move into a smaller place, I was surprised at how difficult that move was for me as an adult son.

Today we're a nation of nomads. On the average, we make 11.7 moves in a lifetime.[1] Something within us, however, always looks back. Even now, when I return to the village of Cedarville, I always try to drive by that house where I grew up and remember how special that place really was. I loved that house and love it still. Love always pulls us home.

I sense that our home in El Cajon is just as important to our four children and eleven grandchildren. We have shared many celebrations in that place and, after what I experienced with the closing of my parents' home, I am not thinking about downsizing any time soon. I want my children and grandchildren to live with the security of knowing where their earthly home is—a place where a light is always on and love is ready to be shared.

I know I have one more move left. No matter how much I love these earthly dwellings, no matter how cozy they have been—this last move will redefine my idea of home. It will be my forever home. Far from "downsizing," this time I'll be "upsizing"—moving to a place where my heavenly Father can gather all of His sons and daughters together for a heavenly reunion that will never end.

That place we usually refer to as "heaven" is given a number of different labels in Scripture. My favorite is "the Father's House," the name Jesus used to describe heaven: "In my Father's house are many rooms; if it were not so, I would have told you. I am going there to prepare a place for you" (John 14:2 NIV). In this comforting image we come face-to-face with the closeness, intimacy, and permanency of heaven.

Commenting on this verse, Randy Alcorn, who has written the best and most definitive book on heaven, describes our future home like this:

> *Place* is singular, but *rooms* is plural. This suggests Jesus has in mind for each of us an individual dwelling that's a smaller part of the larger place. This place will be home to us in the most unique sense.
>
> The term *room* is cozy and intimate. The terms *house* or *estate* suggest spaciousness. That's Heaven: a place

both spacious and intimate. Some of us enjoy coziness, being in a private space. Others enjoy a large, wide-open space. Most of us enjoy both—and the New Earth will offer both.

Heaven isn't likely to have lots of identical residences. God loves diversity, and he tailor-makes his children *and* his provisions for them. When we see the particular place he's prepared for us—not just for mankind in general but for us in particular—we'll rejoice to see our ideal home.[2]

C. S. Lewis agrees: "Your place in heaven will seem to be made for you and you alone, because you were made for it—made for it stitch by stitch as a glove is made for a hand."[3]

In Charlotte Brontë's novel *Jane Eyre*, the lonely heroine has never lived in a place she could call home. She has never had a person in her life who loved her enough to know who she truly was until she established a relationship with her employer, Edward Rochester, a relationship that developed into love. When she had to leave for a few weeks to see a dying relative, he didn't want her to leave, fearing she would not return. She replied, "Wherever you are is my home."

When you love someone, you want to be with that person. In fact, you never want to be separated. In the forty-nine years that we have been married, Donna and I have been apart from each other very few times, and now that our children are grown and have their own families, we travel everywhere together and are hardly ever apart. Here's the unvarnished truth: I love her and I want to be with her. Wherever she is, is my home.

And that's the message Jesus was communicating to His

disciples in John 14. As you read the lengthy discourse in the Upper Room, you can't help but notice the intimacy with which Jesus addresses His closest friends, even as His appointment on Calvary draws near. Jesus is telling us He loves us, and that the time will come when we will never be apart. Wherever He is, is our home.

In heaven we are going to be with Jesus forever and we will never be separated. When I began to think about this concept, I started to notice how often the New Testament talked about the importance of our being with *Him*.

For example, after Jesus explained to His disciples about the rooms in heaven, he said: "If I go and prepare a place for you, I will come again and receive you to Myself; *that where I am, there you may be also*" (John 14:3; italics added).

Another example occurred on the cross, where Jesus comforted a thief beside Him: "Assuredly, I say to you, *today you will be with Me* in Paradise" (Luke 23:43; italics added).

Paul explained death in these same terms: "We are confident, yes, well pleased rather to be *absent from the body and to be present with the Lord*" (2 Corinthians 5:8; italics added). In writing to the Philippians about his own death, Paul wrote: "I am hard-pressed between the two, having a desire *to depart and to be with Christ*, which is far better" (Philippians 1:23; italics added).

After going to great lengths to explain the details of the Rapture, this same apostle summarizes it all with these words: "We who are alive and remain shall be caught up together with them in the clouds to meet the Lord in the air. *And thus we shall always be with the Lord*" (1 Thessalonians 4:17; italics added).

We can say a number of things about heaven, but the one

that matters most is that Jesus is there, and that we will be with Him and with the Father. The great Puritan preacher Richard Baxter said it this way:

My Knowledge of that Life is small;
The Eye of Faith is dim:
But it's enough that Christ knows all;
And I shall be with him.[4]

Speaking of heaven, maybe you have noticed that Christians do not talk much about heaven anymore. We used to preach about it and sing about it in our churches. In fact, when I speak each year at the National Quartet Convention, I often remind the attendees that the writers of Southern Gospel music are just about the only ones who still write songs about heaven.

Perhaps today we focus more on this present life because we're self-indulgent and lack vision. Or perhaps we're self-indulgent and lack vision because we don't focus enough on heaven. There's a reason the Scriptures instruct, "Set your mind on things above, not on things on the earth" (Colossians 3:2). Our citizenship is in heaven, and our hearts should yearn for our true homeland.

Some people don't talk about heaven because they don't like to think about death. Philosopher and theologian Dallas Willard tells the story of a woman who refused to talk about life beyond death because she didn't want her children to be disappointed if it turned out no afterlife existed. As Willard points out, if no afterlife exists, no one will have any consciousness with which to feel disappointment! On the other hand, if there is an afterlife, whoever enters that life unprepared may experience far worse than mere disappointment.[5]

In an article in the *Lakeland Ledger*, Cary McMullen mulls over the abandonment of heaven by the contemporary pulpit: "Among mainline Protestants," McMullen writes, "it was thought that speculation about the nature of a personal afterlife was anti-intellectual and belonged to the realm of red-faced, sawdust-floor evangelists. And too much talk of the next world might detract from efforts to relieve suffering in the present."[6] And it's not only mainline Protestants; we hear little of heaven from Catholic or evangelical preachers. Interestingly enough, the subject is more popular than ever with novelists and filmmakers.

I've been approached by believers who questioned the point of focusing on heaven in this life. "We'll have all of eternity to think about that," they say. "Shouldn't our focus be on making this life better?" And we've heard people say, "If you're too heavenly minded, you're of no earthly good." They figure that you can be so consumed with heaven's golden streets that you neglect to fix the potholes on Main Street.[7]

A. W. Tozer would beg to differ. He wrote that Christians of the mid-twentieth century had become so comfortable, so well-situated, that heaven held little appeal for them. Why live in hope for eternity, when you've got everything just the way you want it now?[8]

In his book *The Wonder of It All*, seminary president and author Bryan Chapell tells the story of a young African seminary student who preached a sermon in a preaching class. His subject was the joy Christians will experience when Christ returns and ushers them into heaven. He, too, wondered if prosperity has caused us to neglect the reality of heaven:

> I have been in the United States for several months now. I have seen the great wealth that is here—the fine homes and cars and clothes. I have listened to many sermons in churches here, too. But I have yet to hear one sermon about heaven. Because everyone has so much in this country, no one preaches about heaven. People here do not seem to need it. In my country most people have very little, so we preach on heaven all the time. We know how much we need it.[9]

The more consumed we are with the love of this world, the less we will be consumed with the love of God represented by heaven. In his classic *Mere Christianity*, C. S. Lewis explained: "If you read history you will find that the Christians who did the most for the present world were just those who thought most of the next... It is since Christians have largely ceased to think of the other world that they have become so ineffective in this. Aim at Heaven and you will get earth 'thrown in': aim at earth and you will get neither."[10]

God's love stirs my heart to care deeply about heaven—and yes, the thought of heaven energizes me to live in the current moment with deeper joy, as someone for whom the best is yet to come. The bottom line is this: God loves you, and He wants to share all eternity with you. Christ has gone to prepare a special and lovely place where you can come and live with Him forever.

A Place of Ultimate Residence

Let not your heart be troubled; you believe in God, believe also in Me. In My Father's house are many mansions; if it were not so, I would have told you. I go to prepare a place for you. And if I go and prepare a place for you, I will come again and receive you to Myself; that where I am, there you may be also.

—JOHN 14:1–3

I read about a law firm that sent flowers to an associate in another city to celebrate the opening of its new offices. Through some mix-up, the card that accompanied the floral piece read "Deepest Sympathy." When the florist was informed of his mistake, realizing two cards had been switched, he cried out, "Oh no! That means the card that went to the funeral home reads 'Congratulations on your new location'!"

We can understand the florist's embarrassment, but we would also like to think that the second card was not inappropriate. Congratulations are due to anyone who is en route to the place of one's deepest joy. And yet we expend a great amount of prayer in holding people back from it. Of course we love them, and we don't want to be parted in the interim. But how can we ever treat heaven as some kind of consolation prize for having to leave this present life?

I think the main reason we feel sorry for those who die—especially those who "die before their time"—is that we don't have a strong concept of the solid reality of heaven. Charles F. Ball pointed out that some think of heaven as they do of Santa's North Pole, or Peter Pan's Never-Never Land. They speak with a nod and a wink, as if to say, "You and I both know that's all fairy tale stuff. Thinking adults don't believe it for a minute."[11]

Then there are those who foresee heaven as something vague, puffy, dehumanized, and barely real. Others believe in a heaven that has no objective reality but is merely a state of consciousness.

But heaven is none of these things. It is not a children's story, a trance state, or an emotion. It is a destination so real that this present reality will seem like a children's story. It is a place so personal that the Father, the Son, and the Holy Spirit dwell there. Dr. Steven J. Lawson says heaven is real enough that Christ came into the world from it and departed again to it when His body left this earth. And someday, we will do the same.[12]

Both Old and New Testament Scriptures treat heaven as both real and important. In fact, the Bible refers to heaven more than five hundred times. The Hebrew word translated "heaven"—*shamayim*—literally means "the heights." The Greek word for "heaven" is *ouranos*, which inspired the name of the planet Uranus. The word refers to that which is raised up or lofty.

As the following Scriptures reveal, heaven is the home of our God:

For Christ has not entered the holy places made with hands, which are copies of the true, but into heaven itself, now to appear in the presence of God for us.

— HEBREWS 9:24

Let your light so shine before men, that they may see your good works and glorify your Father in heaven.

— MATTHEW 5:16

The Lord is in His holy temple, the Lord's throne is in heaven.

—PSALM 11:4

As Canadian pastor Bruce Milne tells us, the book of Revelation speaks of heaven as a place where you will find "God's throne, God's river, God's tree, God's service, God's face, God's seal, God's reign: such are the features of the life of the people of God in the coming Holy City...It is life totally centered on God. That is the deepest and most glorious prospect imaginable, for there is no reality comparable to the triune God, the ever-blessed Father."[13]

My primary goal for this chapter is that you will grasp once and for all that heaven is real. It is an actual location, and it is the future for everyone who knows and loves the Lord Jesus Christ. It is a place of reunion with those we've lost, and it is a place where we will no longer see through the dim glass, but we will regard our Savior face-to-face.

A Place of Ultimate Rejoicing

You will show me the path of life;
In Your presence is fullness of joy;
At Your right hand are pleasures forevermore.

—PSALM 16:11

Huckleberry Finn didn't think much of heaven. In the opening chapter of Mark Twain's classic, *The Adventures of Huckleberry Finn*, Huck is living with the spinster Miss Watson, a starchy, crabby old woman who is bent on his reform. She is going to knock the wildness out of the boy and stuff him full of manners, using the lethal weapon of enforced religion. She bludgeons him with Bible verses. She threatens him with hell. And she coaxes him with heaven. In his streetwise, cocky, cock-eyed way, Huck tells us what he thinks of that: "She went on and told me all about the good place. She said all a body would have to do there was go around all day long with a harp and sing, forever and ever. So I didn't think much of it...I asked her if she reckoned Tom Sawyer would go there, and she said, not by a considerable sight. I was glad about that, because I wanted him and me to be together."[14]

Twain is writing satire, of course, but he touches a real nerve. We've all met people who feel exactly that way. Talk to a nonbeliever, who has given little thought to the matter, and you're apt to get a predictable response. He screws up his face into a scowl and says, "Boooooring!"

In one of his *Far Side* cartoons, Gary Larson captured this common misconception about heaven. In the cartoon, Larson pictures a man with angel wings and a halo sitting on a cloud, doing nothing, with no one nearby. He has the expression of someone utterly bored. The caption under the cartoon reads "Wish I'd brought a magazine."

Pastor and author Mark Buchanan admits to the fear that heaven might just be the extension of a particularly dull church service. He admits to getting a little antsy after an hour of church. He yawns, his backside aches, and his stomach growls—and *he's* the pastor!

Then he thinks about heaven as often presented in all kinds of art: plump, cute angels whizzing around on silken wings or kicking back on fluffy clouds; people playing their harps and singing really old music. "Everything is soft, wispy, dainty, pastel, languid," he writes. "And this is supposed to inspire us?"[15]

These dull images of heaven do many the disservice of allowing even hell to appear more attractive than heaven. We've all heard it; maybe you've even said it yourself: "I don't want to go to heaven and be bored every day. I'd rather be in hell with all my friends and party forever and ever!" I shudder when I hear that. It's another of the devil's lies. Hell will have no friendships, no fun and games, no relationships at all. The rich man in Hades (Luke 16) is completely alone—isolated from all humanity forever. Think what it would be like to be locked up in solitary confinement forever, never again to have any friendships or relationships with anyone, anywhere.

This is what the Bible says about those who miss heaven: "They will be punished with everlasting destruction and shut out from the presence of the Lord and from the majesty of His power" (2 Thessalonians 1:9 NIV). As George MacDonald said, "The one principle of hell is—'I am my own.'"[16] Hell is the one place where God allows one to live that prideful principle throughout all eternity, living with nothing but regrets and memories of missed opportunities.

Could heaven possibly be boring? To make such an assertion, Randy Alcorn suggests, is to imply that God Himself is boring. That's utter nonsense, because God Himself placed within us our very ideas of excitement and pleasure. He made our minds; He shaped our interests, our drives, and our emotions. Alcorn writes:

God is the master artist who created the universe, the inventor of music, the author and main character of the unfolding drama of redemption. Head of state? He's king of the universe. Yet if someone says, "I want to go to Heaven to be with God forever," others wonder, *Wouldn't that be boring?*

What are we thinking?

The very qualities we admire in others—every one of them—are true of God. He's the source of everything we find fascinating. Who made Bach, Beethoven and Mozart? Who gave them their gifts? Who created music itself and the ability to perform it? All that is admirable and fascinating in human beings comes from their creator.[17]

You can be sure that neither God nor heaven will be boring—and neither will you.

In his letter to the Christians in Philippi, Paul describes what is going to happen to us before we enter Paradise. Christ "will transform our lowly body that it may be conformed to His glorious body, according to the working by which He is able even to subdue all things to Himself" (Philippians 3:21).

This transformation will not change who you are; it will make you even more yourself than you are now by removing all the flaws, weaknesses, and incapacities you inherited from the Fall. Even if you are presently the dullest and most boring individual in the neighborhood, in heaven, you will be dynamic!

While our business in heaven is not yet fully revealed, we do have a few hints that we will have meaningful tasks to perform. For example, we are told that we will judge angels (1 Corinthians 6:3), sit on thrones (Revelation 3:21), and reign with

Christ (Revelation 20:4). As you can see, our duties will not be insignificant.

To that end, pastor and writer Douglas Connelly has a suggestion: Why not let the reality of heaven inspire us to greater joy in our gatherings now? If a dull church service points some people to a dull heaven, then the least we can do is take the dullness out of the equation. We need more spontaneity. We need more outright joy and laughter. "You might start a real revolution at your church or in your small group or at the next fellowship dinner if you just smile—or laugh out loud!"[18]

We must banish from our minds those insipid images of heaven that the devil plants in our minds. Instead, we must learn to see heaven through biblical eyes—the heaven too beautiful for human eyes and more thrilling than the most exciting moment any life has ever experienced. As the psalmist reminds us, in God's presence is "fullness of joy," and at His right hand are "pleasures forevermore" (Psalm 16:11).

A Place of Ultimate Recognition

For now we see in a mirror, dimly, but then face to face. Now I know in part, but then I shall know just as I also am known.

—1 CORINTHIANS 13:12

One of the questions most often asked concerning our future home is this: "Will we know one another in heaven?" The answer is a resounding "Yes!"

After His resurrection, Jesus' disciples knew who He was.

They knew that this Jesus who was with them after His death and resurrection was the same Jesus they had known so intimately before. They knew this so deeply in their hearts that they all willingly died as martyrs defending the reality of it.

When Moses and Elijah appeared out of heaven to stand with Christ at His transfiguration, the disciples who were with Christ recognized both the Old Testament saints even though they had never seen them before (Matthew 17)!

When Jesus describes heaven in Matthew 8, He speaks of it as being a real place with real, identifiable people present: "And I say to you that many will come from east and west, and sit down with Abraham, Isaac, and Jacob in the kingdom of heaven" (Matthew 8:11).

Missionary Amy Carmichael points to the simple logic that this issue demands:

> Shall we know one another in Heaven? Shall we love and remember? I don't think anyone need wonder about this or doubt for a single moment…For if we think for a minute, we know. Would you be yourself if you did not remember?…We are told that we shall be like our Lord Jesus…and does He not know and love and remember? He would not be Himself if He did not, and we should not be ourselves if we did not.[19]

Why would God be so intentional about molding who we are in this life, only to scrap the whole thing in the next life? I like the way Tony Evans turns this question around. A woman in his church came to him with the question we're exploring. "Pastor," she asked, "will we know each other in Heaven?"

He smiled and replied, "I would say that we won't really know each other *until* we get to Heaven."[20]

It makes sense, doesn't it? In this world, we only think we know one another. What we see and hear forms our mental portraits of other human beings. But those tangible attributes no more reveal the true complexity of a human being than the tip of an iceberg reveals its total mass. As I noted in the previous section, in heaven we will be fully what God intended us to be. All masks will be removed. We'll see each other face-to-face, with no secrets between us. Our communication will be perfect, rather than marred by the subterfuges and limitations of this fallen world.

Truly, heaven will be ultimate recognition!

A Place of Ultimate Relationships

But you have come to Mount Zion and to the city of the living God, the heavenly Jerusalem, to an innumerable company of angels, to the general assembly and church of the firstborn who are registered in heaven, to God the Judge of all, to the spirits of just men made perfect.

—HEBREWS 12:22–23

This description of the heavenly city was written to believers who were still alive on the earth, yet it is delivered in a way that expresses a future truth already completed. We have not yet arrived in heaven, our future home, but as far as God is concerned, we have already come to the heavenly Jerusalem. We live in an earthly colony of heaven, but we are already given full citizenship in the heavenly kingdom. In this heavenly community, we will live with our fellow Christians—and even angels—for all eternity.

In heaven, our relationships won't be limited to eras of time or boundaries of territory. We'll be able to speak to people from every era of history. We can have friendships with the ancients and, should history continue that long, with people far in the future.

I have many questions for David, Joseph, and Daniel from the Old Testament. I look forward to finding out if I got it right when I preached about them. I would love to be introduced to Jabez and ask him if he ever dreamed Bruce Wilkinson would make him so famous. And of course, I would like to sit with Paul of Tarsus, the wonderful apostle, for hours on end. "Tell me now, Paul, what was that thorn in the flesh? What happened after the conclusion of Acts? Can you fill in those 'blank' years just after your conversion and before your ministry began?" I'll be hanging on his every word.

And then I would have to seek out certain individuals: C. S. Lewis, Charles Haddon Spurgeon, Andrew Murray, A. W. Tozer, to name a few. I owe them a debt of gratitude for the things they wrote and for their quotations that graced my sermons.

Randy Alcorn has had the same thoughts. He imagines friends and loved ones who followed Jesus for a lifetime and are now in His presence. He thinks about reunions with friends, walking along in resurrection bodies more powerful and perfect than the greatest Olympic decathlete. We laugh, we shout for sheer joy, we share ourselves—and everywhere we go we meet new and wonderful and absolutely perfect new friends;

new places to explore; new wonders to behold. Here a feast, there a great discussion among heroes of the Bible. No matter where we go, we are heartily welcomed.[21]

And yet, even as we make new and incredible friendships, none will compare to the greatest privilege of heaven, which is to be in the presence of God, and of His Son, Jesus Christ. Neither you, nor I, nor any living person can begin to imagine how wonderful that will be.

A Place of Ultimate Responsibility

Well done, good and faithful servant; you have been faithful over a few things, I will make you ruler over many things. Enter into the joy of your lord.

—MATTHEW 25:23

For years I have been collecting the sayings that people put on their tombstones. Here is one that expresses what some people think about heaven:

Here lies a poor woman who always was tired,
For she lived in a place where help wasn't hired.
Her last words on earth were, "Dear Friends, I am going
Where washing ain't done, nor sweeping, nor sewing;
And everything there is exact to my wishes,
For where they don't eat, there's no washing of dishes.
Don't weep for me now, don't weep for me ever;
For I'm going to do nothing forever and ever."[22]

It sounds a little more like a nursing home than the biblical conception of heaven. I suppose it's natural for an overworked person to think of heaven as a place of rest. But it reveals another misconception about heaven. When we enter into heaven, we are not put on some kind of heavenly Social Security list. On the contrary, the Bible says a great deal about service in heaven—our tasks and responsibilities—particularly in Revelation:

Therefore they are before the throne of God, and serve Him day and night in His temple. And He who sits on the throne will dwell among them."

—REVELATION 7:15

Then a voice came from the throne, saying, 'Praise our God, all you His servants and those who fear Him, both small and great!'"

—REVELATION 19:5

And there shall be no more curse, but the throne of God and of the Lamb shall be in it, and His servants shall serve Him."

—REVELATION 22:3

As you can see, people seem to keep busy in heaven. Service and reward are important themes in the next life. But these hints of heavenly activity are so broad and general that we cannot help but wonder just what work and service might be like in a place of perfection. "It is work...free from care and toil and fatigue," writes David Gregg. "It is work according to one's tastes and delight and ability. If tastes vary there, if abilities vary there, then occupations will vary there."[23]

Author Larry Dick adds that we need to imagine "a working environment free from the restrictions of time, money, selfishness, greed, sickness, tiredness, laziness, pain, frustration and even mistakes. How incredibly satisfying and rewarding work will be in heaven, doing what you love doing with people who love you and all for the glory of God."[24]

Who knows what awe-inspiring tasks await us there? Wilbur Smith speculates that we'll be permitted to finish the worthy, incomplete tasks we dreamed of wrapping up while on earth.[25] The late pastor, author, and teacher Ray Stedman was willing to let his imagination soar even higher: "There will be new planets to develop, new principles to discover, new joys to experience. Every moment of eternity will be an adventure of discovery."[26]

And theologian Michael E. Wittmer adds:

There will always be some new joy to discover, some place to visit or revisit, some new dish to create, a new flower to breed, a new song to sing, a new poem to write... something new in our relationship with God. And this stretching and growing will go on forever.

Imagine what we will accomplish after working a few million years without the limitations of sin! If you enjoy culture, technology, and the triumph of the human spirit, you are really going to feel at home on the new earth.[27]

Thus both the Bible and Christian theologians help us to correct the misunderstanding of heaven as a boring place of rest where we will have nothing to do. Indeed, the opposite is true. When God created man and woman, He knew they needed meaningful work to validate their significance. Thus He gave them full dominion over the earth and the creatures in it. It will still be true in heaven. God has great plans for us to participate with Him in executing enormous tasks with eternal significance. Not only does He want us with Him forever; He wants us to find immense joy and satisfaction in our new home.

A Place of Ultimate Reality

For in this we groan, earnestly desiring to be clothed with our habitation which is from heaven... We are confident, yes, well pleased rather to be absent from the body and to be present with the Lord.

—2 CORINTHIANS 5:2, 8

We who are believers *groan* knowing that there is still something more, something that we have yet to experience that is not being experienced in our earthly life. There is something more that we have not known—something we long for. And heaven is the answer to the eternal quest of our souls. Heaven is what we have been waiting and longing for. It is the fulfillment of our dreams.

At the beginning of time, God's creation was perfect. And so it would have remained had not Adam and Eve chosen to reject God's command, causing Him to withdraw His intimate companionship with them. This withdrawal allowed evil and sin to invade their lives and the earth itself, afflicting the entire planet with death, disease, hurricanes, tsunamis, earthquakes, and droughts. We are born into this fallen world and suffer all the consequences of the Fall.

Yet, as Ecclesiastes affirms, God has placed eternity in our hearts (3:11). We know that what we see and what we experience are not what was *intended*. Even unbelievers unwittingly know this when they are outraged by evil. They could not complain of evil unless they sensed that it is a violation of what they felt ought to be.

When we go too long without eating, our stomachs groan; when we live in an imperfect world, our spirits do the same. And the world itself, God's creation, groans for the perfection that God will someday bring about (Romans 8:22).

Just as food is the prescription for hunger, air for our lungs, and love for our loneliness, heaven is the prescription for the craving of our spirits. But we often do not recognize our desire for pleasure as a longing for the joy of heaven, so we try to satisfy it with all kinds of earthbound pleasures. Yet no earthly pleasure can truly satisfy the longing. As the late British theologian Peter Toon explains, "The things for which men strive hardly ever turn out to be as satisfying as they expected, and in the rare cases in which they do, sooner or later they are snatched away."[28]

Solomon's book of Ecclesiastes is a journal of his attempt to find heaven on earth. It chronicles his pursuit of fulfillment through work and wealth and pleasure—only to find that only God could fill the void inside.

Mark Buchanan tells us that we need that empty spot at the center of our souls. God put it there as a homing device. If our bodies didn't remind us to eat, we would starve to death. If our bodies forgot to breathe, we would suffocate. The spirit has its own craving, which works to keep our souls from withering inside us. God made us to be pursuers of something the earth can't supply so that in the end we'll look beyond earth. He set us up for disappointment here, in order that we may finally look for joy in the one place it can be found. "Yearning itself is healthy—a kind of compass inside us, pointing to True North," writes Buchanan. "[God] put in me, in you, a homing device for Heaven. We just won't *settle* for anything less."[29]

There's a reason that we feel nostalgia for the things of childhood, the particular aromas of our mothers' cooking, the delight of the family Christmas tree, or the feeling of playing in the deep woods back behind the house. It's because we are homesick for heaven as surely as we get homesick for our childhood homes. That emotional tug toward an earthly home is just an expression of a deeper tug toward the heavenly one; it's just that we have no physical memory of what it is that we really want. Our spirits understand that it has to do with being a child, with being joyful, with being with a loving parent, with innocence and hope. It all points to our experiences in childhood, so we think we long to return to it. In truth, however, we want a more wonderful kind of childhood; a deeper joy; a perfect, profoundly more loving Parent, and a perfect innocence and fulfilled hope that this fallen earth can never provide.

I know that Toledo, Ohio, where I was a little boy, is not heaven. It's just that in some ways, it's the closest to heaven I've been. I also realize that our family home in El Cajon, brimming with grandchildren, is not quite heaven. But when we're all together enjoying a Thanksgiving feast, I think God is showing me how He feels about gathering all of His beloved children around Him. Someday I'll know exactly what it's like to be God's child living in His home, and having my family all around me.

In our deepest cravings, we are hearing the still, small voice of God slipping in through the din and clamor of our lives and saying, "Come and see! Come and enjoy what I've prepared for you!"

So, will heaven be boring? Solemn? Will it be the place that Huckleberry Finn wanted to avoid at all costs? Absolutely not! It will be a deeper, fuller, and more exhilarating gladness than you or I can even begin to fathom. David sensed the real truth when he wrote, "One thing I ask of the Lord, this is what I seek: that I may dwell in the house of the Lord all the days of my life, to gaze upon the beauty of the Lord and to seek him in his temple" (Psalm 27:4 niv).

Heaven will be the answer to the deepest longings in your heart. It will be what you and I have really wanted all our lives, the object of that intense, unidentified desire that we could never fully articulate. Only in heaven will we finally feel the completeness that we were created to enjoy! Christian psychologist Mark McMinn explains,

> However messed up our abnormal world may be, the story is not over yet. The Christian story is ultimately a comedy and not a tragedy; it ends as it began. Someday, there will be a new heaven and a new earth. Birds will really sing. Lions and lambs will tumble and play in grass that is truly green. Our bodies won't be riddled with wrinkles, muscle spasms and cancer. There will be pure joy and beauty and goodness. And God, who longs to be with us, will walk with us in the Garden.

That may sound frightening or intimidating now—but it won't then. No ecstasy in this broken world will ever compare with our joy then, as we walk with God. We will be home. And it won't just be a story about a prodigal son or daughter who could never be good enough to earn God's favor. It will be a story about a loving God who delights in offering lavish, exuberant love. The depth of God's love will be seen everywhere.[30]

Dwight L. Moody, the greatest evangelist of the nineteenth century, became fatally ill in December of 1899. In the midst of a preaching tour, he canceled his itinerary and returned to his home, where his loved ones were called to his side. It was evident he was close to the end. On the evening of December 22, he was suddenly awake and alert. "Earth recedes!" he exclaimed. "Heaven opens before me."

William, his oldest son, smiled and said, "Father, you've been having a dream."

"This is no dream, Will," Moody replied. "It is beautiful! It is like a trance! If this is death, it is sweet! God is calling me, and I must go!"

Soon the rest of the family surrounded the bed. The great man was still speaking. "This is my triumph!" he said. "This is my coronation day! I have been looking forward to it for years." And then, a new light came into his eyes. "Dwight! Irene!" he said. "I see the children's faces!" These were the names of grandchildren who had died.

The family kept its vigil as Moody drifted in and out of consciousness. Sometime later, he raised up on one elbow, noted the people in the room, and seemed puzzled. He asked, "What does all this mean? What are you all doing here?"

"You haven't been well, dear," said his wife. "We wanted to be with you and pray for you."

Moody said, "This is very strange. I've been beyond the gates of death to the very portals of Heaven." He soon surprised everyone by rising and walking across the room to a chair. He spoke of recovery. But soon, he was back in bed, and he breathed his last.[31]

Why do so few believers long for heaven? We might as well be children unmoved by the anticipation of Christmas morning; young couples apathetic about their wedding day; the sick indifferent to the morning they will wake up whole and restored. On the day we finally see Him face-to-face, we will know beyond all doubt just how much God loves us—how much He always has, and how much He always will.

As we kneel in His presence, tears of joy staining our faces, we'll finally understand how much He has longed to be with us. We'll then hear those two words that every soul longs to hear above any words imaginable:

Welcome home.

TEN

God's Love Changes Everything

❧

Rick Garmon opened his gun cabinet and took a long look at the weapons within it. He lifted his best rifle and began polishing it. He had been doing all he could to hide the rage inside him, but people knew.

What they could not know was that the fantasy of vengeance that had crept into his mind months ago had put down roots and grown into a genuine intention. He was going to take this gun, place it on the floor of his car, and drive slowly through the college campus. Sooner or later he would see him—the student who had raped his daughter Katie. Then he would calmly pick up the gun, aim it, and deliver justice.

His sweet Katie had been only eighteen, a college freshman. She couldn't tell anyone for a long time. Instead, she switched schools, developed eating disorders, and fought severe depression. It was Katie's mother—Rick's wife—who finally got the truth out of her. She told her mother about the date rape and gave her the name of the boy. But it didn't help. Katie became more and more withdrawn. It took a year of prayer and therapy before she finally began to turn the corner and get on with her life.

But her protective father did not turn that corner. He seethed with ever-deepening fury over the punk who had devastated his daughter. First Rick merely daydreamed about revenge, but at some point he found himself making solid plans.

Now he stood at the gun cabinet, ready to turn those plans into action. That's when his young son Thomas came up behind him. "You going hunting, Dad? Cleaning your guns? Can I help you?"

For a moment Rick just stood without responding. When he turned around, he saw tears in his son's eyes. *He knows*, Rick thought. *Dear God, I think my son knows my plan.*

Some kind of spell broke at that moment. "Come here, son. Give me a hug."

Thomas ran over to his dad and then wrapped his arms around his father, hugging him with all the love and affection he could muster. And that was when the father realized the truth. He had thought his bitterness defined him—that nothing could stop the overwhelming hatred from growing stronger in his heart. Now he knew he was wrong. Love was stronger. A son's love. A Savior's love. It took a great deal more strength to restrain one's rage than it did to act it out. That strength could be found only in love.

As Rick replaced the gun and locked the cabinet decisively, he also locked away something within himself. He would not exercise his anger. He would not be judge and jury; he would be a servant of God instead, and that meant forgiving. It would be the hardest thing he had ever done, and it might take several months, and innumerable prayers. But through the power of God's love, Rick Garmon was going to forgive the man who had violently abused his daughter.[1]

That day Rick Garmon encountered God's transforming love in his son's embrace. God's love is more than just talk. It is *real*. It completely changes the way we think, the way we see others, the way we live each day. Love delivers us from the vicious cycle of vengeful retaliation. It makes life worth living. It changes everything.

I have been preaching the Gospel for several decades now; and with every year that moves by, I am more and more convinced that my mission in life is to help people understand God's love for them. I've grown less interested in the side issues, the niceties, and the doctrinal trivia. This world desperately needs for us to keep the main thing the main thing. So today my central message is God's astounding love. It's a message that's always new, never old, never dusty or musty.

In many ways I am inspired by John, the last living apostle. His great topic, needless to say, was love. He featured love in his Gospel, and love dominated his first Epistle. They say that as he got older, he reached the point where he preached of nothing else. Occasionally, some impatient member of the audience would interrupt him: "Brother John, you've already preached that one. Tell us something new!"

"Very well," the beloved disciple would say with a smile. "A new commandment I give to you—that you love one another."

John was not senile. He simply understood more deeply than the rest of us that there is one item of news that never stops being new: the life-changing love of God.

After focusing for nine chapters on the glorious love of God, I would like to spend the last pages of this book suggesting a few ways in which change can now begin in your life. I have spent so many words on God's love for a reason. I often wonder if we get it backward, spending 90 percent of our time demanding that we love one another and only 10 percent of our time reminding ourselves of God's love for us. Perhaps, love would flow more abundantly from our lives if we reversed this ratio.

Whatever the ratio needs to be, God's love should flow from us in practical and real ways. In every relationship we have—with God, self, friends, neighbors, and enemies—Christians have a foundational, nonnegotiable responsibility spelled l-o-v-e. There is no person in the world—including God Himself—whom God does not expect us to love.

And that is why I say that God's love changes everything. Think of it: What is life except relationships? And what are relationships without love? If we lack the ability to love, we lack the ability to live. Or, at least, to live the "more abundant" life God wants us to enjoy (John 10:10b).

Because God Loves Us, We Can Love Him

In this is love, not that we loved God, but that He loved us and sent His Son to be the propitiation for our sins... We love Him because He first loved us.

—1 JOHN 4:10, 19

We didn't love God, but He loved us. We didn't deserve this gift of love. In fact, we proved by our actions to be God's enemies. Every gift, every blessing He offered, we threw back in His face. He offered affection; we countered with rebellion. Yet He proved the greatness of His love by continuing to lavish it on us in spite of our rebellion, even sending His Son to take the punishment for our sins.

Just as the sun is our only source of daylight, God is our only source of love. Sunrays reflect from all objects they strike, permeating the air with light and making it possible for us to see. In a similar way, God's love enters the world and reflects off our hearts, making it possible for us to love Him and others. We have no innate capacity, no self-originating store of love to give. We can give only what we receive from Him.

When we receive God's love, it does not merely lie inert on our hearts as a warm, fuzzy feeling. That same Son who gave His life for us also shows us a new way to live. Through the indwelling Holy Spirit, He lives within us and makes it possible for us to return love to Him as He originally created us to do. Because He first loved us, we are enabled to love Him.

Because God Loves Us, We Can Love Ourselves

You shall love your neighbor as yourself.

—MATTHEW 19:19

For some, there is no person more difficult to love, to forgive, to tolerate than the person who appears before us in the mirror. Yet when Jesus says, "You shall love your neighbor *as yourself*," the clear implication is that proper self-love is good. In fact, it is necessary. We will never love outside of ourselves as long as we're at war within ourselves. We cannot give to others what we refuse to accept.

To have contempt for someone Christ died for (including yourself) is an insult to God. He died for *you*, and you are precious to Him, so you must regard yourself as highly valued—not arrogantly, but realistically. Paul instructs the believer "not to think of himself more highly than he ought to think, but to think soberly, as God has dealt to each one a measure of faith" (Romans 12:3). We can have personal peace because God loves us. We are new creations in Christ; the old is gone, the new has come (2 Corinthians 5:17).

The whole notion of "self-love" has been seriously abused in the self-absorbed, narcissistic culture in which we live. And even some well-intentioned Christians have used the term "self-love" in ways that can be confusing.

But what did Christ mean by loving ourselves? He simply meant that we are to love ourselves the same way God loves us—as creatures made in His image, for His purposes, and for His glory. To love ourselves as God loves us means we seek after His best for our lives; we conform ourselves to His expectations; we live according to His guidelines; and we learn, over time, to yield our natural, carnal impulses to the control and counsel of the Spirit of God in us. When we do that, we begin to live *functional*, instead of *dysfunctional*, lives. We find peace and joy—indeed, all the fruit of the Holy Spirit begins to characterize our lives (Galatians 5:22–23).

Once we have a proper self-love, based on our identity in Christ and the fact that we are being gradually remade in His image, then the good part begins. We can become distributors of the most powerful force in the universe—the love of God for His children.

Because God Loves Us, We Can Love One Another

Beloved, if God so loved us, we also ought to love one another.

—1 JOHN 4:11

Here is the progression of love we have explored so far: God first loves us, which empowers us to love Him in return, and then to love ourselves. This progression is to continue. Loving ourselves is a necessary step, but we don't live in isolation; we live in community. As we look through the lens of love at the faces surrounding us, we see them in an entirely new light. These are people for whom Christ died. Now that we have received God's love, we are empowered to love, and we even *want* to love. We long to embody Christ and take His love to those around us.

The New Testament is an "us" book written for people together, not for individuals in isolation. This becomes apparent as we consider the "one another" concept that is so very significant in the New Testament Epistles. That phrase occurs some sixty-one times, almost all of which have to do with how Christians relate to one another. For example, we read that we are to *pray for* one another, *encourage* one another, *greet* one another, and *forgive* one another. These statements form a kind of road map of godly relationships, showing the little highways of caring that connect us. All those roads lead to this destination: "Love one another."

In Jesus' last great address to His disciples, delivered in that Upper Room with His closest companions, "Love one another" was a major theme. In fact, He established it as "a new commandment" (John 13:34–35). What was new about it? It was the fact that the source of all love had personally modeled the way to love. Jesus practiced "loving one another" perfectly in His three years with those men. He cut a highway of love through the wilderness of a broken world and demonstrated the sacrificial nature of love for others.

Now, on His last night on earth, Jesus urges His disciples to carry this love forward. He repeats the commandment (John 15:12–13) and tells His disciples (and us as well) to imitate Him in our love for one another. "I have shown you My love," He is saying. "Now, you follow My lead. You love one another in the same way." He is identifying love for others as the trademark of His true disciples. In other words, people will know we are Christians by our love.

Peter, who was present for this discussion, got the point. Later he wrote, "Above all things have fervent love for one another, for 'love will cover a multitude of sins'" (1 Peter 4:8). Peter learned the truth of this verse through a bitter experience he would never forget. In a moment of fear, he denied that he even knew Jesus. The overcoming power of love was driven home when Jesus later sought him out and forgave him.

It's obvious that Jesus' command to love one another also deeply impressed John. After reiterating the commandment twice in chapter 3 of his first letter (1 John 3:11, 23), he says in chapter 4, "If God so loved us, we also ought to love one another. No one has seen God at any time. If we love one another, God abides in us, and His love has been perfected in us" (vv. 11–12).

In other words, God is invisible, but His love flowing through us makes His presence tangible to others, much like the rustling of leaves gives tangible evidence to the presence of wind. When we truly love, John says, God lives within us and builds up our capacity for love, making it more powerful and dynamic all the time.

Clearly, Peter and John came away from that evening with Jesus with the impression that love was their lifetime assignment. They were to reach the nations with the message, and love would be the wind that carried it from God to an inattentive world. If we love, it will get people's attention. If we don't, they will never listen.

According to John, there is no alternative to love. It is no less than a litmus test for our faith. He who does not love his brother is simply "not of God" (1 John 3:10). Even more clearly, "he who does not love does not know God, for God is love" (4:8). Twelve verses later, unloving believers are called "liars." Such people are walking "in darkness" (2:11) and abiding "in death" (1 John 3:14).

Loving one another, in other words, is not a discipline reserved for advanced Christians or a gift belonging to naturally tolerant people. It's not an option or an extra or a frilly wrapping to make religion more attractive. Love is the heartbeat of our faith; and if we detect no pulse, there is no faith.

In his book *The Mark of a Christian*, the late Francis Schaeffer pointed out that Jesus gives the world the right to judge believers by their love for one another:

Jesus says, "By this shall all men know that you are my disciples, if you have love one to another." In the midst of the world, in the midst of our present dying culture, Jesus is giving a right to the world. Upon his authority he gives the world the right to judge whether you and I are born-again Christians on the basis of our observable love toward all Christians.

That's pretty frightening. Jesus turns to the world and says, "I've something to say to you. On the basis of my authority, I give you a right: you may judge whether or not an individual is a Christian on the basis of the love he shows to all Christians."

In other words, if people come up to us and cast in our teeth the judgment that we are not Christians because we have not shown love toward other Christians, we must understand that they are only exercising a prerogative which Jesus gave them.

And we must not get angry. If people say, "You don't love other Christians," we must go home, get down on our knees, and ask God whether or not they are right. And if they are, then they have a right to have said what they said.[2]

This means our number one priority in fulfilling our commission to bring the world to Christ is to love one another.

This can turn out to be a pretty tough task. We can heartily agree with one Christian writer who describes how nothing in the world is more important *or* more difficult than truly loving other people:

That odorous person with the nasty cough who sat next to you on the plane, shoving his newspaper into your face; those crude louts in the neighborhood with the barking dog, that smooth liar who took you in so completely last week—by what magic are you supposed to feel toward these people anything but revulsion, distrust and resentment, and justified desire to have nothing to do with them?[3]

Of course it's possible to *put up with* people. We can manage to keep our mouths shut, perhaps, when certain folks annoy us. But Christ did not command us to "put up with one another." He specifies *love*, and love is not passive or restrained. It's a powerful, aggressive, positive force that serves, affirms, cares, persists, and gives of itself. We all agree that we *should* love. But given the presence of all these unlovable people who surround us, how exactly do we get there?

We Love One Another by Encouraging One Another

> *Therefore comfort [encourage] each other and edify one another, just as you also are doing.*
>
> —1 THESSALONIANS 5:11

The New Testament word most often translated "encouragement" is *parakaleo*. This term comes from two Greek words: *para*, meaning "alongside of"; and *kaleo*, meaning "to call." When people come alongside us during difficult times to

give us renewed courage, a renewed spirit, and renewed hope—
that's encouragement. That is love, pure and refined.

William Barclay tells us that *parakaleo* is a call to arms, a
rallying cry from a sergeant leading us into battle. The encour-
ager sees hesitation and fear and he comes alongside and says,
"Follow me." He exhorts ordinary people to perform noble
deeds. Life, Barclay says, "is always calling us into battle." And
for us, it is *parakletos*, the Holy Spirit, who leads and encourages us to move from the ordinary to the extraordinary.[4]

The most powerful source of encouragement is the Bible.
Paul tells us that those ancient chapters of the Old Testament
inspire and encourage us for today's living. "For whatever
things were written before were written for our learning, that
we through the patience and comfort [encouragement] of the
Scriptures might have hope" (Romans 15:4). The New Testament also is jam-packed with inspiration and encouragement
for Christians. It contains a number of passages exhorting us to
encourage others. For example:

> *Now we exhort you, brethren, warn those who are unruly,*
> *comfort [encourage] the fainthearted, uphold the weak, be*
> *patient with all.*
>
> —1 THESSALONIANS 5:14

> *But exhort [encourage] one another daily, while it is called*
> *"Today," lest any of you be hardened through the deceitful-*
> *ness of sin.*
>
> —HEBREWS 3:13

*And let us consider one another in order to stir up love and
good works ... exhorting [encouraging] one another, and so
much the more as you we see the Day approaching.*

—HEBREWS 10:24–25

We are to soak up God's Word in order to maintain our
own courage and keep in step with the Spirit. And we are to be
diligent in passing on that encouragement to others.

In his book *A Simple Blessing*, singer Michael W. Smith
tells of Justin, a high school freshman who was walking home
from school one day when he saw a group of students bullying
a smaller boy. They knocked him to the ground, scattering his
books and sending his glasses flying. Justin started to walk on,
but when he saw the hurt in the boy's eyes, he stopped, found
his glasses, and helped him pick up his books. The boy was so
overloaded with books that Justin offered to help him carry
them home. On the way, he learned that the boy, Kyle, was
a recent transfer to the school, had no friends, and was often
harassed by those bullies.

Out of sheer pity, Justin invited Kyle to come over and toss
a football with him. The two became fast friends, and at the
end of their senior year Kyle emerged as valedictorian of the
graduating class. As he began his valedictory speech, Justin was
stunned. Kyle told of his early misery. Uprooted, friendless, bul-
lied, and hopeless, he had decided to end his life and was taking his books home so his mother would not have to clean out
his locker. But this time when the bullies attacked, Justin came
along with kindness and encouragement, which turned Kyle
away from despair and gave him a new grip on life and hope.[5]

Encouraging words carry a special power, and it's a power you can exercise every day. Think of those around you who may have a deep need for one word of positive inspiration that you, in the service of God, could provide. How many of these opportunities do we tragically overlook every day? I am constantly thankful for those who encourage me in my life. I can think of many times when someone sent me a note or called me to offer a word of loving encouragement precisely when my spirit was dragging and I was down and out. Their words lifted me from drudgery, fueled me in the Spirit, and spurred me onward. Encouragement puts the wind in our sails.

Wouldn't you like to be that person for someone? Enlist today. Simply tell God you're ready for service, and I guarantee that He will show you the when and the where. Be a blessing, and He will bless you.

We Love One Another by Edifying One Another

Let no corrupt word proceed out of your mouth, but what is good for necessary edification, that it may impart grace to the hearers.

—EPHESIANS 4:29

We can better understand the word *edification* if we take it apart and put it back together again. In Greek the word is *oikodome*, which is a combination of two words: *oikos*, meaning "house"; and *domeo*, meaning "to build." So to edify means "to build the house."

Paul took this common Greek term and applied it meta-phorically. We are called to *edify*, to build up one another just as a house is built brick by brick. We are called to promote spiritual development in other believers.

Along the roads of our culture we encounter decrepit, decaying lives. They can't fix themselves; they need people filled with the love of Christ to come along and perform the ministry of holy renovation. Sadly, I have seen too many churches filled with demolishers instead of renovators. They judge, they exclude, they condemn. Like residents of exclusive neighborhoods, they tolerate no substandard structures within their borders. Tearing things down requires no thought, no skill, no care. A few angry vandals can do it. We who have received the love of Christ must be builders and not demolishers.

Even believers who have been renovated need continual repair. The building that is my life needs your hammer and nails, and the building that is yours needs mine. We must help each other simply because God designed the church to work that way.

We flourish when we are under the loving care of each other and we wither away when we try to go it alone. We must be about the intentional business of renovating one another. As Paul said, "Let us pursue the things which make for peace and the things by which one may edify another...Let it be for the edification [building up] of the church that you seek to excel" (Romans 14:19; 1 Corinthians 14:12).

Erwin McManus observes that we seem to have lost sight of this core value of the church, allowing the self-absorption of the world to infiltrate the body of Christ. People want to talk only about themselves, and they're interested only in the parts of the church experience that do something for them. They seek tingling sensations in worship, classes that help them cope with their problems, and sermons that make them feel good about themselves. It's a consumer mentality based on *what's in it for me*. Though we are sheep needing to be fed, we also must learn to be shepherds who feed others.

McManus pleads for us to get away from the "meet my needs" mentality, stop church-shopping, and start looking for ways to minister to others. Our battle cry should be, "We are the church, here to serve a lost and broken world," and not, "What can your church do for me?" Just as we are a physically obese society, we may also be a spiritually gluttonous one fixated on consuming rather than serving.[6]

The ultimate tool for building one another up is the unchanging Word of God. The immortal book has changed lives for thousands of years, and it has lost none of its power. When we feel ineffective and fear that we have no encouragement to offer those whose heads are down and hearts are broken, maybe the problem is that our Bibles are closed.

We Love One Another by Entertaining One Another

Be hospitable to one another without grumbling.
—1 PETER 4:9

I don't know what you thought when you read the word *entertaining* in the subheading above. You may have begun to put on your dancing shoes, pick up your harmonica, or dust off your old *Reader's Digest* book of jokes. That's because we've lost the primary meaning of the word. Today, *entertainment* brings to mind "amusement." The classic sense of the word, however, has more to do with the ministry of hospitality.

Paul uses an interesting word when he encourages the Roman Christians to be "given to hospitality" (Romans 12:13). *Given* is the word for "pursue." It is an active, energetic idea. The church father Origen wrote about Paul's use of the word for "pursue" in this context:

> How finely does Paul sum up the generosity of the man who pursues hospitality in one word! For by saying that hospitality is to be pursued, he shows that we are not just to receive the stranger when he comes to us, but actually to inquire after, and look carefully for strangers, to pursue them and search them out everywhere.[7]

I like Paul's phrase "given to hospitality." It's not something we force ourselves to do; we are driven by a passion for the welfare of others. We go above and beyond the required minimum and dedicate ourselves to meeting the needs of those who come into our midst.

When we are given to hospitality, we see beyond the road-ragged clothing and travel dust on our guests and recognize them as eternal creatures whom God loves and created in His own image. C. S. Lewis eloquently made this point in his famous observation from *The Weight of Glory*:

> It is a serious thing to live in a society of possible gods and goddesses, to remember that the dullest, most uninteresting person you talk to may one day be a creature which,

if you saw it now, you would be strongly tempted to worship, or else a horror and a corruption such as you now meet, if at all, only in a nightmare. All day long we are, in some degree, helping each other to one or the other of these destinations. It is in the light of these overwhelming possibilities, it is with the awe and the circumspection proper to them, that we should conduct all of our dealings with one another, all friendships, all loves, all play, all politics. There are no *ordinary* people. You have never talked to a mere mortal. Nations, cultures, arts, civilizations—these are mortal, and their life is to ours as the life of a gnat. But it is immortals whom we joke with, work with, marry, snub, and exploit—immortal horrors or everlasting splendors.[8]

It's an astounding observation. How would we treat other people if we fully realized that we were "helping each other to one or the other of these destinations"? Would we offer more hospitality? Would we be a bit more patient with people in traffic? With coworkers? Family members? It's not always easy, but Peter tells us to muster up a little humility and do it: "Be hospitable to one another without grumbling" (1 Peter 4:9).

You may feel that you stack up pretty well in this department. Most of us believe ourselves to be loving people. When I preach a "love one another" sermon, I never get the idea that people think I'm stepping on their toes. The first generation of Christians in the early church probably felt the same way. Yet Paul challenged them to increase and perfect their love for one another. To the Philippians he wrote: "And this I pray, that your love may abound still more and more" (Philippians 1:9). He wrote a similar message to the Christ-followers of Thessalonica: "You yourselves are taught by God to love one another... But we urge you, brethren, that you increase more and more" (1 Thessalonians 4:9–10).

Alexander Maclaren, one of the great preachers of nineteenth-century England, described what happened when the followers of Jesus began to live out His commandment to love one another. Maclaren's oft-quoted words have been called the most eloquent portrayal of Christian love found outside Scripture itself. He first described the terrible gulfs of language, nationality, gender, and philosophy that separated people in the ancient world. It was a world of unveiled hostility. Then Jesus came and told us to love one another:

Barbarian, Scythian, bond and free, male and female, Jew and Greek, learned and ignorant clasped hands and sat down at one table, and felt themselves all one in Christ Jesus. They were ready to break all other bonds, and to yield to the uniting forces that streamed out from His Cross. There never had been anything like it. No wonder that the world began to babble about sorcery, and conspiracies, and complicity in unnamable vices. It was only that the disciples were obeying the new commandment, and a new thing had come into the world— a community held together by love and not by geographical accidents or linguistic affinities, or the iron fetters of the conqueror... The new commandment made a new thing, and the world wondered."[9]

Because God Loves Us, We Can Love Our Neighbor

Jesus said to him, "'You shall love the LORD your God with all your heart, with all your soul, and with all your mind.' This is the first and great commandment. And the second is like it: 'You shall love your neighbor as yourself.'"

—MATTHEW 22:37–39

I'm confident that every believer knows that we Christians are commanded to love our neighbor. And most understand that this does not mean just the family next door. Who does it include? When Jesus was asked that question, He answered by telling the parable of the good Samaritan. Your neighbor is anyone you encounter who has a need that you can fulfill.

Here Jesus greatly expands the field on which our love is to operate. Love is not limited to God, yourself, your family, or your church. It must be freely extended to everyone you encounter. No longer must you confine your love only to those who love you and can repay it; it must be given even to those who can never repay it.

Peter Kreeft observes that godly love changes the rules for loving one another. We don't worry about the results because we have no motive other than to spread the love that God has given to us. We are not manipulating or trying to earn points or even loving for our own personal gratification. We are simply treating others in the light of how God sees them. We can love "from sheer bounty, just as we have been loved. We become channels of this new living water."[10]

The apostle Paul knew just how critical loving our neighbor is to the authenticity of our Christian life. He twice repeated Jesus' command in his letters. To the Romans he wrote, "He who loves another has fulfilled the law...'You shall love your neighbor as yourself'" (Romans 13:8–9). And to the Galatians, he stressed the overarching importance of this command: "For all the law is fulfilled in one word, even in this: 'You shall love your neighbor as yourself'" (Galatians 5:14).

Because God Loves Us, We Can Love Our Enemies

You have heard that it was said, "You shall love your neigh-bor and hate your enemy." But I say to you, love your ene-mies, bless those who curse you, do good to those who hate you, and pray for those who spitefully use you and perse-cute you, that you may be sons of your Father in heaven... Therefore you shall be perfect, just as your Father in heaven is perfect.

—MATTHEW 5:43–45, 48

In this chapter, we've seen the circle of love expand step-by-step. First, we love God, then ourselves, then our fellow believers, and then our neighbors. Now Jesus tells us to take one more step and love our enemies. This is where it gets interesting. For many, it's a step too far.

Knowing the difficulty in loving our enemies, Jesus gives us an excellent rationale for the command. He says that if we love

only our friends and family, we are no different from unbelievers who don't know Jesus or His commandments. What we can
offer that they cannot is love for our enemies.

If I knew the name of your worst enemy and suggested that
you go serve that person in some good way, you might say, "I
just can't!" But Jesus knows it can be done because He did it.
He found a way to love that race of enemies known as humanity, and we must be eternally grateful that He did.

Christ could have said, "Those men are driving nails into
My hands. They've beaten Me, gambled for My clothing, and
deeply grieved those who love Me. I just can't love them!" No
one would have blamed Him—or remembered Him.

Instead, from the agony of the cross, Christ looked down on
those who had brutalized Him and asked God to forgive them
(Luke 23:34). Stephen, the first martyr, did the same (Acts
7:60). Peter points out that Jesus, "when He was reviled, did
not revile in return; when He suffered, He did not threaten,
but committed Himself to Him who judges righteously"
(1 Peter 2:23). Because Jesus loved His enemies, we live forever.
Because Jesus loved His enemies, we can love ours.

As Jesus pointed out, God sends sunshine and rain to both
the good and the bad—to those who love Him and those who
don't (Matthew 5:45). It's known as God's common grace. He
does not shut out people who might be deemed unworthy, so we
don't have that right either. We love people not for who they are,
but for who they can become—not for the value of their behavior, but for the value of their souls. That's when the world knows
we are serious.

Paul, who built friendships with his prison guards, wrote:
"Bless those who persecute you; bless and do not curse...If

your enemy is hungry, feed him; if he is thirsty, give him a drink; for in so doing you will heap coals of fire on his head" (Romans 12:14, 20). It may seem that Paul is urging us to be "passive-aggressive," until we understand a certain custom of the day. As an act of public contrition, some Egyptians wore a pan of burning coals like a hat to express their shame and guilt. Paul is simply urging a bit of human psychology: Return gentleness for aggression, and your persecutor will be shamed into being contrite. It will be as if he is wearing such a hat.

One of the most inspiring stories of a man loving his enemies is that of John Perkins. John grew up as a black man in Mississippi. He dropped out of school in the third grade, and in his teen years he headed for California, seeking better employment. While there he became a Christian. Perkins soon came to believe that God was calling him to preach the Gospel and develop black leadership for the poor black people he'd been raised with. So he returned to Mississippi.

On February 7, 1970, a Saturday night, police arrested a group of black college students. Perkins and two of his associates went immediately to the jailhouse to post bail. But when they spoke up, five deputy sheriffs and highway patrolmen surrounded them, placed them under arrest, and began beating them violently. Perkins had done nothing wrong. He didn't even have a police record. But he was a black leader trying to help young African Americans, and that was all it took in that particular town.

The beating went on for most of the night. The aggressors stomped on Perkins and kicked him in the head, ribs, and groin. One officer picked up a fork and jammed it first up his nose and then down his throat.

John Perkins was unconscious most of that interminable evening. He was so swollen and mutilated that the helpless students around him were sure that he was either dead or approaching death. But by the grace of God alone, he did not die.

A nonbeliever reacting to such a beating would have been embittered. He would have sworn revenge and used every recourse, legal or possibly otherwise, to strike back at his attackers and perhaps at others he perceived to be of the same ilk. A person could merely ride his rage and seethe with anger for a lifetime after such an experience. He could work out his revenge on a lot of people, and there would always be more yet to inflict.

John Perkins did not choose that road. He had come to Mississippi on a mission for black people. They needed his support and guidance, and that guidance had to begin right now with his example.

He later wrote of his attackers, "I remembered their faces—so twisted with hate. It was like looking at white-faced demons. For the first time, I saw what hate had done to those people. These policemen were poor. They saw themselves as failures. The only way they knew how to find a sense of worth was by beating us. Their racism made them feel like 'somebody.'"[11]

As a Christian, Perkins could not receive hate and deal it back. Such an option was not open to a disciple of Jesus Christ, the Prince of Peace. Even as he lay on the floor of the jail cell, crimson puddles around him, welts rising on his body—he was in prayer. *Lord God*, he murmured, *if You will only get me out of this place alive...*

He knew he shouldn't be bargaining with the Lord, but he couldn't stop the pleadings that rose from his heart. *I want to preach to these people, too. I want to preach to those driven by hatred, and I want to drive out that hatred forever.*

Perkins refused to hate. All he felt was pity.

It required months for his battered body—and his emotions—to heal. Two doctors, one white and one black, labored over the physical wounds gently and compassionately. And Jesus Christ, the Physician of hearts, labored over his mangled emotions. In body and spirit, Perkins healed and regained full strength, and the changes within him would soon be channeled into a ministry he wouldn't have been capable of without suffering.

He knew now that it wasn't just "his" people who needed to be free; it was everyone. The age-old prison of racial hatred had to be opened by more than just laws and movements. There could be no real reconciliation unless Christ was the reconciler. "Now that God had enabled me to forgive the many whites who had wronged me, I found myself able to truly love them," recalls Perkins. "I wanted to return good for evil."[12]

He knew the Spirit of God was moving within him, for a vivid image began to fill his mind: an image of Christ suffering on the cross. Christ knew what Perkins was feeling. He knew what twisted justice felt like. He knew about the punches, the kicks. And His response was "Father, forgive them, for they don't know what they're doing."

Evil draws its power from its viral nature. It spreads the disease of anger and vengeance. You hurt me, and I either hurt you back or take it out on someone else—maybe a series of someone elses. Sin is born into us, but it is reinforced by the spread of its billions of malignant missionaries in the world. It is stopped when we refuse to pass the infection, when we let Christ heal us and we deal out blessing rather than reprisal. And then, through the power of God, love can spread virally, too.

John Perkins said, "Let it stop with me." They hated him; he forgave them. They cursed; he blessed. He didn't do it because he was some kind of saint; in fact, the opposite was true. God had shown him that he was no better than those who had assaulted him. The sin in his heart was not of any higher-quality blend; it was the same nasty stuff. In the eyes of God—the only standard that matters—he had no high ground to claim. He needed forgiveness, too. So John Perkins set out on his long journey of reconciliation, of bridge-building between black and white, of defusing hatred, of living the miracle of grace.

John Perkins went on to become a successful pastor and founder of the Voice of Calvary Ministries, dedicated to racial reconciliation. He has received many awards and honorary degrees and even served on a presidential commission on inner-city problems under President Ronald Reagan.[13]

Let Love Change Your World

The great question that faced John Perkins also faces us: Can we let love change everything in our world? Can we stop living in an endless cycle of evil for evil, or even of apathy for apathy? What would happen if we actually began to treat people as lost members of God's family?

Some people will always seem unlovable to you. And maybe from your standpoint, they are. But before you get too sure of yourself, remember that to someone else, you may also be unlovable.

If you have chosen to follow Christ, the Holy Spirit has come to live within you—to guide you and empower you, to fill you with the love of Christ. When you feel anger or resentment rising in your heart, I challenge you to ask God to help you love and forgive in the power of the Spirit. He will answer that prayer every time. There is no occasion when it's not God's will for you to love. On your own, all things are difficult; in the power of the Spirit, all things are possible.

Well over a century ago, Henry Drummond preached a classic message on love called "The Greatest Thing in the World." In one section, Drummond deals with how Christ's love becomes our own. He points out that a magnet will pass its charge into a piece of ordinary iron that is left near it long enough.[14] There is no force in the world more magnetic than the love of Christ. You can't be exposed to it for long without its taking you over. He has loved us; now we can love Him. We can love ourselves. We can love others. We can love our neighbors. We can even love our enemies.

But will we? Will you? Christ has come down from heaven to show you what love is and how to live in its power. Now it is up to you and to me to go out and love a world tearing itself to pieces for want of it.

Our task is a daunting one, but in the power of Christ through the work of the Holy Spirit, we can do it. We will do it.

Let's make waves, you and I. Waves can begin with ripples. If enough of us send out ripples, if enough of us show what the love of God means to this world, those waves will touch the shores of eternity itself.

I'm ready for action. How about you?

In his famous novel *The Fountain*, which explored the themes of love, art, and death, English novelist Charles Morgan wrote, "There is no surprise more magical than the surprise of being loved; it is God's finger on man's shoulder."[1]

That is a beautiful way of expressing the reality of the image of God in man. When we are in a genuinely loving relationship on earth, it is as if God is tapping us on the shoulder and saying, "There is more. Revel in the earthly love you have found, but don't settle for it as if it is the pinnacle of love. There is more. There is My love for you."

An author never knows into whose hands his or her books may fall. Therefore, I don't know what your relationship is to the love of God. You could be a follower of Christ who has spent years enjoying the loyal, unconditional love of God. Or you could be a Christian, new or old, who thinks of God's love in purely human terms, believing that God loves you in exactly the same way others have. Perhaps you have been abused by someone who used "love" as a pretense for his or her own agenda—and you have sworn never to trust the words "I love you" again.

Regardless of your relationship to love, you may be a read-the-last-chapter-first kind of person and so you turned to the conclusion of this book to see what the bottom line is before committing to the whole thing. If you have read the title, you have read the concluding line as well: God loves you—He always has and He always will. That's not true because I say it is. It's true because that is the "conclusion" of the Bible.

I gave my life to God as a young person, and I've lived as a follower of Jesus Christ for many decades now. I know God is real, and I know He loves me. I know that He loves you, too, whoever you are, whatever your circumstances may be.

I've been through the good times and the bad times of life, and God has always been there for me. He has never failed me. But neither has He kept me free of problems or heartbreak. In this world, we must contend with them. But He has always been with me; He has always given me the wisdom to take the next step. He has blessed me in more ways than I could write down. I can't imagine what life would be without Him.

You can know Him, too. Again, let's forget your history and your present circumstances. God's love is not conditioned by anything you are or anything you have done. God loves you because it is His nature to love you. But God does not force His love on anyone. He created us to be creatures of free will. He makes His love available to each of us, but we must take the initiative to receive it.

But how do you open your heart and life to receive that love? I would like to take these final paragraphs to walk you through that process, and encourage you to take the most wonderful step life can afford. If you have already read the book, you will remember some of these truths from previous chapters. If you jumped to the conclusion, you will want to go back and review. Either way, let's bring them all together now. Let's find out what they mean for you, in your desire to accept God's love and begin to know Him personally.

First, you need to acknowledge that you are a sinner. *All* of us are. This just means we are fallible human beings, imperfect, prone to doing things that separate us from God. The Bible says it this way: "For all have sinned and fall short of the glory of God" (Romans 3:23).

God's love is perfect. But everything about God is perfect, including His holiness and His justice. Because He loves us, He wants to forgive us. Because He is holy and just, He must deal with our sin. And the Bible says that "the wages of sin is death" (Romans 6:23).

Unless God were to find a way to intervene on our behalf, unless He were to devise a plan to bring us together that would satisfy both His love and His justice, we would be doomed to an eternity of separation and punishment.

But here is the Gospel—the good news of God's plan: God sent His only Son to this earth to give Himself as a sacrifice for our sin: "But God demonstrates His own love toward us, in that while we were still sinners, Christ died for us" (Romans 5:8).

Jesus Christ is the only One who has ever walked upon this earth and lived a perfect, sinless life. As the spotless Lamb of God, He died on the cross in our place, and the punishment of our sin was placed upon Him. That means that at the time of judgment, as God prepares to judge the sins you've committed, Christ steps forward and says, "This person's sin-debts are paid in full."

On the cross, God looked at His Son and saw your sin,

which Christ had taken upon Himself. At judgment, God looks at you and sees Christ's righteousness, which has been thrown over you like a white robe. Because Christ takes *your* sin and gives you *His* righteousness, the problem of your acceptability to a holy God has been resolved.

Second, you must accept God's gift of love. The entire message of this book has been that God loves you—He always has and He always will. But it's not enough to say, "Great to hear," and walk away. To know about God's love and not accept it changes nothing in your life. A gift that you do not receive is of no value. God has paid the price for your sin, and eternal life is now available to you; but you must receive it!

At this very moment, Christ stands at the door of your heart and waits for you to invite Him in: "Behold, *I* stand at the door and knock. If anyone hears My voice and opens the door, *I* will come in" (Revelation 3:20; italics added).

Finally, ask God to forgive your sin, and invite Christ into your heart. Tell Him that you want the forgiveness that only He can give. Here is a simple suggestion for your prayer:

Dear God,

I know I am a sinner. I need Your forgiveness. I freely lay all my sin before You, and I know that because of what Your Son did for me, my sins will be separated from me as far as the East is from the West. Lord Jesus Christ, I ask You to come into my heart and life. I accept You as my Savior and my only hope of heaven. Only You can make me pure and clean, and I ask You to do that. I love You, Lord, and I give You my life. Thank You for hearing my prayer. Amen.

That's all it takes. Own your sin, disown it through laying it before Christ, and determine to follow the One who loves you perfectly.

One final request. Let us know about your decision. We would love to send you some printed material that will help you grow in your new relationship with Jesus Christ. As you begin this new life, never forget:

GOD LOVES YOU
HE ALWAYS HAS—HE ALWAYS WILL.

NOTES

Chapter 1: *God Is Love*

1. Adapted from Reuben Archer Torrey, *Anecdotes and Illustrations* (New York: Revell, 1907), 35–36.
2. Trula Cronk, *Over Mountain or Plain or Sea* (Nashville: Randall House, 2003), 162.
3. Max Lucado, *In the Grip of Grace* (Dallas: Word, 1996).
4. Charles Ryrie, *Basic Theology: A Popular Systematic Guide to Understanding Biblical Truth* (Wheaton, IL: Victor Books, 1986), 35.
5. John R. W. Stott, *The Epistle of John* (Grand Rapids: Eerdmans, 1964), 160.
6. John Bartlett, *Bartlett's Familiar Quotations* (New York: Hachette, 1891).
7. Peter Kreeft, *The God Who Loves You: Love Divine, All Loves Excelling* (San Francisco: Ignatius Press, 1988), 49–50.
8. Frederick M. Lehman, "The Love of God," 1917.
9. Henri J. M. Nouwen, *The Return of the Prodigal Son: A Story of Homecoming* (New York: Image Books/Doubleday, 1994), 42.
10. John Ortberg, *Love Beyond Reason* (Grand Rapids: Zondervan, 1998), 180.
11. Brennan Manning, "Living as God's Beloved: An Interview with Brennan Manning About How We Can Experience God's Love," *Discipleship Journal*, July/August 1997, accessed December 28, 2012, http://www.navpress.com/magazines/archives/article.aspx?id=11697.
12. J. I. Packer, *Knowing God* (Downers Grove, IL: InterVarsity Press, 1973), 41–42.
13. John Piper, *The Pleasures of God: Meditations on God's Delight in Being God* (Sisters, OR: Multnomah, 2000), 188.
14. Michael B. Brown, *God's Man: A Daily Devotional Guide to Christlike Character,* ed. Don M. Aycock (Grand Rapids: Kregel, 2000), 15.
15. Adapted from Mark Galli, "The End of Christianity as We Know It," *Christianity Today*, April 15, 2010, accessed February 29, 2012, http://www.christianitytoday.com/ct/2010/aprilweb-only/25-41.0.html?start=3.

16. Packer, *Knowing God*, 124.
17. A.W. Tozer, *The Knowledge of the Holy* (New York: HarperCollins, 1961), 102.
18. Brennan Manning, *The Wisdom of Tenderness: What Happens When God's Fiery Mercy Transforms Our Lives* (New York: HarperCollins, 2002), 25–26.

Chapter 2: *God Loved You Before You Were Born*

1. Henri J. M. Nouwen, *The Return of the Prodigal Son: A Story of Home-coming* (New York: Image Books/DoubleDay, 1992), 105–6.
2. Alexander Tsiaras, *TED Talks*, "Conception to Birth—Visualized," November 2011, accessed March 6, 2012, http://www.ted.com/talks/alexander_tsiaras_conception_to_birth_visualized.html.
3. John Phillips, *Exploring Psalms, Volume Two: An Expository Commentary* (Grand Rapids: Kregel, 1988), 597–98.
4. Quoted in Scott L. Klusendorf, *The Case for Life: Equipping Christians to Engage the Culture* (Wheaton, IL: Crossway, 2009), 36.
5. Ibid., 36.
6. Ibid., 36–37.
7. Mother Teresa, "Whatsoever You Do…," February 3, 1994, accessed April 4, 2012, http://www.priestsforlife.org/brochures/mtspeech.html.
8. John Ortberg, *Love Beyond Reason* (Grand Rapids: Zondervan, 1998), 20.
9. Warren W. Wiersbe, *Wiersbe's Expository Outlines on the Old Testament* (Wheaton, IL: Victor B, 1993), 20.
10. Taken from *Celebrate Life*, (c) 2010 by Good News Tracts. Used by permission. For more information, visit www.goodnewstracts.org.
11. Marvin Olasky, "After-Birth Abortion: A New Argument Calls for New Decisions," *World*, March 24, 2012.
12. Peter Kreeft, *The God Who Loves You: Love Divine, All Loves Excelling* (San Francisco: Ignatius Press, 1988), 61.
13. Tim Muldoon, "March for Love: Abortion Is an Interruption of the Potential for Love," *Patheos.com*, January 24, 2012, accessed April 20, 2012, http://www.patheos.com/Resources/Additional-Resources/March-for-Love-Tim-Muldoon-01-24-2012.html.
14. Jeanne Monahan, "Ultrasound Policy," *Family Research Council*, accessed April 26, 2012, http://www.frc.org/onepagers/ultrasound-policy.
15. Gianna Jessen, testimony before a subcommittee of the U.S. House of Representatives Judiciary Committee, *AbortionFacts.com*, April 22, 1996, accessed April 9, 2012, http://www.abortionfacts.com/survivors/giannajessen.asp.
16. *Celebrate Life* (Wheaton, IL: Good News Tracts).
17. Adapted from Norma McCorvey and Gary Thomas, *Won by Love: Norma McCorvey, Jane Roe of Roe v. Wade, Speaks Out for the Unborn*

as She Shares Her New Conviction for Life (Nashville: Thomas Nelson, 1998). Quoted excerpt Norma McCorvey with Gary Thomas, *Roe No More Ministry*, accessed April 20, 2012, http://www.leaderu.com/norma/nmtestimony.html.

Chapter 3: *God Carved His Love in Stone*

1. Turner has since apologized for this statement. See *Ted Turner, Call Me Ted* (New York: Hachette Book Group, 2008), 361.
2. Irene Lacher, "Ted Turner's 10 Commandments," *LA Times*, May 4, 1990.
3. Adapted from Steve Chalke and Alan Mann, *The Lost Message of Jesus* (Grand Rapids: Zondervan, 2003), 51.
4. Ron Mehl, *The Tender Commandments* (Sisters, OR: Multnomah, 1998), 14.
5. Charles Spurgeon, "God's Love to the Saints," October 26, 1905, accessed April 26, 2012, http://spurgeongems.org/vols49-51/chs2959.pdf.
6. Peter Kreeft, *The God Who Loves You: Love Divine, All Loves Excelling* (San Francisco: Ignatius Press, 1988), 123–24.
7. Martin H. Fischer, *The Large Catechism of Martin Luther* (Philadelphia: Fortress Press, 1959), 9.
8. Owen M. Weatherly, *The Ten Commandments in Modern Perspective* (Richmond, VA: John Knox Press, 1961), 11.
9. T. S. Eliot, *Four Quartets* (New York: Harcourt, 1943), 120.
10. Jerry Vines, *Basic Bible Sermons on the Ten Commandments* (Nashville: Broadman Press, 1992), 24.
11. Mehl, *Tender Commandments*, 76.
12. Leslie B. Flynn, *Come Alive with Illustrations* (Grand Rapids: Baker, 1987), 193–94.
13. Jacob and Wilhelm Grimm, *The Complete Grimm's Fairy Tales* (Digireads .com, 2009), 185.
14. For statistics, see http://www.abort73.com/abortion_facts/us_abortion _statistics/; http://www.nimh.nih.gov/health/publications/suicide-in-the -us-statistics-and-prevention/index.shtml; http://www.disastercenter.com/ crime/uscrime.htm.
15. Diana Kendall, *Sociology in Our Times* (Belmont, CA: Wadsworth, Cengage Learning, 2011), 220.
16. Tim Keller, *Counterfeit Gods* (New York: Dutton, 2009), 52.
17. C. S. Lewis, "The Weight of Glory," in *The Weight of Glory and Other Addresses* (New York: Macmillan, 1975, 1980), 10.
18. Dorothy Sayers, *The Mind of the Maker* (San Francisco: Harper & Rowe, 1941), 4.
19. John Killinger, *To My People with Love* (United Kingdom: Abingdon, 1998), 13–14.

Chapter 4: *God's Love Never Quits*

1. Skye Jethani, *With: Reimagining the Way You Relate to God* (Nashville: Thomas Nelson, 2011), 80–82.
2. Blaise Pascal, *Pensees*, 1670.
3. Quoted by Gerald H. Twombly, *Major Themes from the Minor Prophets* (Winona Lake, IN: BMH Books, 1981), 18.
4. Elizabeth Edwards, *Resilience* (New York: Broadway Books, 2009), 178–79.
5. Frederick A. Tatford, *Prophet of a Broken Home: Exposition of Hosea* (Sussex, England: Prophetic Witness, 1974), 20.
6. Roy Clements, "The Love of God: A Sermon on Hosea 11," in *Nothing Greater, Nothing Better: Theological Essays on the Love of God*, ed. Kevin J. Vanhoozer (Grand Rapids: Eerdmans, 2001), 204.
7. Clements, "Love of God," 206–7.
8. Associated Press, "Weeks After Wife's Death, Ex-Detroit Lions Linebacker Chris Spielman Enters College Football Hall of Fame," December 9, 2009, accessed February 7, 2012, http://www.mlive.com/lions/index.ssf/2009/12/former_detroit_lions_linebacke.html.
9. Gary V. Smith, *The NIV Application Commentary: Hosea* (Grand Rapids: Zondervan, 2001), 161.
10. G. Campbell Morgan, *Hosea: The Heart and Holiness of God* (Grand Rapids: Baker, 1974), 128.
11. D. A. Carson, *The Difficult Doctrine of the Love of God* (Wheaton, IL: Crossway, 2000), 47.
12. Clements, "Love of God," 206–7.
13. The first article of chapter 2 of the *Westminster Confession of Faith* reads: "There is but one only, living, and true God, who is infinite in being and perfection, a most pure spirit, invisible, without body, parts, or passions."
14. Morgan, *Hosea*, 133.
15. Ibid.,133.
16. John Phillips, *Exploring Psalms* (Grand Rapids: Kregel, 1988), 705.
17. Claudine Zap, "Paralyzed Bride to Marry One Year After Accident," *Yahoo! News*, July 18, 2011, accessed April 6, 2012, http://news.yahoo.com/blogs/upshot/paralyzed-bride-marry-one-accident-175440457.html.

Chapter 5: *God Wrote His Love in Red*

1. Paul Lee Tan, *Encyclopedia of 7700 Illustrations: Signs of the Times* (Garland, TX: Bible Communications, 1996).
2. Elizabeth Tenety, "Tim Tebow's 316 Yards Inspire 'John 3:16' Searches," *Washington Post*, January 8, 2012, accessed April 24, 2012, http://www

.washingtonpost.com/blogs/under-god/post/tim-tebows-316-yards-fans
-keep-the-faith-after-broncos-win/2012/01/08/gIQAYNLOkP_blog
.html.

3. G. Campbell Morgan, "Preaching by G. Campbell Morgan," *The G. Campbell Archive*, accessed May 7, 2012, http://www.gcampbellmorgan.com/preaching.pdf.

4. Scholars debate whether John 3:16–21 is a direct quote from Jesus or a reflection from the pen of John, summarizing Jesus' words. In either case, it is clear that the teaching came from the lips of Jesus.

5. William Barclay, *The Gospel of John*, vol. 1 (Edinburgh: Saint Andrews Press, 1964), 128.

6. Leon Morris, *The Gospel According to John* (Grand Rapids: Eerdmans, 1995), 229.

7. C. S. Lewis, *The Four Loves* (New York: Harcourt, Brace, 1960).

8. James Montgomery Boice, *The Gospel of John* (Grand Rapids: Baker, 2005), 287.

9. Ira D. Sankey, *My Life and the Story of Gospel Hymns and of Sacred Songs and Solos* (London: Sunday School Times, 1906), 345.

10. Ryle, *Gospel of John*, 160.

11. John Phillips, *Exploring John* (Grand Rapids: Kregel, 1969), 75.

12. R. Kent Hughes, *John: That You May Believe* (Wheaton IL: Crossway, 1999), 85.

13. Arthur Miller, *Timebends* (New York: Penguin, 1987), 482.

14. Adapted from Douglas W. Mize, "As *Titanic* Sank, He Pleaded, 'Believe in the Lord Jesus!'" Baptist Press, April 13, 2012, accessed April 25, 2012, http://www.bpnews.net/printerfriendly.asp?ID=37601.

Chapter 6: *God Loves You Even When You Don't Love Him*

1. George Murray, *Jesus and His Parables* (Edinburgh: T&T Clark, 1914), 163.

2. George Arthur Buttrick, *The Parables of Jesus* (New York: R. R. Smith, 1930), 194.

3. Kenneth Bailey, *Poet and Peasant and Through Peasant Eyes: A Literary-Cultural Approach to the Parables in Luke* (Grand Rapids: Eerdmans, 1983), 161–62.

4. John MacArthur, *The Prodigal Son: An Astonishing Study of the Parable Jesus Told to Unveil God's Grace for You* (Nashville: Thomas Nelson, 2008), 45.

5. Kenneth E. Bailey, *The Cross and the Prodigal: Luke 15 Through the Eyes of Middle Eastern Peasants* (Downers Grove, IL: InterVarsity Press, 2005), 52–53.

6. Hannah More, *The Complete Works of Hannah More*, vol. 1 (New York: Harper & Brothers, 1935), 381.

7. Henri J. M. Nouwen, *The Return of the Prodigal Son: A Story of Homecoming* (New York: Image Books/Double Day, 1994), 36.

8. *Real Sports with Bryant Gumble*, episode 179, February 22, 2012.

9. Nouwen, *Return of the Prodigal Son*, 48.

10. Ibid., 53.

11. Kenneth E. Bailey, "The Pursuing Father: What We Need to Know About This Often Misunderstood Middle Eastern Parable," *Christianity Today*, October 26, 1998, accessed April 18, 2012, http://www.ctlibrary.com/ct/1998/october26/8tc034.html.

12. Bailey, "Pursuing Father."

13. MacArthur, *Prodigal Son*, 136.

Chapter 7: *God Loves You When He's Correcting You*

1. "Kick Save: With Their Freight Train Hurtling Toward Certain Disaster, Two Brave Railroad Men Sweep a Toddler Off the Tracks," *People*, June 1, 1998, accessed April 24, 2012, http://www.people.com/people/archive/article/0,,20125421,00.html.

2. C. S. Lewis, *The Problem of Pain* (New York: Macmillan, 1973), 31–32, 40.

3. Charles Ryrie, *Basic Theology* (Wheaton, IL: Victor, 1986), 39.

4. Author unknown.

5. Theodore Laetsch, *Bible Commentary Jeremiah* (St. Louis: Concordia, 1965), 234–35.

6. Lewis, *The Problem of Pain*, 91.

7. "Notebook," *Time*, February 6, 2006, 15.

8. Malcolm Muggeridge, *Jesus Rediscovered* (Glascow: Collins, 1974), 102.

9. John Piper and Justin Taylor, eds., *Suffering and the Sovereignty of God* (Wheaton, IL: Crossway, 2006), 224–25.

10. Rebecca Manley Pippert, *Hope Has Its Reasons* (Downers Grove, IL: InterVarsity Press), 100.

11. Ibid., 101.

12. Eugene H. Peterson, adapted from foreword of Alan E. Nelson, *Embracing Brokenness: How God Refines Us Through Life's Disappointments* (Colorado Springs: NavPress, 2002).

13. Quoted by Gordon MacDonald in *The Life God Blesses* (Nashville: Thomas Nelson, 1994), 25–26.

14. Hilary Stout, "For Some Parents, Shouting Is the New Spanking," *New York Times*, October 21, 2009, accessed April 10, 2012, http://www.nytimes.com/2009/10/22/fashion/22yell.html?pagewanted=all.

15. "Joni Eareckson Tada," an interview with Kim Lawton on the website *Religion and Ethics Newsweekly*, September 24, 2010, accessed April 27,

2012, http://www.pbs.org/wnet/religionandethics/episodes/september-24-2010/joni-eareckson-tada/7074/.

16. John Ortberg, "Don't Waste a Crisis," *Leadership Journal* (Winter, 2011).

17. Leonard Sweet, *Learn to Dance the Soul Salsa: 17 Surprising Steps for Godly Living in the 21st Century* (Grand Rapids: Zondervan, 2002), 7.

Chapter 8: *God's Love Will Never Let You Go*

1. Karl Taro Greenfeld/Kathmandu, "Adventure: Blind to Failure," *Time*, June 18, 2001, accessed March 14, 2012, ttp://www.time.com/time/magazine/article/0,9171,1000120 7,00.html.

2. Erik Weihenmayer and Paul Stoltz, *The Adversity Advantage: Turning Everyday Struggles into Everyday Greatness* (New York: Simon & Schuster/Touchstone, 2010), 4.

3. John Stott, *Romans: God's Good News for the World* (Downers Grove, IL: InterVarsity Press, 1994), 259.

4. James Montgomery Boice, *Romans, Vol. 2: The Reign of Grace* (Grand Rapids: Baker, 1992), 1001.

5. Paraphrased from R. Kent Hughes, *Romans: Righteousness from Heaven* (Wheaton, IL: Crossway, 1991), 171.

6. D. Martyn Lloyd-Jones, *Romans: Final Perseverance of the Saints—Exposition of Chapter 8:17-39* (Grand Rapids: Zondervan, 1975), 448.

7. William Hendricksen, *New Testament Commentary: Exposition of St. Paul's Epistle to the Romans* (Grand Rapids: Baker, 1980), 301.

8. Adapted from J. C. Macaulay, *Expository Commentary on Acts* (Chicago: Moody Press, 1978), 130-31.

9. Elie Wiesel, *Night* (New York: Hill and Wang, 2006), xix.

10. Corrie ten Boom, *The Hiding Place* (Grand Rapids: Chosen Books, 2006), 206.

Chapter 9: *God Loves You and Wants You with Him Forever*

1. *United States Census*, accessed May 7, 2012, http://www.census.gov/population/www/pop-profile/geomob.html.

2. Randy Alcorn, *Heaven* (Wheaton, IL: Tyndale House Publishers, Inc., 2004), 321-22.

3. C. S. Lewis, *The Problem of Pain* (New York: MacMillan, 1962), 147.

4. Richard Baxter, *Poetical Fragments: Heart Imployment with God and Itself* (London: Black Raven, 1689), 62.

5. Quoted in Philip Yancey, "What's a Heaven For?" *Christianity Today*, October 26, 1998, accessed April 22, 2012, http://www.christianitytoday.com/ct/1998/october26/8tc104.html.

6. Cary McMullen, "Heaven: A Lot of Questions, but No One Really Knows the Answers," *TheLedger.com*, March 27, 2005, accessed May 7, 2012, http://

www.theledger.com/article/20050327/NEWS/503270394?template=
printart.

7. Wayne Martindale, *Beyond the Shadowlands: C. S. Lewis on Heaven and Hell* (Wheaton, IL: Crossway, 2005), 46–47.

8. A. W. Tozer and H. Verploegh, *The Quotable Tozer II: Wise Words with a Prophetic Edge* (Camp Hill, PA: WingSpread, 1977), 102.

9. Bryan Chapell, *The Wonder of It All: Rediscovering the Treasures of Your Faith* (Wheaton, IL: Crossway Books, 1999), 189.

10. C. S. Lewis, *Mere Christianity*, in *The Complete C. S. Lewis Signature Classics* (New York: HarperCollins, 2007), 112.

11. Charles F. Ball, quoted by Oswald Sanders in *Heaven: Better by Far* (Grand Rapids: Discovery House, 1994), 57.

12. Steven J. Lawson, *Heaven Help Us!* (Colorado Springs: NavPress, 1995), 16.

13. Bruce Milne, *The Message of Heaven and Hell* (Downers Grove, IL: InterVarsity Press, 2002), 327.

14. Mark Twain, *The Adventures of Huckleberry Finn* (New York: Fawcett Columbine, 1996), 6.

15. Mark Buchanan, *Things Unseen* (Sisters, OR: Multnomah, 2002), 66–67.

16. *George MacDonald Anthology*, ed. C. S. Lewis (London: Geoffrey Bless, 1946; Repr. 1970), 85.

17. Alcorn, *Heaven*, 184.

18. Douglas Connelly, *The Promise of Heaven* (Downers Grove, IL: InterVarsity Press, 2000), 116.

19. Amy Carmichael, "Thou Givest...They Gather," quoted in *Images of Heaven: Reflections on Glory*, comp. Lil Copan and Anna Trimiew (Wheaton, IL: Harold Shaw, 1996), 111.

20. Tony Evans, *Tony Evans Speaks Out on Heaven and Hell* (Chicago: Moody Press, 2000), 10.

21. Randy Alcorn, *We Shall See God: Charles Spurgeon's Devotional Thoughts on Home* (Carol Stream, IL: Tyndale, 2011), 11–12.

22. Author unknown.

23. David Gregg, *The Heaven-Life or Stimulus for Two Worlds* (Charleston, SC: Nabu Press, 2012), 62.

24. Larry Dick, *A Taste of Heaven* (Victoria, BC: Trafford, 2002), 103.

25. Wilbur M. Smith, *The Biblical Doctrine of Heaven* (Chicago: Moody, 1968), 195.

26. Ray Stedman, "The City of Glory," accessed April 23, 2012, http://www.pbc.org/system/message_files/5774/4211.pdf.

27. Michael E. Wittmer, *Heaven Is a Place on Earth: Why Everything You Do Matters to God* (Grand Rapids: Zondervan, 2004), 272.

28. Peter Toon, *Heaven and Hell: A Biblical and Theological Overview* (Nashville: Thomas Nelson, 1986), 204.

29. Buchanan, *Things Unseen*, 51, 54.

30. Mark McMinn, *Why Sin Matters: The Surprising Relationship Between Our Sin and God's Grace* (Wheaton, IL: Tyndale, 2004), 53.

31. Robert J. Morgan, *Nelson's Complete Book of Stories, Illustrations, and Quotes* (Nashville: Thomas Nelson, 2000), 188–89.

Chapter 10: *God's Love Changes Everything*

1. Rick Garmon, "My Secret Hate," *Today's Christian* (May–June 2006). Cited in Craig Brian Larson and Phyllis Ten Elshof, *1001 Illustrations That Connect* (Grand Rapids: Zondervan, 2008), 226–27.

2. Francis Schaeffer, *The Mark of a Christian* (Downers Grove, IL: Inter-Varsity Press, 1970), 13.

3. Quoted in Ray Stedman, "The One Commandment," May 10, 1985, accessed May 21, 2012, http://www.pbc.org/system/message_files/4298/3867.html.

4. William Barclay, *More New Testament Words* (New York: Harper & Brothers, 1958) 134–35.

5. Michael W. Smith, *A Simple Blessing* (Grand Rapids: Zondervan, 2011), 145–46.

6. Erwin Raphael McManus, *An Unstoppable Force: Daring to Become the Church God Had in Mind* (Loveland, CO: Group Publishing, 2001), 29–31.

7. C.E.B. Cranfield, *A Critical and Exegetical Commentary on the Epistle to the Romans: Volume 2* (Edinburgh: T. & T. Clark Limited, 1979), 640.

8. C. S. Lewis, *The Weight of Glory* (New York: HarperCollins, 2001), 45–46.

9. Alexander Maclaren, *Expositions of Holy Scripture*, vol. 10 (Grand Rapids: Baker, 1974), 227, 228.

10. Peter Kreeft, *The God Who Loves You: Love Divine, All Loves Excelling* (San Francisco: Ignatius Press, 1988), 25.

11. John Perkins, *With Justice for All* (Ventura, CA: Regal Books/GL, 1982), 107.

12. Ibid., 111.

13. Ibid., 98–103.

14. Henry Drummond, "The Greatest Thing in the World," 1880, accessed June 6, 2012, http://henrydrummond.wwwhubs.com/greatest.htm.

Conclusion

1. Charles Morgan, *The Fountain* (Hesperides Press, 2008).

Stay connected to the teaching series of
DR. DAVID JEREMIAH

Publishing

Radio

Television

Online

FURTHER YOUR STUDY OF THIS BOOK

God Loves You: He Always Has—He Always Will Resource Materials

To enhance your study on this important topic, we recommend the correlating audio message album, study guide, and DVD messages from the *God Loves You: He Always Has—He Always Will* series.

Audio Message Album

The material found in this book originated from messages presented by Dr. David Jeremiah at the Shadow Mountain Community Church where he serves as Senior Pastor. These ten messages are conveniently packaged in an accessible audio album.

Study Guide

This 128 page study guide correlates with the *God Loves You: He Always Has—He Always Will* messages by Dr. Jeremiah. The lessons provide an outline, overview, and application questions for each chapter.

DVD Message Presentations

Watch Dr. Jeremiah deliver the ten *God Loves You: He Always Has—He Always Will* original messages in this special DVD collection.

To order these products, call us at 1-800-947-1993 or
visit us online at www.DavidJeremiah.org.

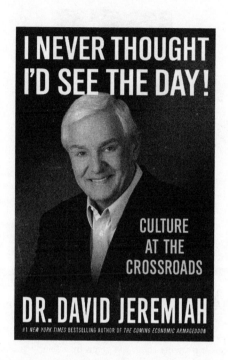

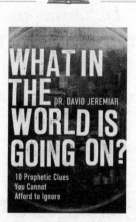

Turning Point
with Dr. David Jeremiah

Delivering the

UNCHANGING WORD OF GOD

to an

EVER-CHANGING WORLD

Dr. Jeremiah *on* Radio

Dr. Jeremiah's English radio program, *Turning Point*, was launched in 1982 and is now transmitted over 1,300 stations, with over 2,000 daily broadcasts heard in the United States, Canada, the Caribbean, Central America, the South Pacific, Europe, and Africa. The thirty-minute radio programs are also available worldwide via the Internet.

In addition, *Turning Point*'s Spanish programming, *Momento Decisivo,* reaches all 23 Spanish speaking countries with nearly 50 translated series. On any given day there are more than 799 programs airing from 573 transmitters around the world, 79 of which are in the United States.

As of March 2011, *Turning Point* is also broadcasting in China, potentially reaching 780 million Mandarin Chinese speakers. Turning Point is currently working toward translating and transmitting radio programs into ten other languages including Punjabi, Tagalog, and Farsi, seeking to deliver biblical truth to people around the world.

For more information, and to find a station in your area that carries *Turning Point*, visit the Turning Point website at www.DavidJeremiah.org/radio.

Dr. Jeremiah *on* Television

Dr. Jeremiah's ministry, Turning Point, also features weekly television programming. Senior Pastor at Shadow Mountain Community Church, Dr. Jeremiah's Sunday sermons are recorded live and adapted for hour- and half-hour-long telecasts.

Launched in 29 cities in April of 2000, *Turning Point* telecasts can now potentially be viewed from every household in America. *Turning Point* Television is carried by Lifetime, ION TV, Trinity Broadcasting Network, FamilyNet, DayStar, Faith TV, and Inspirational Network in the United States, Vision TV in Canada, Trinity Broadcasting in Europe and the United Kingdom, Shine TV in New Zealand and Australia, and METV in the Middle East. Arabic translations are also available in the Middle East via Kingdom Satellite.

Turning Point Television continues to grow and expand, reaching more local stations in cities across the United States in order to minister more directly to receiving communities.

For more information on *Turning Point* Television, go to www.DavidJeremiah.org/Television.

Dr. Jeremiah Online

Dr. Jeremiah's website offers up-to-date information on ministry happenings including current television and radio series, available resources, upcoming live events, and articles by Dr. Jeremiah. You can also read daily devotionals, learn about Turning Point's global outreach, and shop at the online bookstore.

From the Turning Point bookstore you can purchase all resources offered through Turning Point, including books by Dr. Jeremiah, teaching series on CD and DVD, pamphlets, study guides, and many other resources.

Shop today at www.DavidJeremiah.org/Shop.

Stay connected to the teaching of

DR. DAVID JEREMIAH

Take advantage of two great ways to let Dr. David Jeremiah give you spiritual direction every day! Both are absolutely FREE.

Turning Points Magazine and Devotional

Receive Dr. Jeremiah's magazine, *Turning Points* each month:

- Monthly study focus
- 48 pages of life-changing reading
- Relevant articles
- Special features
- Humor section
- Family section
- Daily devotional readings for each day of the month
- Bible study resource offers
- Live event schedule
- Radio & television information

Your Daily Turning Point E-Devotional

Start your day off right! Find words of inspiration and spiritual motivation waiting for you on your computer every morning! You can receive a daily e-devotional from Dr. Jeremiah that will strengthen your walk with God and encourage you to live the authentic Christian life.

There are two easy ways to sign up for these free resources from Turning Point. Visit us online at **www.DavidJeremiah.org** and select **"Subscribe to *Turning Points* Magazine"** or visit the home page and find Daily Devotional to subscribe to your daily e-devotional.